Catherine N. Dulmus, PhD
Karen M. Sowers, PhD
Editors

Kids and Violence: The Invisible School Experience

Kids and Violence: The Invisible School Experience has been co-published simultaneously as *Journal of Evidence-Based Social Work*, Volume 1, Numbers 2/3 2004.

Pre-publication REVIEWS, COMMENTARIES, EVALUATIONS . . .

"A MUST-READ for any social worker, especially school social workers, and other professional youth workers. This is an eye-opening work that provides much-needed grounding for practice frameworks and program development. The contributors are noted national social work scholars. This book makes a significant contribution to our understanding of the issues behind youth violence and bullying, and the concluding chapter provides clear discussion and an empirical assessment of school violence prevention programs."

Ira C. Colby, DSW
Dean and Professor of Social Work
Graduate School of Social Work
University of Houston

More Pre-publication
REVIEWS, COMMENTARIES, EVALUATIONS . . .

"IMPORTANT. . . . WILL BENEFIT SCHOOL ADMINISTRATORS, COUNSELORS, TEACHERS, AND PERSONNEL as they come to identify, understand, and act on violence in school settings. This is a timely publication, coming as society attempts to come to terms with ever-increasing reports of all forms of school-based violence."

Peter A. Newcombe, PhD, BEd, BA (Hons)
Acting Program Director
Behavioural Studies
School of Social Work
and Applied Human Sciences
The University of Queensland
Australia

"EXCEPTIONAL. . . . BURSTING WITH VALUABLE INFORMATION on violence, youngsters, and our aggressive society. The chapters are all well written, thoughtful, informative, and–best of all–practical. The editors, who also author many of the chapters, have done a marvelous job, providing the field with REQUIRED READING FOR SOCIAL WORKERS in schools and every other setting serving youth in these seemingly endless times of violence."

Kevin Corcoran, PhD, JD
Professor
Graduate School
of Social Work
Portland State University

The Haworth Social Work Practice Press
An Imprint of The Haworth Press, Inc.

Kids and Violence: The Invisible School Experience

Kids and Violence: The Invisible School Experience has been co-published simultaneously as *Journal of Evidence-Based Social Work*, Volume 1, Numbers 2/3 2004.

The *Journal of Evidence-Based Social Work*™ Monographic "Separates"

Below is a list of "separates," which in serials librarianship means a special issue simultaneously published as a special journal issue or double-issue *and* as a "separate" hardbound monograph. (This is a format which we also call a "DocuSerial.")

"Separates" are published because specialized libraries or professionals may wish to purchase a specific thematic issue by itself in a format which can be separately cataloged and shelved, as opposed to purchasing the journal on an on-going basis. Faculty members may also more easily consider a "separate" for classroom adoption.

"Separates" are carefully classified separately with the major book jobbers so that the journal tie-in can be noted on new book order slips to avoid duplicate purchasing.

You may wish to visit Haworth's website at . . .

http://www.HaworthPress.com

. . . to search our online catalog for complete tables of contents of these separates and related publications.

You may also call 1-800-HAWORTH (outside US/Canada: 607-722-5857), or Fax 1-800-895-0582 (outside US/Canada: 607-771-0012), or e-mail at:

docdelivery@haworthpress.com

Kids and Violence: The Invisible School Experience, edited by Catherine N. Dulmus, PhD, and Karen M. Sowers, PhD (Vol. 1, No. 2/3, 2004). *"Important . . . . will benefit school adminstrators, counselors, teachers, and personnel as they come to identify, understand, and act on violence in school settings." (Peter A. Newcombe, PhD, BEd, BA (Hons), Acting Program Director, Behavioural Studies, School of Social Work and Applied Human Sciences, The University of Queensland, Australia)*

Kids and Violence: The Invisible School Experience

Catherine N. Dulmus, PhD
Karen M. Sowers, PhD
Editors

Kids and Violence: The Invisible School Experience has been co-published simultaneously as *Journal of Evidence-Based Social Work*, Volume 1, Numbers 2/3 2004.

The Haworth Social Work Practice Press
An Imprint of The Haworth Press, Inc.

Published by

The Haworth Social Work Practice Press, 10 Alice Street, Binghamton, NY 13904-1580 USA

The Haworth Social Work Practice Press is an imprint of The Haworth Press, Inc., 10 Alice Street, Binghamton, NY 13904-1580 USA.

Kids and Violence: The Invisible School Experience has been co-published simultaneously as *Journal of Evidence-Based Social Work*, Volume 1, Numbers 2/3 2004.

Cover design by Marylouise E. Doyle

Library of Congress Cataloging-in-Publication Data

Kids and Violence: The Invisible School Experience /Catherine N. Dulmus, PhD, and Karen M. Sowers, PhD, editors.

p. cm.

"Co-published simultaneously as Journal of evidence-based social work, Volume 1, numbers 2/3 2004."

Includes bibliographical references and index.

ISBN 0-7890-2585-X (hard cover : alk. paper)–ISBN 0-7890-2586-8 (soft cover : alk. paper)

1. School violence–United States 2. Children and Violence–United States. 3. Voilence in children–United States . 4. School violence–United States-Prevention 5. Children and violence–United States–Prevention. 6. Violence in children–United States–Prevention I. Sowers, Karen M. (Karen Marlaine) II. Journal of evidence-based social work (Online).

LB3013.32.K52 2004

371.7′82–dc22 2004020032

With affection and gratitude we dedicate this book to "The Group."
You continually embrace us unconditionally in work and in play.
You know who you are.

Catherine and Karen

∞ ALL HAWORTH SOCIAL WORK PRACTICE PRESS
BOOKS AND JOURNALS ARE PRINTED ON
CERTIFIED ACID-FREE PAPER

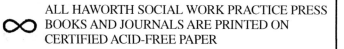

Indexing, Abstracting & Website/Internet Coverage

This section provides you with a list of major indexing & abstracting services and other tools for bibliographic access. That is to say, each service began covering this periodical during the year noted in the right column. Most Websites which are listed below have indicated that they will either post, disseminate, compile, archive, cite or alert their own Website users with research-based content from this work. (This list is as current as the copyright date of this publication.)

Abstracting, Website/Indexing Coverage . . . . Year When Coverage Began

- *CareData: the database supporting social care management and practice <http://www.elsc.org.uk/caredata/caredata.htm>* **2004**
- *EBSCOhost Electronic Journals Service (EJS) <http://ejournals.ebsco.com>* **2004**
- *Family & Society Studies Worldwide <http://www.nisc.com>* **2003**
- *Family Index Database <http://www.familyscholar.com>* **2004**
- *National Center for Chronic Disease Prevention & Health Promotion (NCCDPHP) <http://chid.nih.gov>* **2004**
- *National Clearinghouse on Child Abuse & Neglect Information Documents Database <http://www.nccanch.acf.hhs.gov>* **2004**
- *Sage Family Studies Abstracts (SFSA)* **2004**
- *Social Services Abstracts <http://www.csa.com* **2004**
- *Sociedad Iberoamericana de Información Científica (SIIC) <http://www.siicsalud.com>* **2004**
- *Women, Girls & Criminal Justice Newsletter. Civic Research Institute, 4490 Rte 27 Box 585, Kingston, NJ 08528* **2004**

(continued)

Special Bibliographic Notes related to special journal issues (separates) and indexing/abstracting:

- indexing/abstracting services in this list will also cover material in any "separate" that is co-published simultaneously with Haworth's special thematic journal issue or DocuSerial. Indexing/abstracting usually covers material at the article/chapter level.
- monographic co-editions are intended for either non-subscribers or libraries which intend to purchase a second copy for their circulating collections.
- monographic co-editions are reported to all jobbers/wholesalers/approval plans. The source journal is listed as the "series" to assist the prevention of duplicate purchasing in the same manner utilized for books-in-series.
- to facilitate user/access services all indexing/abstracting services are encouraged to utilize the co-indexing entry note indicated at the bottom of the first page of each article/chapter/contribution.
- this is intended to assist a library user of any reference tool (whether print, electronic, online, or CD-ROM) to locate the monographic version if the library has purchased this version but not a subscription to the source journal.
- individual articles/chapters in any Haworth publication are also available through the Haworth Document Delivery Service (HDDS).

Kids and Violence: The Invisible School Experience

CONTENTS

ABOUT THE EDITORS

Catherine N. Dulmus, PhD, is an Associate Professor in the College of Social Work at the University of Tennessee. She received her baccalaureate degree in Social Work from Buffalo State College in 1989, the Master's Degree in Social Work from the State University of New York in 1991 and the PhD degree in Social Welfare from the State University of New York in 1999. Dr. Dulmus' research focuses on child mental health, prevention, and violence. She has authored or coauthored several journal articles, books, and has presented her research nationally and internationally. Dr. Dulmus is co-editor of *The Journal of Evidence-Based Social Work*, associate editor of *Stress, Trauma, and Crisis: An International Journal*, and sits on the editorial board of the *Journal of Human Behavior in the Social Environment.* In 2002 was awarded an excellence in teaching citation from the University of Tennessee. Prior to obtaining the PhD her social work practice background encompassed almost a decade of experience in the fields of mental health and school social work.

Karen M. Sowers, PhD, was appointed Professor and Dean of the College of Social Work at the University of Tennessee, Knoxville in August 1997. She served as Director of the School of Social Work at Florida International University from June 1994 to August 1997 and as the Undergraduate Program Director of the School of Social Work at Florida International University from 1986 to 1994. She received her baccalaureate degree in Sociology from the University of Central Florida in 1974, the Master's Degree in Social Work from Florida State University in 1977 and the PhD in Social Work from Florida State University in 1986. Dr. Sowers is nationally known for her research and scholarship in the areas of juvenile justice, child welfare, cultural diversity and culturally effective intervention strategies for social work practice, and social work education. Her current research and community interests include the development of initiatives to support responsible and involved fatherhood, the implementation and evaluation of community-oriented policing, welfare reform, school violence and juvenile justice practice. She has authored or co-authored numerous books, book chapters and refereed journal articles. She has served as a founding member of the *Journal of Research on Social Work Practice*, and is currently serving on the editorial boards of the *Journal of Evidence-Based Social Work: Advances in Practice, Programs, Research and Policy* and *Journal of Stress, Trauma and Crisis: An International Journal.*

Introduction

Schools as social institutions may negatively impact child well-being. This special collection demonstrates how school violence takes many forms in relation to time, place, and type of perpetrator. In fact, many articles in this volume indicate that the adults responsible for the well-being of our children may be perpetrating violence, holding silent about the violence, and/or inadvertently supporting a system which supports a violent environment. The title of this publication highlights the "invisible school experience" characterized by a level of violence in the school system that is often hidden, ignored and/or subtly tolerated.

What makes this special collection on school violence unique is its holistic and systemic approach. The lead article by Hilarski, Dulmus, Theriot, and Sowers, focuses on bullying among students, grades 3 through 8, in a rural school district. Results of type and frequency of bully-victimization experienced by male and female students relating to gender and grade level are presented. The second article by Thomlison, Thomlison, Sowers, Theriot, and Dulmus, focuses on school personnel's observations of bullying among elementary and middle school students. They report on analysis of data from a community sample of 70 school personnel as to the sources and types of bullying among children. The third article by Blackburn, Dulmus, Theriot, and Sowers, addresses the importance of communication between school and home in the prevention and intervention of bullying behaviors.

The fourth article by Hilarski focuses on corporal punishment as a cultural norm in the United States, as evidenced by the use of corporal punishment in schools currently being legal in 22 states. She argues that

---

[Haworth co-indexing entry note]: "Introduction." Dulmus, Catherine N. and Karen M. Sowers. Co-published simultaneously in *Journal of Evidence-Based Social Work* (The Haworth Social Work Practice Press, an imprint of The Haworth Press, Inc.) Vol. 1, No. 2/3, 2004, pp.1-3; and: *Kids and Violence: The Invisible School Experience* (ed: Catherine N. Dulmus and Karen M. Sowers) The Haworth Social Work Practice Press, an imprint of The Haworth Press, Inc., 2004, pp. 1-3. Single or multiple copies of this article are available for a fee from The Haworth Document Delivery Service [1-800-HAWORTH, 9:00 a.m. - 5:00 p.m. (EST). E-mail address: docdelivery@haworthpress.com].

http://www.haworthpress.com/web/JEBSW

Digital Object Identifier: 10.1300/J394v1n02_01

corporal punishment is a form of violence against children that affects child development and may possibly be a link to later violent behavior. Through secondary analysis she examines variables that are significant among individuals who support use of corporal punishment. Such knowledge will assist in the development of interventions to address cultural norms that support this type of violence against children. The fifth article in this volume by Theriot, Dulmus, Sowers, and Bowie, examines the *"criminal bully"* which are those bullies whose acts of bullying against other students in schools could be considered criminal in nature. The paper examines such behaviors within a context of delinquency as a continuum. The sixth article by Hopson and Kim provides a description of a solution-focused approach to crisis intervention with adolescents and a review of related efficacy research. They propose this intervention approach to working with adolescents in crisis in both school and community settings.

The seventh article by Edwards, Smokowski, Sowers, Dulmus, and Theriot, examines bullying of children by school personnel as violence and abuse of power. Data was gathered from a sample of school personnel in a rural school district which found 36% of the sample reporting they had observed other school personnel bullying students during the previous three-month period. The eighth article by Rapp-Paglicci, Dulmus, Sowers, and Theriot, explores the location that bullying occurs in schools as reported by elementary and middle school children surveyed in a rural school district. Location was found to be important, with "hotspots" for bullying identified by grade level and gender. Recommendations for school prevention are provided. The ninth article examines adolescent dating violence in the school setting. Ely provides a synthesized literature review that examines risk factors associated with school-aged adolescents and provides suggestions for school personnel in regards to prevention intervention and policy formation.

The tenth article by Rowe, Theriot, Sowers, and Dulmus, provides results from an exploratory study that examined self identified bullies in a sample of elementary and middle school children. Results reported provide some insight into the attitudes and beliefs of children who bully and may be instrumental in the development of effective intervention programs. The last article in this special publication is authored by Molina, Bowie, Dulmus and Sowers, and is a literature review on school violence. The article provides a review of selected school violence prevention programs with empirical effectiveness to guide school social workers and school administrators in their attempts in primary prevention of school violence.

If indeed violence begets violence then our schools and communities are in for a bumpy ride. The time to stop the violence is now and social work should lead the charge. Who better and more uniquely prepared to intervene at a multisystemic level to combat violence in schools than school social workers? Sadly, our author's reviews of the literature indicate that social work academicians, practitioners, and policy makers are part of the problem by their often lack of involvement in the issues. This collection should serve as a call for immediate action for social workers to provide leadership in researching, developing, and delivering empirically-based prevention interventions and development of policies informed by research evidence, in an effort to stop the cycle of violence in our schools. Unfortunately, a cycle that in some cases is perpetuated by the schools themselves.

Catherine N. Dulmus, PhD
Karen M. Sowers, PhD

Bully-Victimization Related to Gender and Grade Level: Implications for Prevention Efforts

Carolyn Hilarski, PhD, CSW, ACSW
Catherine N. Dulmus, PhD
Matthew T. Theriot, PhD
Karen M. Sowers, PhD

SUMMARY. This descriptive study used the Olweus Bully/Victim Questionnaire to obtain data from a convenience sample (N = 192) of three rural public school students in grades 3 through 8. The objectives of the study were to determine the type and frequency of bully-victimization experienced by male and female students relating to gender and grade level. Using frequencies and percentages, elementary school males and females described, weekly or more, *relational (or verbal)* victimization (26%) similar to middle school students (22%); *threatening*

Carolyn Hilarski is Assistant Professor, Social Work Department, College of Liberal Arts, Rochester Institute of Technology, 18 Lomb Memorial Drive, Rochester, NY 14623.

Catherine N. Dulmus is Associate Professor, Matthew T. Theriot is Assistant Professor, Karen M. Sowers is Dean and Professor The University of Tennessee, College of Social Work.

The authors would like to gratefully acknowledge the contributions of Pamela Jinks and David Dupper to the project.

[Haworth co-indexing entry note]: "Bully-Victimization Related to Gender and Grade Level: Implications for Prevention Efforts." Hilarski, Carolyn et al. Co-published simultaneously in *Journal of Evidence-Based Social Work* (The Haworth Social Work Practice Press, an imprint of The Haworth Press, Inc.) Vol. 1, No. 2/3, 2004, pp. 5-24; and: *Kids and Violence: The Invisible School Experience* (ed: Catherine N. Dulmus and Karen M. Sowers) The Haworth Social Work Practice Press, an imprint of The Haworth Press, Inc., 2004, pp. 5-24. Single or multiple copies of this article are available for a fee from The Haworth Document Delivery Service [1-800-HAWORTH, 9:00 a.m. - 5:00 p.m. (EST). E-mail address: docdelivery@haworthpress.com].

http://www.haworthpress.com/web/JEBSW

Digital Object Identifier: 10.1300/J394v1n02_02

bully-victimization (6%) different from middle school youth (3%), and *physical* bully-victimization (17%), quite unlike middle school students (6%). These findings were inconsistent with previous findings that verbal bully-victimization tends to increase as children age. Gender and grade level data identified females as chronically exposed to threatening and physical bully-victimization unlike males; contradicting a common theme in preliminary bully-victim research that males experience greater frequencies of overt bullying than females. Additionally, gender and grade level frequency demonstrated that males, in this study, reported consistent exclusion victimization different from females. A comprehensive system level prevention program should begin with a school wide bullying and victim survey. Once awareness of the extent of the bullying problem occurs, staff training may be required for effective intervention.

KEYWORDS. Bullying, gender, rural schools, grade level

INTRODUCTION

Victims of bullies experience such behaviors as hitting, kicking, pushing, name calling, abusive language, spreading rumors, manipulation of friendships, excluding or ignoring, and threatening by individuals who are older, stronger, and more powerful (Dake, Price, & Telljohann, 2003).

The consequences of this victimization are depression (Bond, Carlin, Thomas, Rubin, & Patton, 2001), loneliness (Nansel et al., 2001), low self esteem (O'Moore & Kirkham, 2001), psychiatric issues (Kumpulainen, Rasanen, & Puura, 2001), aggressive bullying (Austin & Joseph, 1996), anxiety, eating disorders (Salmon, James, & Smith, 1998), absenteeism, and poor academic performance (Roberts & Coursol, 1996). An added dilemma is that student bullying is increasing and becoming more threatening (Olweus, 1991).

The need for appropriate school prevention programs to address bullying victimization is urgent. Since assessment is the first stage of prevention, it is essential to understand the extent of bullying victimization and any influencing factors, such as gender or age. To date, there are no definable estimates, as bullying victimization prevalence data ranges from 5% to greater than 80% (Wolke, Woods, Bloomfield, & Karstadt, 2001). The basis for these varied outcomes may be complex and related to measurement and/or developmental issues. An overall explanation may be that much of the available bullying victimization research comes from international investigations (Boulton, 1994; Genta, Menesini, Fonzi, & ACostabile, 1996; Olweus, 1998; Peterson & Rigby, 1999). Conceptual definitions and measurement of bullying and victimization may not be equivalent from country to country (Wolke et al., 2001).

The United States has only recently begun to research bullying victimization. It is suggested that school professionals and parents may actually be unaware of the extent of bullying victimization happening in U.S. schools (Cavendish & Salomone, 2001). Determining the prevalence of the type of bullying victimization in relation to age/grade issues in youth attending U.S. schools can serve to inform professionals of the extent and influencing factors of the problem, generate further studies, and stimulate appropriate prevention efforts.

RESEARCH PURPOSE AND QUESTIONS

The purpose of this study was to understand the type and frequency of bullying experiences of male and female youth in an elementary and middle rural school population.

The following three research questions were addressed in this study:

1. What is the overall frequency and type of bullying experiences of elementary and middle school students?
2. What is the frequency and type of bullying experiences of students, grade 3 through 5, based on gender?
3. What is the frequency and type of bullying experiences of students, grade 6 through 8, based on gender?

PREVALENCE OF BULLYING VICTIMIZATION AMONG YOUTH

In spite of the current conflicting prevalence data, there are some similarities beginning to appear. First, victimization by bullies seems to be a universal concern. Second, the proportion of youth experiencing victimization appears significant. For example, twenty percent of school children, age 8 to 11, living in central Italy reported being bullied "once a week or more" (Genta et al., 1996) and a comparable sample living near Rome reported similar circumstances (Baldry & Farrington, 1998). Primary school children in Belgium (23%) and Portugal (22%) reported being bullied "regularly or often" (Tomas de Almeida, 1999; Vettenburg, 1999), and an age equivalent sample attending school in the Midwestern U.S. (77%) reported significant bully-victimization in the previous year (Hoover, Oliver, & Hazler, 1992). Other U.S. studies found that one third of the students, grades 4 through 6, were bullied often (Berthold & Hoover, 2000), and, in grades 3 through 5, 10% self reported being highly victimized (Perry, Kusel, & Perry, 1988).

Gender Issues

Victims of bullying are often bullied by others of the same gender, for example, males are victimized by other males and females victimized by other females (Boulton & Underwood, 1992). Research indicates that males bully more often than females (Andreou, 2001). Are males, therefore, bullied more often than females? The evidence is contradictory. Several studies propose that males and females experience bullying similarly (Olweus, 1995; Salmivalli, Lappalainen, & Lagerspetz, 2000; P. K. Smith et al., 2002), and others report that males experience greater bullying victimization than females (O'Moore, Kirkham, & Smith, 1997; Siann, Callaghan, Glissov, Lockhart, et al., 1994). However, there is an implication that females experience more *relational* (verbal teasing and name calling) bullying (Hoover et al., 1992) and males experience greater *physical* bullying (Crick, Bigbee, & Howes, 1996; Crick & Brotpeter, 1995; Crick, Casas, & Ku, 1999). The gender inconsistency may be the result of fear based underreporting (Cowie, 2000). This reluctance to report may have several foundations; however, one explanation relates to the *process* of the bullying experience. To illustrate, males self report often being bullied by *one* other male (Genta et al., 1996) and females report being bullied by *several other females rather than one* (Rivers & Smith, 1994). Research suggests that male bullying behavior is generally overt whereas female bullying is more covert (Borg, 1999). Covert, or indirect, forms of aggression are more harmful than direct (Hawker & Boulton, 2000). Thus, females, who are most often bullied covertly by other females *in a group*, fear reporting such perceived serious violence exposure (Menesini, Eslea, Smith, Genta, et al., 1997). Indeed, underreporting is thought common because students are afraid of the unavailability of school professionals to assist in preventing retaliatory aggression (Olweus, 1993), especially females (Noaks & Joaks, 2000).

Age/Grade Issues

In relation to age when bullying victimization might occur, some researchers indicate that youth as young as 4 or 5 years experience bullying (Crick et al., 1999). Others propose that being bullied begins in elementary school, then declines in grade 7 (Olweus, 1991; Peterson & Rigby, 1999). Olweus (1991) relates that students in grades 2 through 6 are significantly more likely to be bullied than those in grades 7 through 9. Still, others advise that bullying victimization remains constant through childhood and adolescence, it just changes form, from overt to more covert (e.g., verbal) behaviors (Borg, 1999), particularly in females (Galen & Underwood, 1997). Explanations for the decrease or change in victimization in relation to grade level or age may be that as youth evolve they acquire skills of reframing and empathy that encourage less internalizing of potential verbal assaults (P. K. Smith et al., 2002). Further, as children move through school there are simply fewer older and more powerful individuals to bully them (P. K. Smith et al., 2002).

IN CONCLUSION

Bully-victimization prevalence data and age/grade trends in male and female youth are inconsistent. The greater part of the bully-victimizing data comes from outside the U.S. and may not be comparable (Wolke et al., 2001). Bully-victimization and gender issue variations may be the result of underreporting in one or both gender groups (Cowie, 2000), or, the fact that bully victims are a more heterogeneous group than bullies are (Wolke et al., 2001). This study attempts to further understand the extent and type of bullying victimization that U.S. elementary and middle school male and female students are exposed. These findings will enable those professionals interacting with bullied youth to assess and intervene more effectively. Further, school administrators may use these findings to propose future preventive programs.

METHODOLOGY

Study Design

This study utilized a survey research design to gather information from students as to their self-reported bullying victimization during the three month period prior to data collection. The IRB at a large university in the Southeastern United States granted permission to conduct the research before the start of the project. Parental consent was obtained for all student subjects whose participation was voluntary and confidential.

Study Sample

Letters to parents were sent home with students to recruit subjects. Subjects were recruited from three rural public schools (an elementary school, a middle school, and a school that housed grades K-8) located within the same school district in a Southeastern rural region of the United States. The school district is located in a county characterized by high rates of poverty as evidenced by 43% to 61% of students receiving free or reduced lunches and 12% of the population still not having a telephone. The school district reports 98% of its students as Caucasian and the dominant culture as Appalachian.

The letter sent home to parents included information related to the study and a consent form for parents to complete to allow their child to participate in the study. A self-addressed stamped envelope was provided for parents to mail the consent form back to the principal investigator at the university. Ultimately, the convenience sample consisted of 192 students in grades three through eight, representing an 18.4% response rate. Data collection occurred in the fall of 2002. A team of researchers conducted data collection in the school setting for all children who met inclusion criteria and for whom written parental consent was obtained. Since all subjects were measured at one point in time, no follow-up was necessary. Thus, attrition was not problematic.

Inclusion criteria were as follows: (a) subjects had to be students enrolled in the school where data collection occurred, and (b) subjects had to be in grades three through eight. Written parental consent was obtained for each subject prior to their participating in the study. In addition, all children completed an individual assent form.

Measure

Each subject completed the Olweus Bully/Victim Questionnaire (Olweus, 1986). This 56-item, self-administered questionnaire, designed for grades 1 through 10, asks questions specific to student's experiences and participation in various aspects of bullying in the school setting.

For the purposes of this study and as per the Olweus questionnaire, we defined and explained bullying to the students as being when another student or several other students do the following:

- completely ignore or exclude him or her from their group of friends or leave him or her out of things on purpose
- hit, kick, push, shove around, or lock him or her inside a room
- tell lies or spread false rumors about him or her or send mean notes and try to make other students dislike him or her
- and other hurtful things like that

In addition, we explained that a student is being bullied when the above things happen repeatedly, and it is difficult for the student being bullied to defend him or herself. We further explained that bullying is when a student is teased repeatedly in a mean and hurtful way, but that bullying was not when teasing was done in a friendly or playful way.

Data Collection Procedures

A team of researchers collected data in the school setting over a period of two days. Students whom parental consent had been obtained were called to the cafeteria during the school day to complete the assent form and questionnaire. Definition of bullying used for this study and directions for completion of the questionnaire were provided. Data collectors were trained to use appropriate and consistent responses to student questions and to utilize the study's definition of bullying. They also assisted students with the reading of questions as necessary. Upon completion of the questionnaires, students were given a pencil and key chain as a thank you gift and sent back to their classrooms. All subjects were assured of the confidentiality of their responses throughout the study. There were minimal physical, psychological, legal, or social risks for participants. To ensure confidentiality and protection of subjects they were instructed not to put their names or any identifying information on the questionnaire.

Data Analysis

All data were coded directly from respondent's answers to specific questions asked on the survey instrument. The data for these bullied students are displayed on four tables. Table 1 presents the frequency and type of bullying experienced by elementary school versus middle school students. Table 2 reports this information for male and female students. Tables 3 and 4, then, combine these paths of comparison. Specifically, Table 3 looks at the frequency and type of bullying experienced by male versus female elementary school students while Table 4 illustrates similar gender-stratified data for middle school students. Consistent with the structure of the school district from which this information was gathered, students in grades 3, 4, and 5 are elementary school students while those in grades 6, 7, and 8 are middle school students. On all 4 tables, the categorical data are presented in frequencies and percentages.

Limitations

This exploratory research provides beginning knowledge as to children's bullying victimization in a rural school setting. Generalizability is limited by the lack of random assignment, no control group, subjects coming from only one region of the country, and the lack of diversity among students in the school district. In addition, the low response rate of 18.4% is certainly a limitation, but the result of only surveying those students whom formal, written parental consent was granted. The questionnaire used in this study also limited statistical analysis. The purpose of this study was exploratory, focusing only on bullying victimization, so the myriad of psychosocial factors that may be involved in bullying and being bullied were not examined.

RESULTS

Among the 192 children surveyed, 158 responded that they have experienced some form of being bullied in the past three months. One student did not identify their gender, so the final sample consists of 157 students. Within this group there are 89 elementary school students, 68 middle school students, 80 males and 77 females. Table 1 shows several differences in frequency and type of bullying experienced by elementary and middle school students. Most noticeably, the incidence of theft or property damage, the use of threats and force, and the occurrence of

TABLE 1. Frequency and Type of Bullying Experienced by Elementary and Middle School Students (N = 157)

Types of Bullying	Elementary School Students (n = 89)					Middle School Students (n = 68)				
	Has Not Happened in Past 3 Months Freq. (%)	Happened Only Once or Twice Freq. (%)	Happened 2-3 Times a Month Freq. (%)	Happened About Once a Week Freq. (%)	Happened Several Times a Week Freq. (%)	Has Not Happened in Past 3 Months Freq. (%)	Happened Only Once or Twice Freq. (%)	Happened 2-3 Times a Month Freq. (%)	Happened About Once a Week Freq. (%)	Happened Several Times a Week Freq. (%)
Called Mean Names, Made Fun of, or Teased	25 (28.1)	33 (37.1)	8 (9.0)	10 (11.2)	13 (14.6)	18 (26.5)	33 (48.5)	2 (2.9)	7 (10.3)	8 (11.8)
Excluded or Ignored by Others	44 (50.0)	24 (27.3)	3 (3.4)	5 (5.7)	12 (13.6)	38 (55.9)	21 (30.9)	2 (2.9)	0 (0.0)	7 (10.3)
Hit, Kicked, Shoved, or Assaulted	45 (50.6)	22 (24.7)	7 (7.9)	8 (9.0)	7 (7.9)	48 (70.6)	14 (20.6)	2 (2.9)	3 (4.4)	1 (1.5)
Others Told Lies or Spread False Rumors	34 (38.2)	30 (33.7)	7 (7.9)	7 (7.9)	11 (12.4)	23 (33.8)	31 (45.6)	8 (11.8)	4 (5.9)	2 (2.9)
Had Money or Items Taken or Damaged	56 (62.9)	21 (23.6)	7 (7.9)	3 (3.4)	2 (2.2)	49 (72.1)	15 (22.1)	1 (1.5)	2 (2.9)	1 (1.5)
Threatened or Forced to Do Things	61 (68.5)	15 (16.9)	7 (7.9)	3 (3.4)	3 (3.4)	59 (86.8)	6 (8.8)	1 (1.5)	1 (1.5)	1 (1.5)
Heard Comments or Called Names Based on Race or Color	58 (65.9)	13 (14.8)	9 (10.2)	3 (3.4)	5 (5.7)	58 (85.3)	5 (7.4)	2 (2.9)	1 (1.5)	2 (2.9)
Bullied with Sexual Comments, Names, or Gestures	53 (59.6)	23 (25.8)	5 (5.6)	3 (3.4)	5 (5.6)	44 (64.7)	18 (26.5)	3 (4.4)	2 (2.9)	1 (1.5)
Bullied in Other Ways	56 (62.9)	19 (21.3)	3 (3.4)	7 (7.9)	4 (4.5)	47 (70.1)	15 (22.4)	1 (1.5)	3 (4.5)	1 (1.5)

Column percentages may not total 100% because of rounding.

racial bullying are more common among elementary school students than among their middle school counterparts. For example, 37.1% of bullied elementary school students have had their money or property stolen or damaged compared to 27.9% of bullied middle school students. Additionally, while more than 30% of the elementary school group have been threatened or forced to do things or have been bullied with racial comments and names, less than 15% of the middle school group has experienced such bullying. More elementary students have also experienced physical bullying and assault (49.4% compared to 29.4% of the middle school students).

The interaction of bullying with student's grade level is complicated regarding the incidence and frequency of lies and false rumors. A majority of both groups have experienced this form of bullying. Yet, 57.4% of the middle school group experienced this bullying less than weekly (versus 41.6% of bullied elementary school students). Comparatively, 20.3% of the elementary group has been victimized by lies or false rumors at least weekly (versus only 8.8% of the middle school group). Finally, it is important to recognize that the most frequent type of bullying experienced by both groups is being teased or called mean names and being excluded or ignored.

These two types of bullying are also the most frequently occurring types when bullying is assessed by gender rather than by grade level. Further, regarding frequency, for five of the nine types of bullying listed on Table 2, a larger percentage of males are bullied several times a week than the female group is. Also concerning gender, more females experienced being called mean names or teased (80% versus 64.9% males), being excluded or ignored (54.4% versus 40.3% of the males), and being threatened or forced to do things (27.5% versus 19.5%). Conversely, more males experienced having money and items taken or damaged (37.7% versus 28.7%) and racial name-calling (28.6% versus 22.8%).

It is difficult to detect differences in bullying frequency as reported on Tables 3 and 4. Perhaps, this is due to the utilization of smaller sub-groups. Nonetheless, there do appear to be noticeable differences in the types of bullying that students have experienced in the past three months. Specifically, among those students who have experienced being bullied, more elementary school females have been victimized by name-calling and teasing (81% compared to 63.8% for males) or exclusion (56.1% compared to 44.7%). On the other hand, fewer females have been bullied with lies and false rumors (57.1% for females compared to 66.0% for males), have had money or property taken or dam-

TABLE 2. Frequency and Type of Bullying Experienced by Gender (N = 157)

Types of Bullying	Males (n = 77)					Females (n = 80)				
	Has Not Happened in Past 3 Months Freq. (%)	Happened Only Once or Twice Freq. (%)	Happened 2-3 Times a Month Freq. (%)	Happened About Once a Week Freq. (%)	Happened Several Times a Week Freq. (%)	Has Not Happened in Past 3 Months Freq. (%)	Happened Only Once or Twice Freq. (%)	Happened 2-3 Times a Month Freq. (%)	Happened About Once a Week Freq. (%)	Happened Several Times a Week Freq. (%)
Called Mean Names, Made Fun of, or Teased	27 (35.1)	28 (36.4)	7 (9.1)	6 (7.8)	9 (11.7)	16 (20.0)	38 (47.5)	3 (3.8)	11 (13.8)	12 (15.0)
Excluded or Ignored by Others	46 (59.7)	18 (23.4)	2 (2.6)	2 (2.6)	9 (11.7)	36 (45.6)	27 (34.2)	3 (3.8)	3 (3.8)	10 (12.7)
Hit, Kicked, Shoved, or Assaulted	46 (59.7)	15 (19.5)	6 (7.8)	4 (5.2)	6 (7.8)	47 (58.8)	21 (26.3)	3 (3.8)	7 (8.8)	2 (2.5)
Others Told Lies or Spread False Rumors	28 (36.4)	34 (44.2)	6 (7.8)	3 (3.9)	6 (7.8)	29 (36.3)	27 (33.8)	9 (11.3)	8 (10.0)	7 (8.8)
Had Money or Items Taken or Damaged	48 (62.3)	20 (26.0)	4 (5.2)	2 (2.6)	3 (3.9)	57 (71.3)	16 (20.0)	4 (5.0)	3 (3.8)	0 (0.0)
Threatened or Forced to Do Things	62 (80.5)	9 (11.7)	2 (2.6)	1 (1.3)	3 (3.9)	58 (72.5)	12 (15.0)	6 (7.5)	3 (3.8)	1 (1.3)
Heard Comments or Called Names Based on Race or Color	55 (71.4)	11 (14.3)	6 (7.8)	1 (1.3)	4 (5.2)	61 (77.2)	7 (8.9)	5 (6.3)	3 (3.8)	3 (3.8)
Bullied with Sexual Comments, Names, or Gestures	46 (59.7)	22 (28.6)	3 (3.9)	1 (1.3)	5 (6.5)	51 (63.8)	19 (23.8)	5 (6.3)	4 (5.0)	1 (1.3)
Bullied in Other Ways	53 (68.8)	18 (23.4)	1 (1.3)	3 (3.9)	2 (2.6)	50 (63.3)	16 (20.3)	3 (3.8)	7 (8.9)	3 (3.8)

TABLE 3. Frequency and Type of Bullying at Elementary Schools by Gender (N = 89)

Types of Bullying	Males (n = 47)					Females (n = 42)				
	Has Not Happened in Past 3 Months Freq. (%)	Happened Only Once or Twice Freq. (%)	Happened 2-3 Times a Month Freq. (%)	Happened About Once a Week Freq. (%)	Happened Several Times a Week Freq. (%)	Has Not Happened in Past 3 Months Freq. (%)	Happened Only Once or Twice Freq. (%)	Happened 2-3 Times a Month Freq. (%)	Happened About Once a Week Freq. (%)	Happened Several Times a Week Freq. (%)
Called Mean Names, Made Fun of, or Teased	17 (36.2)	13 (27.7)	5 (10.6)	4 (8.5)	8 (17.0)	8 (19.0)	20 (47.6)	3 (7.1)	6 (14.3)	5 (11.9)
Excluded or Ignored by Others	26 (55.3)	13 (27.7)	1 (2.1)	2 (4.3)	5 (10.6)	18 (43.9)	11 (26.8)	2 (4.9)	3 (7.3)	7 (17.1)
Hit, Kicked, Shoved, or Assaulted	25 (53.2)	9 (19.1)	5 (10.6)	3 (6.4)	5 (10.6)	20 (47.6)	13 (31.0)	2 (4.8)	5 (11.9)	2 (4.8)
Others Told Lies or Spread False Rumors	16 (34.0)	20 (42.6)	3 (6.4)	2 (4.3)	6 (12.8)	18 (42.9)	10 (23.8)	4 (9.5)	5 (11.9)	5 (11.9)
Had Money or Items Taken or Damaged	27 (57.4)	12 (25.5)	4 (8.5)	2 (4.3)	2 (4.3)	29 (69.0)	9 (21.4)	3 (7.1)	1 (2.4)	0 (0.0)
Threatened or Forced to Do Things	33 (70.2)	8 (17.0)	2 (4.3)	1 (2.1)	3 (6.4)	28 (66.7)	7 (16.7)	5 (11.9)	2 (4.8)	0 (0.0)
Heard Comments or Called Names based on Race or Color	30 (63.8)	8 (17.0)	5 (10.6)	0 (0.0)	4 (8.5)	28 (68.3)	5 (12.2)	4 (9.8)	3 (7.3)	1 (2.4)
Bullied with Sexual Comments, Names, or Gestures	25 (53.2)	14 (29.8)	2 (4.3)	1 (2.1)	5 (10.6)	28 (66.7)	9 (21.4)	3 (7.1)	2 (4.8)	0 (0.0)
Bullied in Other Ways	31 (66.0)	11 (23.4)	1 (2.1)	2 (4.3)	2 (4.3)	25 (59.5)	8 (19.0)	2 (4.8)	5 (11.9)	2 (4.8)

aged (31.0% versus 42.6%), and have been subjected to sexual name-calling or gesturing (33.3% versus 46.8%).

Moving to similar comparisons of middle school males and females (as presented on Table 4), a larger percentage of females have experienced a variety of different types of bullying. For example, more females have experienced name-calling and teasing (78.9% versus 66.7%), exclusion (52.6% versus 33.3%), and lies and false rumors about them (71.1% versus 60.0%). More females have also been threatened or forced to do things (21.1% versus 3.3%), bullied in a sexual manner (39.5% versus 30.0%), or bullied in another, unspecified way (32.4% versus 26.7%).

DISCUSSION

Prevalence of Type of Bully-Victimization Relating to Gender and Grade Level

Physical Bully-Victimization

A disturbing number (17%) of elementary school students reported weekly or more *physical* victimization (hit, kicked, shoved, or assaulted) (see Table 1). This finding is far higher than Olweus's (1991) outcome where 3% of the students, grades two through six, were bullied one or more times a week and Whitney and Smith's (1993) findings of 10% for similar circumstances; although, considerably lower than several European studies of primary school students (Baldry & Farrington, 1998; Genta et al., 1996; Vernberg, Jacobs, & Hershberger, 1999).

In middle school, the reported weekly or more *physical* bully-victimization frequency declined to 6%; agreeing with several studies that older children report less physical bullying victimization than younger youth (Peterson & Rigby, 1999; Salmivalli, Kaukiainen, & Lagerspetz, 2000).

Gender and grade level issues regarding weekly or more *physical* bullying showed no differences (see Tables 3 and 4). These results support previous similar findings (Olweus, 1995; Salmivalli, Lappalainen et al., 2000; P. K. Smith et al., 2002) and contradict others, where girls were found to be bullied more often than boys (Genta et al., 1996; Kumpulainen et al., 1998) and boys found victimized more frequently than girls (O'Moore et al., 1997; Siann et al., 1994).

TABLE 4. Frequency and Type of Bullying at Middle Schools by Gender (N = 68)

Types of Bullying	Males (n = 30)					Females (n = 38)				
	Has Not Happened in Past 3 Months Freq. (%)	Happened Only Once or Twice Freq. (%)	Happened 2-3 Times a Month Freq. (%)	Happened About Once a Week Freq. (%)	Happened Several Times a Week Freq. (%)	Has Not Happened in Past 3 Months Freq. (%)	Happened Only Once or Twice Freq. (%)	Happened 2-3 Times a Month Freq. (%)	Happened About Once a Week Freq. (%)	Happened Several Times a Week Freq. (%)
Called Mean Names, Made Fun of, or Teased	10(33.3)	15(50.0)	2(6.7)	2(6.7)	1(3.3)	8(21.1)	18(47.4)	0(0.0)	5(13.2)	7(18.4)
Excluded or Ignored by Others	20 (66.7)	5 (16.7)	1 (3.3)	0 (0.0)	4 (13.3)	18 (47.4)	16 (42.1)	1 (2.6)	0 (0.0)	3 (7.9)
Hit, Kicked, Shoved, or Assaulted	21 (70.0)	6 (20.0)	1 (3.3)	1 (3.3)	1 (3.3)	27 (71.1)	8 (21.1)	1 (2.6)	2 (5.3)	0 (0.0)
Others Told Lies or Spread False Rumors	12 (40.0)	14 (46.7)	3 (10.0)	1 (3.3)	0 (0.0)	11 (28.9)	17 (44.7)	5 (13.2)	3 (7.9)	2 (5.3)
Had Money or Items Taken or Damaged	21 (70.0)	8 (26.7)	0 (0.0)	0 (0.0)	1 (3.3)	28 (73.7)	7 (18.4)	1 (2.6)	2 (5.3)	0 (0.0)
Threatened or Forced to Do Things	29 (96.7)	1 (3.3)	0 (0.0)	0 (0.0)	0 (0.0)	30 (78.9)	5 (13.2)	1 (2.6)	1 (2.6)	1 (2.6)
Heard Comments or Called Names based on Race or Color	25 (83.3)	3 (10.0)	1 (3.3)	1 (3.3)	0 (0.0)	33 (86.8)	2 (5.3)	1 (2.6)	0 (0.0)	2 (5.3)
Bullied with Sexual Comments, Names, or Gestures	21 (70.0)	8 (26.7)	1 (3.3)	0 (0.0)	0 (0.0)	23 (60.5)	10 (26.3)	2 (5.3)	2 (5.3)	1 (2.6)
Bullied in Other Ways	22 (73.3)	7 (23.3)	0 (0.0)	1 (3.3)	0 (0.0)	25 (67.6)	8 (21.6)	1 (2.7)	2 (5.4)	1 (2.7)

Threatening Bully-Victimization

Weekly or more, *threatening* (threatened or forced to do things) victimization, in males and females, declined in middle school (3%) from elementary school (6%) supporting the preliminary assertion that overt abusive bullying lessens as students age (Nansel et al., 2001). However, when looking at gender/grade level differences, a more descriptive picture emerges; almost twice as many males self reported weekly or more threatening victimization than females (9% and 5%, respectively) in elementary school (see Table 3). Yet, in middle school, weekly or more victimization by threats remained stable for females (5%), while males self reported none (see Table 4). This finding is significant as it contradicts a common theme in preliminary bully-victim research that males experience greater frequencies of overt bullying than females (Batsche & Knoff, 1994; Vernberg et al., 1999), and that the number of bully-victims decrease with age (Salmivalli, Lappalainen et al., 2000). It suggests that females in this study were exposed to chronic, weekly or more, overt bullying-victimization in comparison to males.

Relational Bully-Victimization

Weekly, or more, *relational* (or verbal) victimization (e.g., being called mean names or teased) remained a stable weekly or more self-report (see Table 1) in elementary (26%) and middle school (22%) students. This disagrees with Borg (1999) and Boulton and Underwood's (1992) findings that verbal bully-victimization tends to increase as children age.

When looking at gender and age/grade issues (see Table 3), both the male (25%) and female (26%) elementary school students expressed similar weekly or more occurrences of relational bullying. However, in middle school (see Table 4), males (10%) reported considerably less weekly or more *relational* bullying than females (32%), agreeing with Olweus (1993) and Hoover et al. (1992) that females are exposed to greater verbal bullying experiences than males.

Weekly or more, other relational victimization, such as, *exclusion* declined in middle school self report (10%) from elementary school (19%) students (see Table 1). Interestingly, the male's description of weekly or more exclusion frequency did not change from elementary school to middle school (14% and 13%, respectively, see Table 3 and 4) in comparison to the females, which declined (23% and 7%, respectively) considerably.

IN CONCLUSION

In this study, elementary school males and females described a disconcerting picture of relational (verbal), threatening, and physical bully-victimization exposure that, overall, appeared to decline in middle school; supporting several studies that younger youth experience a greater prevalence of bully-victimization that appears to decline in frequency as children age (Nansel et al., 2001; Peterson & Rigby, 1999). Explanations for this circumstance propose that younger children may understand bullying in a different way than older youth, that younger youth are naturally exposed to scores of older and stronger youth who have the opportunity to bully, or, that younger youth lack effective social interaction skills (P.K. Smith & Madsen, 1999).

The current findings also identified concerns relating to gender, age, and type of bullying experience. Namely, females may be chronically exposed to *threatening* and *physical* bully-victimization frequencies that males do not experience (see Graph 1). Second, males may experience consistent types of relational bullying (exclusion) that is different from females, in opposition to a frequent theme that males do not experience *relational* bullying as females do (Batsche & Knoff, 1994).

Effects of Chronic Bully-Victimization on Youth

Chronic bully-victimization is associated with higher levels of depressive symptoms and lower levels of self-esteem in youth (Egan & Perry, 2001; Kochenderfer & Ladd, 1997). Academically, victims often report feeling insecure and abandoned by school officials (Olweus, 1994), and perceive their school experience as fearful (Roberts & Coursol, 1996). The covert or 'psychological' types of bully-victimization that females are proposed to experience more than males is described as much more destructive than *physical* bullying and may cause children to choose to not attend school because of debilitating fear (Olweus, 1991). This decision affects the student's intellectual achievement in addition to social development (Crick & Brotpeter, 1995). For example, in late elementary to early middle school, youth are working towards developing a cohesive ego identity. Bully-victimization can severely interfere with this developmental effort (Cleary, 2000) in both males and females (Crick & Brotpeter, 1995).

PREVENTION AND INTERVENTION

Teachers and parents report being generally unaware of the extent and the problems caused by bullying behavior (Charach & Pepler, 1995). School professionals will often state that they have no confirmation of bullying and are found to intervene in only 4% of bullying cases (O'Connell, Pepler, & Craig, 1999). In many instances, bullying is ignored and even tolerated by educators (O'Connell et al., 1999). Only a small percentage of students believe that a school professional would solve their bullying problem and most students feel that school staff intervention would be useless (Charach & Pepler, 1995).

It is crucial to raise the awareness level of school personnel, children, and parents regarding the negative consequences (e.g., other violent behaviors) of bullying (Espelage & Swearer, 2003). School administrators and teachers need additional data on the prevalence and types of bullying behaviors to understand the magnitude of the problem and to design effective interventions. Educators must then be willing to intervene when bullying occurs. Intervention by adults in bully/victim conflicts is crucial (Espelage & Swearer, 2003).

A comprehensive system level prevention effort should begin with a school wide survey to assess the extent of the bullying problem (Olweus, 1994). Selecting a working group for bullying prevention and a coordinator of core curriculum activities is suggested for the success of the program (Garrity & Jens, 1997). Once awareness of the extent of bullying problem occurs, staff training may be required for effective intervention.

When developing programs to address bullying behaviors, it is important to consider three criteria: the program should be supported by research, based on sound behavior principles, and focused on skills training for teaching pro-social behaviors to replace the existing bullying behaviors (Garrity & Jens, 1997). The most effective programs are all-inclusive in scope and include awareness and involvement by all concerned (Garrity & Jens, 1997). Some programs teach assertiveness skills to victims, and provide family counseling for the bully's family (Garrity & Jens, 1997). Since group treatment is not effective for bullies, teaching self-control skills and empathy for others, and incorporating sanctions that include loss of privileges for breaking the rules is essential (Garrity & Jens, 1997). An additional component is bringing the bully and the victim together to resolve their conflicts in a Shared Concern method (Garrity & Jens, 1997).

Schools have a responsibility to protect students while they are at school and to provide age appropriate programs aimed at reducing victimization (Fitzpatrick & Boldizar, 1993). Safety and order are necessary for children's social, emotional, and academic development. Once school professionals become aware of the prevalence of bullying behaviors, and how to intervene effectively, children will be more willing to report the bullying incidents they witness (Clarke & Kiselic, 1997). The school environment that is positive and supportive of students while nurturing a sense of belonging and connection to the school is on its way to preventing bully-victimization (Clarke & Kiselic, 1997).

REFERENCES

Andreou, E. (2001). Bully/Victim problems and their association with coping behavior in conflictual peer interactions among school-age children. Educational Psychology, 12 (1), 59-66.

Austin, S., & Joseph, S. (1996). Assessment of bully/victim problems in 8 to 11 year-olds. British Journal of Educational Psychology, 66 (Pt 4), 447-456.

Baldry, A. C., & Farrington, D. P. (1998). Parenting influences on bullying and victimization. Legal and Criminological Psychology, 3 (2), 237-254.

Batsche, G. M., & Knoff, H. M. (1994). Bullies and their victims: Understanding a pervasive problem in the schools. School Psychology Review, 23 (2), 165-174.

Berthold, K., & Hoover, J. (2000). Correlates of bullying and victimization among intermediate students in the midwestern USA. School Psychology International, 21 (1), 65-79.

Bond, L., Carlin, J. B., Thomas, L., Rubin, K., & Patton, G. (2001). Does bullying cause emotional problems? A prospective study of young teenagers. British Medical Journal, 323 (7311), 480-484.

Borg, M. G. (1999). The extent and nature of bullying among primary and secondary school children. Educational Research, 41, 137-153.

Boulton, M. J. (1994). The extent and nature of bullying among primary and secondary schoolchildren. British Journal of Developmental Psychology, 12, 315-329.

Boulton, M. J., & Underwood, K. (1992). Bully/victim problems among middle school children. British Journal of Educational Psychology, 62 (Pt 1), 73-87.

Cavendish, R., & Salomone, C. (2001). Bullying and sexual harassment in the school setting. *Journal School Nursing, 17*(1), 25-31.

Charach, A., & Pepler, D. (1995). Bullying at school. *Educationa Canada, 35* (1), 12-19.

Clarke, E. A., & Kiselic, M. S. (1997). A systematic counseling approach to the problem of bullying. *Elementary School Guidanance & Counseling, 31* (4), 310-326.

Cleary, S. D. (2000). Adolescent victimization and associated suicidal and violent behaviors. *Adolescence, 35* (140), 671-682.

Cowie, H. (2000). Bystanding or standing by: Gender issues in coping with bullying in English schools. *Aggressive Behavior, 26* (1), 85-97.

Crick, N. R., Bigbee, M. A., & Howes, C. (1996). Gender differences in children's normative beliefs about aggression: how do I hurt thee? Let me count the ways. *Child Development, 67* (3), 1003-1014.

Crick, N. R., & Brotpeter, J. K. (1995). Relational aggresion, gender, and social-psychological adjustment. *Child Development, 66* (3), 710-722.

Crick, N. R., Casas, J. F., & Ku, H. C. (1999). Relational and physical forms of peer victimization in preschool. *Developmental Psychology, 35* (2), 376-385.

Dake, J. A., Price, J. H., & Telljohann, S. K. (2003). The nature and extent of bullying at school. *J Sch Health, 73* (5), 173-180.

Egan, S. K., & Perry, D. G. (2001). Gender identity: a multidimensional analysis with implications for psychosocial adjustment. *Dev Psychol, 37* (4), 451-463.

Espelage, D. L., & Swearer, S. M. (2003). Research on school bullying and victimization: What have we learned and were do we go from here? *School Psychology Review, 32* (3), 365-384.

Fitzpatrick, K. M., & Boldizar, J. P. (1993). The prevalence and consequences of exposure to violence among African-American youth. *J Am Acad Child Adolesc Psychiatry, 32* (2), 424-430.

Galen, B. R., & Underwood, M. K. (1997). A developmental investigation of social aggression among children. *Developmental Psychology, 33* (4), 589-600.

Garrity, C., & Jens, K. (1997). Bully proofing your school: Creating a positive climate. *Intervention in School and Clinic, 32* (4), 235-244.

Genta, M. L., Menesini, R., Fonzi, A., & ACostabile, A. e. a. (1996). Bullies and victims in schools in central and southern Italy. *European Journal of Psychology of Education, 11* (1), 97-110.

Hawker, D. S., & Boulton, M. J. (2000). Twenty year's research on peer victimization and psychosocial maladjustment: a meta-analytic review of cross-sectional studies. *Journal of Child Psychology Psychiatry and Allied Disciplines, 41* (4), 441-455.

Hoover, J. H., Oliver, R., & Hazler, J. (1992). Bullying: Perceptions of adolescent victims in the Midwestern USA. *School Psychology International, 13* (1), 5-15.

Kochenderfer, B. J., & Ladd, G. W. (1997). Victimized children's responses to peer's aggression: behaviors associated with reduced versus continued victimization. *Dev Psychopathol, 9* (1), 59-73.

Kumpulainen, K., Rasanen, E., Henttonen, I., Almqvist, F., Kresanov, K., Linna, S. L., et al. (1998). Bullying and psychiatric symptoms among elementary school-age children. *Child Abuse Negl, 22* (7), 705-717.

Kumpulainen, K., Rasanen, E., & Puura, K. (2001). Psychiatric disorders and the use of mental health services among children involved in bullying. *Aggressive Behavior, 27*, 102-110.

Menesini, E., Eslea, M., Smith, P. K., Genta, M. L., et al., (1997). Cross-national comparison of children's attitudes towards bully/victim problems in schools. *Aggressive Behavior, 23* (4), 245-257.

Nansel, T. R., Overpeck, M., Pilla, R. S., Ruan, W. J., Simons-Morton, B., & Scheidt, P. (2001). Bullying behaviors among US youth: prevalence and association with psychosocial adjustment. *Journal of American Medical Association, 285* (16), 2094-2100.

Noaks, J., & Joaks, L. (2000). Violence in school: Risk, safety and fear of crime. *Educational Psychology in Practice, 16* (1), 69-73.

O'Connell, P., Pepler, D., & Craig, W. (1999). Peer involvement in bullying: insights and challenges for intervention. *J Adolesc, 22* (4), 437-452.

Olweus, D. (1986). The Olweus Bully/Victim Questionnaire. Mimeo. Bergen, Norway: University of Bergen.

Olweus, D. (1993). *Bullying at school: What we know and what we can do.* Oxford, England: Blackwell Publishers, Inc.

Olweus, D. (1994). Bullying at school: Basic facts and effects of a school based intervention program. *Journal of Child Psychology & Psychiatry & Allied Disciplines, 35* (7), 1171-1190.

Olweus, D. (1995). Bullying or peer abuse at school: Facts and interventions. *Current Directions in Psychological Science, 4*, 196-200.

Olweus, D. (1998). Bully/victim problems in school: Knowledge base and an effective intervention program. *Irish Journal of Psychology, 18* (2), 1997.

Olweus, D. (Ed.). (1991). *Bully/victim problems among school children: Basic facts and effects of a school-based intervention program.* Hillsdale, N.J.: Er;bai,.

O'Moore, A. M., & Kirkham, C. (2001). Self-esteem and its relationship to bullying behavior. *Aggressive Behavior, 27*, 269-283.

O'Moore, A. M., Kirkham, C., & Smith, M. (1997). Bullying behavior in Irish schools: A nationwide stud. *Irish Journal of Psychology, 18* (2), 141-169.

Perry, D. G., Kusel, S., & Perry, L. (1988). Victims of peer aggression. *Developmental Psychology, 24* (6), 807-814.

Peterson, L., & Rigby, K. (1999). Countering bullying at an australian secondary school with students as helpers. *Journal of Adolescence, 22* (4), 481-492.

Rivers, I., & Smith, P. K. (1994). Types of bullying behavior and their correlates. *Aggressive Behavior, 20* (5), 359-368.

Roberts, W. B., & Coursol, D. H. (1996). Strategies for intervention with childhood adolescent victims of bullying, teasing, and intimidation in school settings. *Elementary School Guidance & Counseling, 30*, 201-212.

Salmivalli, C., Kaukiainen, A., & Lagerspetz, K. (2000). Aggression and sociometric status among peers: do gender and type of aggression matter? *Scandinavian Journal of Psychology, 41* (1), 17-24.

Salmivalli, C., Lappalainen, M., & Lagerspetz, K. M. (2000). Stability and change of behavior in connection with bullying in schools: A two year follow up. *Aggressive Behavior, 24* (3), 205-218.

Salmon, G., James, A., & Smith, D. M. (1998). Bullying in schools: Self-reported anxiety, depression, and self esteem in secondary school children. *British Medical Journal, 317*, 924-925.

Siann, G., Callaghan, M., Glissov, P., Lockhart, R., & al., e. (1994). Who gets bullied? The effect of school, gender and ethnic group. *Educational Research, 36* (2), 123-134.

Smith, P. K., Cowie, H., Olafsson, R. F., Liefooghe, A. P., Almeida, A., Araki, H., et al. (2002). Definitions of bullying: a comparison of terms used, and age and gender differences, in a fourteen-country international comparison. *Child Development, 73* (4), 1119-1133.

Smith, P. K., & Madsen, K. C. (1999). What causes the ge decline in reportes of being bullied at school? Towards a developmental. *Educational Research, 41* (3), 267-286.

Tomas de Almeida, A. M. (1999). Portugal. In P. K. Smith, Y. Morita, J. Junger_Tas, D. Olweus, R. Catalano & P. Slee (Eds.), *The nature of school bullying: A cross-national perspective* (pp. 174-186). London: Routledge.

Vernberg, E. M., Jacobs, A. K., & Hershberger, S. L. (1999). Peer victimization and attitudes about violence during early adolescence. *Journal of Clinical Child Psychology, 28* (3), 386-395.

Vettenburg, N. (1999). Belgium. In P. K. Smith, Y. Morita, J. Junger-Tas, R. C. D. Olweus & P. Slee (Eds.), *The Nature of School Bullying: A cross-national perspective* (pp. 187-204). London: Routledge.

Wolke, D., Woods, S., Bloomfield, L., & Karstadt, L. (2001). Bullying involvement in primary school and common health problems. *Arch Dis Child, 85* (3), 197-201.

School Personnel's Observations of Bullying and Victimization Among Rural Elementary and Middle School Children

Ray J. Thomlison, PhD
Barbara Thomlison, PhD
Karen M. Sowers, PhD
Matthew T. Theriot, PhD
Catherine N. Dulmus, PhD

SUMMARY. School bullying and aggression is recognized as a public health problem and appears to be the most prevalent form of school vio-

---

Ray J. Thomlison is Professor and Director, School of Social Work, Criminal Justice, and Policy Administration, Barbara Thomlison is Professor and Director the Institute for Children & Families at Risk, School of Social Work, Florida International University.

Karen M. Sowers is Dean, Matthew T. Theriot is affiliated with the College of Social Work, Catherine N. Dulmus is an Associate Professor, College of Social Work, University of Tennessee.

Address correspondence to: Ray J. Thomlison, PhD, Director, School of Social Work, Criminal Justice, and Policy Administration, Florida International University, University Park, 11200 SW 8th Street, ECS Room 457, Miami, FL, 33199 (E-mail: thomlisr@fiu.edu).

The authors would like to gratefully acknowledge the contributions of Pamela Jinks and David Dupper to the project.

[Haworth co-indexing entry note]: "School Personnel's Observations of Bullying and Victimization Among Rural Elementary and Middle School Children." Thomlison, Ray J. et al. Co-published simultaneously in *Journal of Evidence-Based Social Work* (The Haworth Social Work Practice Press, an imprint of The Haworth Press, Inc.) Vol. 1, No. 2/3, 2004, pp. 25-43; and: *Kids and Violence: The Invisible School Experience* (ed: Catherine N. Dulmus and Karen M. Sowers) The Haworth Social Work Practice Press, an imprint of The Haworth Press, Inc., 2004, pp. 25-43. Single or multiple copies of this article are available for a fee from The Haworth Document Delivery Service [1-800-HAWORTH, 9:00 a.m. - 5:00 p.m. (EST). E-mail address: docdelivery@haworthpress.com].

http://www.haworthpress.com/web/JEBSW

Digital Object Identifier: 10.1300/J394v1n02_03

lence in elementary and middle schools (Olweus, 1993). Bullying behavior among peers has detrimental effects for the bully and the victim as well as others who witness it. Research has shown that children who are involved in school bullying or are victims are at risk of developing problems later in life (Craig, Peters, & Konarski, 1998; Farrington, 1993). The problem is often exacerbated by the fact that family, school and peer culture do not recognize bullying behavior. This paper reports on analysis of data from a community sample of 70 school personnel in three rural elementary and middle schools to better understand the sources and types of bullying occurring as part of a pilot project on prevention of school violence. Transforming the family, school, and destructive peer culture is an important step in intervening and modifying the bullying behaviors. Effective intervention programs are identified.

KEYWORDS. Bullying, victimization, school personnel, violence in schools, school and peer culture

Children are among the most highly victimized segments of the population and they suffer much victimization during childhood by bullies at school (Finkelhor & Hashima, 2001; Luster, Small, & Lower, 2002). National survey research suggests that school bullying and aggressive behavior is thought to be one of the causes of violence in school settings and a problem of cross-cultural concern (Craig & Pepler, 1995; Olweus, 1993; 1994; 1996; Perry, Kusel, & Perry, 1988; Rigby & Slee, 1991; Whitney & Smith, 1993). The extent to which victims report school bullying occurring weekly or more frequently ranges from 5-15 per cent of elementary school children and 10-20 per cent of adolescents in high school (Farrington, 1993; Kaltiala-Heino, Rimpela, Rantanen, & Rimpela, 2000). Up to 96% of elementary students surveyed reported witnessing multiple instances of harassment and bullying at school each year (Smith & Sprague, 2000). In the same survey (Smith & Sprague, 2000) 86% of elementary school children reported being harassed or bullied at school over the year. Similarly, school principals, in a national survey of school violence (Heaviside et al., 1998), report physical fights between students as the most pressing discipline issue in middle schools (35%) and somewhat less of a concern by principals in elementary schools (18%).

Many individuals do not recognize the full range of bullying and harassment behaviors as detrimental and therefore cannot identify these factors as contributing to the development of aggressive and antisocial behavior in childhood. These behaviors are not normal or natural developmental behaviors and interactions in peer and social situations (Craig, Peters, & Konarski, 1998), although often the bullying behavior is made to look social in nature (Smith & Sprague, 2000). School bullying and aggression appears to be the most prevalent form of school violence in elementary schools (Olweus, 1993) and occurs in nonclassroom spaces such as hallways, playgrounds, lunchrooms, and entrance/exit areas (Meyer, Astor, & Behre, 2004). These are locations where adult surveillance is low and few people may observe it.

Bullying behavior has detrimental effects for both the bully and the victim. Research has shown that children who are involved in school bullying or are victims are at risk of developing problems in later in life (Craig, Peters, & Konarski, 1998; Farrington, 1993). Delinquencies, criminality, antisocial behavior, school failure and drop out, with suicide being one of the most drastic repercussions; as well as unemployment, depression, anxiety, and reduced attainment and competence in adulthood are some of the problems that result from being bullied or victimized by bullies (Craig, Peters, & Konarski, 1998; Finkelhor & Hashima, 2001; Fonzi et al., 1999; Riittakerttu, Rimplela, Rantanen, & Gimpela, 2000). The outcomes of bullying behavior are considered to be serious with 60% of boys having at least one criminal conviction, and 40% having three or more arrests by age 24 (Olweus, 1991; Committee for Children, 2001). Craig et al. (1998) state "there is little overlap in these children so that, bullies are not victims at other times and victims tend not to bully others" (pg. 3). More boys are bullies than girls, and more girls report victimization than boys (Craig, Peters, & Konarski, 1998; Finkelhor & Hashima, 2001).

BULLYING BEHAVIORS

Bullying behavior can take many forms. Although numerous definitions of bullying have been developed, bullying among children is commonly defined as repeated, negative acts committed by one or more children against another. It is a form of aggressive behavior involving coercions, intimation, and threats to one's safety or well being (Walker, Colvin, & Ramsey, 1995). These aggressive and anti-social negative acts may be direct physical or verbal actions (overt behaviors), and/or indirect actions (covert behaviors), physical and verbal actions, such as the destruction of property, anonymous thefts, lying, manipulation of friendships, gossip, and the exclusion from groups and friendships (social bullying), and more often are subtle and concealed actions excluding victims from activities (Olweus, 1991). Direct forms of bullying behavior include physical aggression (e.g., kicking, hitting, taking or damaging belongings); verbal aggression (e.g., name-calling, insulting, repeated teasing, racist remarks, verbal assaults meant to cause mental or emotional stress). Indirect forms of bullying include psychological and verbal forms of attack such as intimidation (e.g., spreading nasty rumours, threatening; actively alienating or isolating someone from social groups).

Bullying involves an imbalance of power, is repeated over time and is intended to cause harm or fear to the victim (Farrington, 1993). When bullying is repeated over time, the bully acquires power over the victim and the behaviors become entrenched, resulting in the victim feeling distress and fear. Those witnessing or observing the victimization are also victims and may experience distress and fear like the victim (Ziegler & Pepler, 1993). Research by Olweus (1994) concluded that bullies are aggressive and physically dominant, perceive themselves as dominant, and feel little empathy with victims.

BULLYING BEHAVIOR AND SCHOOL PERSONNEL

Bullying involves various persons: the perpetrators, victims, and bystanders. The problem of school bullying persists because it is further exacerbated by the fact that school personnel frequently do not recognize bullying behaviours. School personnel are much more likely to respond to physical bullying–that which can be seen. Other forms of bullying such as verbal and emotional bullying (e.g., rejection, taunting, humiliation, and teasing) can be tolerated by school staff because these behaviours are often made to appear "social" in nature. Commonly, adults view bullying and aggressive behavior as "normal" development for boys and girls (Smith & Sprague, 2000). Brendtro (2001) reports that teachers identified bullying behavior but intervened in only one out of 25 (4%) episodes of verbal or emotional bullying. Students report that adults intervene in fewer than 5% of the bullying episodes on playgrounds (Craig & Pepler, 1996). Craig and Pepler (1996) reported that teachers thought they intervened in 70% of the bullying episodes they observed in the playground but in reality they only intervened in 4% of the incidents the researchers recorded on videotape. Similarly, other students are hesitant to intervene or report these incidents to school officials or adults.

Longitudinal studies suggest that conflict with peers, bullying, relational aggression, and physical aggression first begins in preschool (Crick, Casas, & Mosher, 1997) and persists through elementary (Smith & Levan, 1995), middle (Boulton & Smith, 1994; Olweus, 1993), and secondary school years (Whitney & Smith, 1993). Family conditions are thought to contribute to bullying and aggressive behavior. Parenting practices and family management such as poor parent-child interactions, inflexible or inconsistent rules, and aggressive and bullying behaviors lead to the development of aggressive behaviour problems in children (Craig, Peters, & Konarski, 1998; Loeber, Stouthamer-Loeber, 1986; Patterson, Reid, & Dishion, 1992). When both the school and family environments support these behaviors, this then sets in motion the initiation, escalation, and continuation of these behaviors. Then the consequence of not intervening can be serious over time as the likelihood of escalating bullying and aggressional behaviours increases risk of repeated victimization. Bullying behaviours that children learn, practice, and experience from early childhood are a potential antecedent to other forms of interpersonal violence in other relationships (Kaltiala-Heino et al., 2000). Therefore, there is a need to address this behaviour early and consistently.

Research to date has focused primarily on identifying bullying behaviours in school settings, the individual characteristics of bullies and victims and the social contexts in which bullying occurs (family, peer group school, and community). It is therefore important to understand how best to support teacher and school personnel to identify and recognize bullying and victimization among school children. Training and education is one element in the development of interventions with bullying and its unique issues and problems. Only a few intervention programs make school personnel training mandatory for delivery of an anti-bullying program. The perceptions, beliefs about their role, or responsibility to monitor and intervene in bullying victimization episodes may be a key element in reducing school bullying and victimization episodes. The aim of this study is to further explore school personnel perceptions of bullying behaviours as first steps to documenting perceptions of school bullying as a beginning to understanding how school personnel may arrive at judgments for intervention. This may provide informational assumptions for the development of further research on training for school personnel and intervention program content for positive school climate and effective anti-bullying school interventions.

METHOD

The present study utilized an exploratory research design to study school personnel perceptions and observations of bullying and victimization among rural elementary and middle school children. Data was gathered from a survey administered to a community convenience sample of school personnel in three rural elementary schools in one school district from a southeastern county in the United States. The survey instrument was designed to obtain from school personnel their observations and perceptions during the three previous months of bullying behavior among students in their school. Participation was voluntary and completely anonymous.

PARTICIPANTS

Participants were located in a county characterized by high rates of poverty as evidenced by 43% to 61% of students receiving free or reduced lunches, and 12% of the population still not having a telephone. The school district's students and employees are 98% Caucasian and the dominant culture is Appalachian.

An inclusion protocol was developed to identify the participants for the study. Inclusion criteria were as follows: (a) participants had to be employees of the school district and have contact with students enrolled in the study schools, and/or (b) participants had to be subcontracted by the school district to provide services to the student population in the study schools.

Participants were a community convenience sample of school personnel recruited from three rural public schools (an elementary school, a middle school, and a school with combined grades K-8) located within the same school district in a Southeastern rural region of the United States. School personnel were adult employees, in contact with students in the school setting and included administrators, teachers, teacher's aides, ancillary professionals (e.g., nurses, librarians, social workers, counselors), secretaries, lunchroom workers, janitors, and bus drivers.

The community sample qualities are arrayed in Table 1: School Personnel Characteristics and Bullying Experiences. A total of 70 school personnel participated in the study, representing a 33.7% response rate. A profile of the teachers and administrator participants (n = 41) shows they were 85% (n = 35) female, 14.6% (n = 6) male, and they were approximately 40 years of age and had an average of 12.6 years of experience in the education system. A profile of other school staff participants (n = 29) shows they were 75.9% (n = 22) female, 24.1% (n = 7) male, and were approximately 44 years of age and had an average of 12.3 years of experience in the education system.

MEASURE

Each participant completed the Olweus School Personnel Observation and Awareness of Bullying Between Students at School Questionnaire (Olweus, 1986), further adapted for school personnel. This revised 71-item, self-administered questionnaire included questions specific to school personnel perceptions and observations of student bullying in the school setting. For the purposes of this study the Olweus (1991) definition of bullying was provided to the participant with the questionnaire.

Bullying was defined as behaviors of a student or several students who engage in the following:

- Completely ignore or exclude a student from his or her group of friends or leave him or her out of things on purpose;
- Hit, kick, push, shove around, or lock him or her inside a room;
- Tell lies or spread false rumors about him or her or send mean notes and try to make other students dislike him or her; and
- Other hurtful things like that.

In addition, the researchers explained to participants that a student is being bullied when the above things happen over and over again, and it is difficult for the student being bullied to defend himself or herself. We further explained that bullying is when a student is teased over and over in a mean and hurtful way, but that bullying was not when teasing was done in a friendly or playful way.

DATA COLLECTION PROCEDURES

The questionnaires were introduced to school personnel during school hours in the fall of 2002. School personnel were invited to participate in the study by a member of the research team. When approached, each individual was given an envelope that included information about the study and its purpose. The envelope contained the following four items: (1) information about the study purpose and a definition of bullying used for this study, (2) a statement of informed consent indicating that only the research team would see their individual responses; information that the questionnaire was anonymous, and a form for the participants signature; (3) instructions for completing the questionnaire and a questionnaire; and (4) a self-addressed and stamped envelope to return the materials by mail directly to the principal investigator within a 2-week period. In addition, each participant was given a thank you gift of a coffee mug for participation in the study. Questionnaires were coded to protect anonymity and no personal or identifying information was included.

One week later a follow-up letter was placed in all school personnel mailboxes, emphasizing the importance of the study and encouraging participants to complete the questionnaire and other materials and mail them back.

DATA ANALYSIS

All data were coded directly from participant's responses to the specific questions asked on the survey instrument. Descriptive statistics were used to analyze the data. All categorical data are shown as frequencies and percentages. Continuous variables are reported as means ($\pm$ standard deviations). In the rare instance that study participants did not respond to any survey question, participants are excluded for that particular variable and all frequencies and percentages have been adjusted accordingly.

Survey findings are presented on Tables 1 through 5. Table 1 shows School Personnel Characteristics and Bullying Experiences divided into two groups–teachers and administrators, and other school staff and included counselors, secretaries, janitors, bus drivers, lunchroom workers, aides, and other school employees. Table 2 and Table 3 includes only those participants who reported that they have directly observed students bully other students. Table 2 presents information on the type and frequency of bullying observed, and Table 3 displays data on the location of these bullying behaviors. Table 4 and Table 5 include only those school personnel who have been made aware of bullying in the previous three months. Table 4 displays data on the type and frequency of the bullying behaviors school personnel have been made aware of. Likewise, Table 5 shows the locations of bullying behaviors.

RESULTS

Table 1, School Personnel Characteristics and Bullying Experiences shows differences between the teachers and administrators and other school staff. Three questions regarding bullying experiences of school personnel were included. Participants were asked (1) if they had directly observed students bullying other students; (2) if they had been made aware of such behavior happening at school in the previous three months; and (3) if they had been bullied at school as a child. Among the 70 study participants, 65 (93%) reported that they have directly observed or witnessed bullying between students in the previous three months, and 63 (90%) responded they have been made aware of such bullying in the previous three months.

Table 2, Frequency and Type of Bullying Directly Observed by School Personnel reveals similar findings between the two groups of participants. Specifically, the most common and frequently observed type of bullying across both groups is calling others mean names, making fun of them, or teasing. Though the ordering differs slightly, the next most common and frequently observed types of bullying are intentionally excluding or ignoring others, physically assaulting others, and maliciously spreading false rumors or lies. The least observed type of bullying is threatening or forcing others do things. This is also among the least frequently observed bullying behaviors.

While teachers and administrators recognized hallways and stairwells as the most popular location for observing bullying acts between students (64.1% of the group said they have observed bullying here), the most popular location for school staff was the lunchroom (57.7% of staff have seen bullying occur here). Also shown on Table 3, other common locations among a majority of teachers and administrators included the classroom (56.4%), the playground (53.8%), and the lunchroom (51.3%). After the lunchroom, other popular settings identi-

TABLE 1. School Personnel Characteristics and Bullying Experiences (N = 70)

Characteristics		Teachers and Administrators (n = 41) Frequency (%)or Mean ± SD	Other School Staff (n = 29) Frequency (%) or Mean ± SD
Gender			
	Male	6 (14.6)	7 (24.1)
	Female	35 (85.4)	22 (75.9)
Age		39.49 ± 10.51	44.14 ± 10.83
	Years working in an educational setting	12.60 ± 8.78	12.32 ± 10.60
	I was bullied in school when I was child.	14 (34.1)	18 (62.1)
	I have *directly observed* bullying at school in the previous three months.	39 (95.1)	26 (89.7)
	I have *been made aware of* bullying at school in the previous three months.	38 (92.7)	25 (86.2)

Column percentages may not total 100% because of rounding. SD = standard deviation

fied by a majority of school staff were hallways and stairwells (53.8%) and the classroom (53.8%).

Though not included on the tables, it is useful to report that, within the group that has directly observed bullying, twenty participants (30.8%; 15 teachers and administrators and 5 staff) said that the bullying they have observed occurred between students in the same class. An additional eight people (12.3%; 3 teachers and 5 staff) said that the bully is in a higher grade than the child being bullied. Concerning gender, fourteen teachers and administrators stated that the bullies involved in each bullying incident tended to be both boys and girls (35.9%) while seven (17.9%) said that the bully is usually one boy, five said it is a lone girl (12.8%), and five said that it is a group of several boys (12.8%). The majority of school staff (14 people; 53.8%) stated that both girls and boys bully. The next largest group (4 people; 15.4%) said that one boy is the perpetrator in the bullying that they have observed.

Along the same lines, fourteen teachers and administrators (35.9%) stated that most instances of bullying involved one bully, eleven (28.2%) said the bullying involved 2-3 bullies, and ten (25.6%) said that the bullying involved a group of 4 or more bullies or several different groups of bullies. These percentages are similar to those from members of the school's staff. In this group, eleven (42.3%) said that the bullying acts usually involved 2-3 bullies per incident, five (19.2%) said a single bully was involved in each observed incident, and eight people (30.8%) said that 4 or

TABLE 2. Frequency and Type of Bullying Directly Observed by School Personnel (N = 65)

Types of Bullying	Teachers or School Administrators (n = 39)					Other School Staff (n = 26)				
	Has Not Observed this in Past 3 Months Freq. (%)	Observed Only Once or Twice Freq. (%)	Observed 2-3 Times a Month Freq. (%)	Observed About Once a Week Freq. (%)	Observed Several Times a Week Freq. (%)	Has Not Observed this in Past 3 Months Freq. (%)	Observed Only Once or Twice Freq. (%)	Observed 2-3 Times a Month Freq. (%)	Observed About Once a Week Freq. (%)	Observed Several Times a Week Freq. (%)
Called Mean Names, Made Fun of, or Teased	1 (2.6)	11 (28.2)	12 (30.8)	8 (20.5)	7 (17.9)	2 (7.7)	9 (34.6)	2 (7.7)	7 (26.9)	6 (23.1)
Excluded or Ignored by Others	9 (23.1)	14 (35.9)	5 (12.8)	7 (17.9)	4 (10.3)	9 (36.0)	3 (12.0)	9 (36.0)	2 (8.0)	2 (8.0)
Hit, Kicked, Shoved, or Assaulted	16 (41.0)	7 (17.9)	5 (12.8)	7 (17.9)	4 (10.3)	8 (32.0)	8 (32.0)	3 (12.0)	2 (8.0)	4 (16.0)
Others told Lies or Spread False Rumors	12 (30.8)	10 (25.6)	9 (23.1)	6 (15.4)	2 (5.1)	12 (48.0)	5 (20.0)	3 (12.0)	2 (8.0)	3 (12.0)
Had Money or Items Taken or Damaged	22 (56.4)	7 (17.9)	6 (15.4)	3 (7.7)	1 (2.6)	16 (64.0)	5 (20.0)	3 (12.0)	0 (0.0)	1 (4.0)
Threatened or Forced Others to Do Things	27 (69.2)	8 (20.5)	3 (7.7)	0 (0.0)	1 (2.6)	22 (88.0)	1 (4.0)	2 (8.0)	0 (0.0)	0 (0.0)
Heard Comments or Called Names based on Race or Color	23 (59.0)	13 (33.3)	1 (2.6)	1 (2.6)	1 (2.6)	13 (52.0)	8 (32.0)	1 (4.0)	2 (8.0)	1 (4.0)
Bullied with Sexual Comments, Names, or Gestures	19 (48.7)	9 (23.1)	8 (20.5)	2 (5.1)	1 (2.6)	17 (65.4)	6 (23.1)	1 (3.8)	2 (7.7)	0 (0.0)
Bullied in Other Ways	20 (55.6)	9 (25.0)	1 (2.8)	3 (8.3)	3 (8.3)	14 (58.3)	8 (33.3)	1 (4.2)	1 (4.2)	0 (0.0)

Column percentages may not total 100% because of rounding.

TABLE 3. Location of Bullying Directly Observed by School Personnel (N = 65)

Location of Bullying	Teachers and Administrators (n = 39) Frequency (%)	Other School Staff (n = 26) Frequency (%)
On the playground/athletic field (during recess or break times)	21 (53.8)	12 (46.2)
In the hallways/stairwells	25 (64.1)	14 (53.8)
In the classroom	22 (56.4)	14 (53.8)
In the bathroom	14 (35.9)	8 (30.8)
In gym class or in the gym locker room/shower	6 (15.4)	2 (7.7)
In the lunchroom	20 (51.3)	15 (57.7)
On the way to and from school	0 (0.0)	6 (23.1)
At the school bus stop	2 (5.1)	5 (19.2)
On the school bus	1 (2.6)	7 (26.9)
Somewhere else in school	11 (28.2)	3 (11.5)

Column percentages may not total 100% because of rounding.

more bullies or multiple groups of bullies were involved. Most study participants in both groups (21 teachers and administrators and 15 staff members) responded that the bullying has tended to last 1-2 weeks.

Likewise, twenty-four (61.5%) teachers and administrators and thirteen (50.0%) school staff reported that adults at school almost always try to stop bullying when it is observed. No one responded that adults never try to stop such acts. Conversely, only two teachers (and no staff) said that other students almost always try to stop bullying that they observe. Instead, twenty-three teachers and administrators (59.0%) and nineteen (73.1%) staff members said that students try to stop the bullying of others only sometimes or once in a while. Finally, thirty-four teachers and administrators (87.2%) and twenty-two people in the school staff group (88.0%) said they feel sorry for students who they observe being bullied and they try to help the student. To this end, thirty-four teachers and administrators (88.0%) and sixteen staff (64.0%) stated that they have spoken with bullying students during the previous three months about their behavior.

Moving now to examine the bullying that school personnel have been made aware of (but not directly observed) in the previous three months, once again the most common and frequent type of bullying is the use of mean names and teasing. As shown on Table 4, among those personnel who have been made aware of bullying, 97.4% of teachers and administrators and 88.0% of school staff have been made aware of this bullying act. The other more common and frequent types of bullying include ex-

TABLE 4. Frequency and Type of Bullying that School Personnel Have Been Made Aware of (N = 63)

Types of Bullying	Teachers or School Administrators (n = 38)					Other School Staff (n = 25)				
	Has Not Observed this in Past 3 Months Freq. (%)	Observed Only Once or Twice Freq. (%)	Observed 2-3 Times a Month Freq. (%)	Observed About Once a Week Freq. (%)	Observed Several Times a Week Freq. (%)	Has Not Observed this in Past 3 Months Freq. (%)	Observed Only Once or Twice Freq. (%)	Observed 2-3 Times a Month Freq. (%)	Observed About Once a Week Freq. (%)	Observed Several Times a Week Freq. (%)
Called Mean Names, Made Fun of, or Teased	1 (2.6)	12 (31.6)	10 (26.3)	9 (23.7)	6 (15.8)	3 (12.0)	11 (44.0)	7 (28.0)	3 (12.0)	1 (4.0)
Excluded or Ignored by Others	9 (23.7)	6 (15.8)	13 (34.2)	8 (21.1)	2 (5.3)	6 (24.0)	9 (36.0)	7 (28.0)	2 (8.0)	1 (4.0)
Hit, Kicked, Shoved, or Assaulted	10 (26.3)	8 (21.1)	11 (28.9)	4 (10.5)	5 (13.2)	10 (40.0)	6 (24.0)	5 (20.0)	2 (8.0)	2 (8.0)
Others told Lies or Spread False Rumors	8 (21.1)	11 (28.9)	9 (23.7)	7 (18.4)	3 (7.9)	13 (52.0)	4 (16.0)	2 (8.0)	6 (24.0)	0 (0.0)
Had Money or Items Taken or Damaged	15 (39.5)	15 (39.5)	5 (13.2)	3 (7.9)	0 (0.0)	19 (76.0)	5 (20.0)	1 (4.0)	0 (0.0)	0 (0.0)
Threatened or Forced Others to Do Things	22 (57.9)	11 (28.9)	5 (13.2)	0 (0.0)	0 (0.0)	19 (76.0)	6 (24.0)	0 (0.0)	0 (0.0)	0 (0.0)
Heard Comments or Called Names based on Race or Color	17 (44.7)	14 (36.8)	4 (10.5)	2 (5.3)	1 (2.6)	14 (56.0)	7 (28.0)	2 (8.0)	1 (4.0)	1 (4.0)
Bullied with Sexual Comments, Names, or Gestures	15 (39.5)	9 (23.7)	10 (26.3)	2 (5.3)	2 (5.3)	16 (66.7)	5 (20.8)	3 (12.5)	0 (0.0)	0 (0.0)
Bullied in Other Ways	24 (68.6)	8 (22.9)	2 (5.7)	0 (0.0)	1 (2.9)	19 (79.2)	5 (20.8)	0 (0.0)	0 (0.0)	0 (0.0)

Column percentages may not total 100% because of rounding.

cluding or ignoring others, spreading lies and false rumors, and physically harming other students. Beyond this, there are interesting differences in the frequency of certain bullying behaviors. For example, no school staff reported being made aware of bullying that involved threatening or forcing others to do things or other unspecified forms of bullying occurring more than once or twice in a three month period. In contrast, 13.2% and 8.6% of teachers and administrators, respectively, were made aware of these behaviors occurring with greater frequency. The same differences exist for bullying that involves theft or property damage and bullying of a sexual nature.

The final table, Table 5, shows that, for staff, the most popular location of the bullying that they have been made aware of is the lunchroom (48.0%). For teachers and administrators, this location is the bathroom (73.7%). Other popular locations for both groups are the playground and athletic fields and the hallways and stairwells.

The concluding bits of data reported here are similar to those previously reported for school personnel who directly witnessed bullying between students. Among those personnel who have been made aware of bullying, ten teachers and administrators (26.3%) and five staff (20.0%) said that the bully and the bullied tend to be in the same class. Also, twenty-three teachers and administrators (60.5%) and nine staff members (36.0%) said that that have been made aware of bullying by both boys and girls. The next most common response from the teacher's group was that a single bullying boy was involved in most of the bullying instances that they were made aware of (8 people; 21.1%) while five staff (20.0%) said that several boys were to blame.

As with the bullying that was directly observed, twelve teachers and administrators (31.6%) and five staff (20.0%) reported that the bullying incidents involved one bully. Twelve people in the teacher group (31.6%) and eight staff (32.0%) said that the bullying is usually perpetrated by a group of 4 or more bullies or by several groups of students. The bullying has lasted approximately 1-2 weeks (52.4% of the total sample estimated this length of time). As a final note, twenty-eight teachers and administrators (73.7%) and ten school staff members (40.0%) said that, even though they haven't directly observed the bullying, they have spoken with students about bullying that they have been made aware of.

LIMITATIONS OF THE CURRENT RESEARCH

Although this study suggests that bullying and bullying behaviors are a serious problem in the reported schools, there are several limitations

TABLE 5. Location of Bullying that School Personnel Have Been Made Aware of (N = 63)

Location of Bullying	Teachers and Administrators (n = 38) Frequency (%)	Other School Staff (n = 25) Frequency (%; n)
On the playground/athletic field (during recess or break times)	25 (65.8)	11 (44.0)
In the hallways/stairwells	27 (71.1)	10 (40.0)
In the classroom (with teacher present)	24 (63.2)	8 (32.0)
In the classroom (with teacher absent)	17 (44.7)	6 (24.0)
In the bathroom	28 (73.7)	10 (40.0)
In gym class or in the gym locker room/shower	11 (28.9)	2 (8.0)
In the lunchroom	26 (68.4)	12 (48.0)
On the way to and from school	12 (31.6)	6 (24.0)
At the school bus stop	7 (18.4)	4 (16.0)
On the school bus	20 (52.6)	9 (36.0)
Somewhere else in school	10 (26.3)	1 (4.0)

Column percentages may not total 100% because of rounding.

evident in this study. First, a community convenience sample and a self-administered mailed survey questionnaire were used for data collection, thereby limiting the generalizability of the findings. Second, the study response rate on the mailed questionnaire is low (33.7%) and considered inadequate, thereby adding to the generalizability of the results. The relatively small size of the school sample limits generalizability of the findings. Although participants were reminded to return the questionnaire, this resulted in a smaller than anticipated sample size. It is possible participants thought the questionnaire was not relevant or possibly threatening or too sensitive. Third, the study participants were Caucasian and do no reflect the diversity of other populations in the country. Finally, the responses of the participants in the survey may not accurately represent those of school personnel in other schools or areas.

CONCLUSIONS AND RECOMMENDATIONS

It is recognized that this study cannot tell us everything we need to know about the causes of bullying and victimization, however, it does point out that bullying and aggressive and anti-social behaviours place many children who are the target of bullying at greater risk of violent behaviours. Both the bullies and the victims are likely to suffer academically and socially, and therefore, there is a need to respond early and with pro-active multidimensional approaches using a combination of individual, classroom, and school-wide strategies. It is suggested that efforts to intervene consist of targeting children, teachers, the school climate (policies and procedures), as well as families. This study focused on teachers and therefore suggestions for helping educate teachers through teacher training to identify bullying behaviours, and assist teachers to teach children positive behaviours and thereby reinforcing the students and the school community. Based on this study there is a need to conduct improved research and not rely on survey data alone. This study however, does suggest there are a number of indictors or signs that bullying behavior is observed in the student body and school personnel and students need to be sensitised to the indicators. The teacher and student relationships play a crucial role in school climate and if bullying is ignored this may have a powerful effect on learning. School administrators need to sensitize school personnel through teacher training as an integrated and a required component in anti-bullying programs to change this public health problem. Teachers will then have a greater understanding of their role and responsibilities related to bullying and the person harm, and this will allow them to become more engaged in preventing bullying behaviours and targeting violence prone locations and situations.

What can be done to reduce bullying and victimization in schools? Social policies aimed at school based interventions programs would facilitate reduction of bullying and victimization. Effective prevention and early identification programs must be identified and must require teacher and school personnel training as one focus as mentioned earlier. There are few research or evidence-based anti-bullying interventions available to schools (Center for National Crime Prevention Council, 1997; Center for the Study and Prevention of Violence *http://www.colorado.edu/cspv/blueprints/index.html*). Of those available to reduce bullying and aggressive behaviours, only two evaluations assessed a reduction in verbal bullying and only one looked at "exclusion" behaviours (for a more complete review the reader is referred to Thurston, Meadows, Tutty, & Bradshaw, 1999; *http://www.ucalgary.ca/resolve/violenceprevention/English/ reviewprog/bullyintro.htm*). Most of the interventions suggest multi-component programs, but few positive effects were found in any year and during the time of evaluation in the goals of reducing aggressive behaviours, fights at school, injuries due to fighting, being threatened, or missing classes due to feeling unsafe (see Prevention programs addressing bullying and conflict resolution, *http://www.ucalgary.ca/resolve/violenceprevention/English/reviewprog/bullyintro.htm*). See also Oregon Institute Violence and Destructive Behavior (at *http://darkwing.uoregon.edu/~ivbd/.*), for suggestions of effective programs and curricula:

1. Second Step Violence Prevention Program (available from the Committee for Children, Seattle, WA, *http://www.cfchildren.org*).
2. Steps to respect (anti-bullying program available from the Committee for Children, Seattle, WA, *http://www.cfchildren.org*).
3. Bully Proofing Your School (available from Sopris West Inc., P.O. Box 1890, Longmont, CO 80502-1809).
4. Effective Behavioral Support EEBS). (Contact George Sugai at 541.346.1642 or Rob Horner at 541.346.2460.
5. Building Effective Schools Together (BEST) (contact Jeffrey Sprague at 541.346.3592).

The goal needs to be to create a culture change in which bullying is not accepted in any context and targeting children and adults who influence this behavior. This effort must embody parents, teachers, children and youth, teachers and administrators on a continuing basis.

REFERENCES

Boulton, M. J. & Smith, P. K. (1994). Bully/victim problems in middle-school children: Stability, self perceived competence, peer perceptions and peer acceptance. *British Journal of Developmental Psychology*, 12, 315-329.

Brendtro, L. K. (2001). Worse than sticks and stones: Lesson from research on ridicule. *Reclaiming Children and Youth 10* (1), 47-49.

Center for the Study and Prevention of Violence. Blueprints Model Programs. Available on-line at http://www.colorado.edu/cspv/blueprints/index.html

Committee for Children. (2001). *http://cfchildren.org/568* First Avenue South, Suite 600, Seattle, Washington 98104-2804 | Phone: 1-800-634-4449.

Craig, W. & Pepler, D. J. (1995). Peer processes in bullying and victimization: A naturalistic study. Exceptionality Education in Canada, 4, 81-95.

Craig, W.M., Peters, D., & Konarski, R. (1998). *Bullying and victimization among Canadian school children.* Available online from Applied Research Branch, Strategic Policy, Human Resources Development Canada at *http://www.hrdc-drhc.gc.ca/arb/publications/research/abw-98-28e.shtml.*

Crick, N. R., Casas, J. F. & Mosher, M. (1997). Relational and overt aggression in preschool. *Developmental Psychology*, 33, 579-588.

Farrington, D. P. (1993). Understanding and preventing bullying. In M. Tonry & N. Morris (Eds.), *Crime and justice An annual review of research* (Vol. 17) (pp. 381-458). Chicago: University of Chicago Press.

Finkelhor, D. & Hashima, P. Y. (2001). The victimization of children and youth. A comprehensive overview. In S. O. White (Ed.) *Handbook of Youth and Justice* (pp. 49-78). New York: Kluwer Academic/Plenum.

Fonzi, A., Genta, M. L., Menesini, E., Bacchini, D., Bonino, S., & Costabile, A. (1999). Italy. In P. K. Smith, Y. Morita, J. Junger-Tas, D. Olweus, R. Catalano, & P. Slee (Eds.), *The nature of school bullying* (pp. 140-156). New York: Routledge.

Heaviside, S., Rowand, C., Williams, C., Farris, E., Burns, S., & McArthur, E. (1998). *Violence and discipline problems in U.S. public schools: 1996-1997.* (NCES-98030). Washington, DC: United States Department of Education.

Kaltiala-Heino, R., Rimplela, M., Rantanen, P. & Rimpela, A. (2000). Bullying at school-an indicator of adolescents at risk for mental disorders. *Journal of Adolescence*, 23, 661-674.

Loeber, R., & Stouthamer-Loeber, M. (1986). Family factors as correlates and predictors of juvenile conduct problems and delinquency. In N. Morris & M. Tonry (Eds.), *Crime and justice: An annual review of research*, (Vol. 17). (pp. 29-149). Chicago: University of Chicago Press.

Luster, T., Small, S. A., & Lower, R. (2002). The correlates of abuse and witnessing abuse among adolescents. Journal of Interpersonal Violence, 17 (12), 1323-1340.

Meyer, H. A., Astor, R. A., & Behre, W. J., (2004). Teacher's reasoning about school fights, contexts, and gender: an expanded cognitive developmental domain approach. *Aggression and Violent Behavior*, 9, 45-74

National Crime Prevention Council (1997). Bullying and victimization: The problems and solutions for school-aged children. Available on-line at http://www.crime-prevention.org/english/publications/children/violence/indes.html.

Olweus, D. (1986). *The Olweus Bully-Victim Questionnaire*. Mimeo. Bergen, Norway: University of Bergen.

Olweus, D. (1991). Bully/victim problems among schoolchildren: Basic facts and effects of a school based intervention program. In D. Pepler & K. Rubin (Eds.) *The development and treatment of childhood aggression* (pp. 411-448). Hillsdale, NJ: Erlbaum.

Olweus, D. (1992). Bullying among school children: Intervention and prevention. In R. DeV. Peters, R. J., McMahon & P. Quinsey (Eds.), *Aggression and violence throughout the life span* (pp. 100-125). Newbury Park, CA: Sage.

Olweus, D. (1993). *Bullying at school: What we know and what we can do.* Oxford: Blackwell.

Olweus, D. (1994). Annotation: Bullying at school: Basic facts and effects of a school based intervention program. *Journal of Child Psychology and Psychiatry*, 35, 1171-1190.

Patterson, G. R., Reid, J. B., & Dishion, T. J. (1992). *Antisocial boys*. Eugene, Oregon: Castalia.

Perry, D. G., Kusel, S. J. & Perry, L. C. (1988). Victims of peer aggression. *Developmental Psychology*, 24, 807-814.

Rigby, K. & Slee, P. (1991). Victims in school communities. *Journal of the Australian Society of Victimology*, 25-31.

Smith, P. K. & Levan, S. (1995). Perceptions and experiences of bullying in younger pupils. *British Journal of Educational Psychology*, 65, 489-500.

Smith, S. & Sprague, J. (2000). Bullying and schools: An overview of the problems. Retrieved from *http://darkwind.uoregon.edu?~ivb/index.html*. December 09, 2003.

Thurston, W. E., Meadows, L., Tutty, L. M. & Bradshaw, C. (1999). *A violence reduction health promotion model*. Unpublished manuscript available at Faculty of Medicine, Department of Family Medicine, Calgary, AB: University of Calgary, Canada. Available on line at http:www.ucalgary.ca/resolve/violenceprevention/English/reviewprog/bullyintro.htm.

Whitney, I. & Smith, P. K. (1993). A survey of the nature and extent of bullying in junior/middle and secondary schools. *Educational Research*, 35, 3-25.

Ziegler, S., & Pepler, D. J. (1993). Bullying at school: Pervasive and persistent. *Orbit, 24,* 29-31.

Kids–Parents–School Personnel: Few Are Talking and Even Less Are Listening

James A. Blackburn, PhD
Catherine N. Dulmus, PhD
Matthew T. Theriot, PhD
Karen M. Sowers, PhD

SUMMARY. Teacher awareness and a desire to create a positive environment can result in an atmosphere where caring is the norm and bullying is not tolerated. Yet, if parents and teachers are not communicating, timely and well-reasoned responses to bullying cannot be offered. This study examined communication patterns between children, parents and school personnel in regard to bullying in a rural school setting in the United States. A convenience sample of 494 individuals was surveyed. The sample included 230 parents, 72 school personnel, and 192 students. Findings indicate that school bullying has been and continues to be a serious problem, though communication between children, parents, and

---

James A. Blackburn is Dean and Professor, Hunter College, School of Social Work, 129 E. 79th Street, New York, NY 10021 (james.blackburn@hunter.cuny.edu).

Catherine N. Dulmus, (cdulmus@utk.edu), Matthew T. Theriot, (mtheriot@utk.edu), and Karen M. Sowers are affiliated with The University of Tenneseee, College of Social Work, 109 Henson Hall, Knoxville, TN 37996.

The authors would like to gratefully acknowledge the contributions of Pamela Jinks and David Dupper to the project.

[Haworth co-indexing entry note]: "Kids–Parents–School Personnel: Few Are Talking and Even Less Are Listening." Blackburn, James A. et al. Co-published simultaneously in *Journal of Evidence-Based Social Work* (The Haworth Social Work Practice Press, an imprint of The Haworth Press, Inc.) Vol. 1, No. 2/3, 2004, pp. 45-57; and: *Kids and Violence: The Invisible School Experience* (ed: Catherine N. Dulmus and Karen M. Sowers) The Haworth Social Work Practice Press, an imprint of The Haworth Press, Inc., 2004, pp. 45-57. Single or multiple copies of this article are available for a fee from The Haworth Document Delivery Service [1-800-HAWORTH, 9:00 a.m. - 5:00 p.m. (EST). E-mail address: docdelivery@haworthpress.com].

http://www.haworthpress.com/web/JEBSW

Digital Object Identifier: 10.1300/J394v1n02_04

school personnel did not reflect the reality of the bullying problem. An overview of the findings are presented, along with suggestions for interventions and future research to enhance communication patterns between all parties in an effort to eliminate school bullying.

KEYWORDS. Rural schools, communication, parents, bullying, collaboration, students

INTRODUCTION

As research on the bullying problem at U.S. schools continues to evolve, initial findings suggest that bullying victimization may be more prevalent in the U.S. than in European countries (Hoover, Oliver, & Hazler, 1992). In challenge to the myth that bullying only occurs at large urban schools, a parallel body of literature has begun to explore bullying in rural U.S. schools (Hoover, Oliver, & Hazler, 1992; Olweus, 1993; Dulmus, Theriot, Sowers, & Blackburn, 2004). Hoover and associates (1992), in a study of middle and high school students in small Midwestern U.S. towns found that 72-81% of the students were bullied at some point during their school experience. More recently, a study conducted at rural elementary and middle schools reported that 82% of the students said they were bullied in a three-month period (Dulmus, Theriot, Sowers, & Blackburn, 2004). In light of results such as these, some have concluded that school bullying may be as big or bigger a problem in rural areas than in larger cities and more urban areas (Hoover, Oliver, & Hazler, 1992; Olweus, 1993; Clarke & Kiselica, 1997; Dulmus et al., 2004).

Olweus (1993) has hypothesized that a lack of communication about bullying contributes to these problems in rural areas. In his study of school bullying in Norway, Olweus found that teachers and parents in "big-city" schools talked more often with students about bullying problems than their rural counterparts. Olweus concluded that "big-city" schools have a somewhat greater awareness of bullying problems than schools outside of urban areas.

While research has yet to expand upon Olweus' conclusion in relation to rural schools, other studies have explored school communication and awareness about bullying. For example, Boulton (1997) surveyed 138 teachers working in settings that ranged from preschool to high school. He found that, while teachers considered a wide range of behaviors to be bullying, there was greater consensus that physical aggression or the threat of violence constituted bullying compared to less agreement about such behaviors as "intentionally leaving people out" or "laughing at people." Similarly, Hazler, Miller, Carney, and Green (2001) discovered that teachers and school counselors considered physical aggression to be far more serious than social or emotional bullying.

Despite recognizing the seriousness of such aggression, though, students who have been bullied believe that teachers do not respond to bullying when they see it (Roberts & Coursol, 1996). Instead, teachers only intervene in approximately 4% of such episodes (O'Connell, Pepler, & Craig, 1999). In another, more generous estimate, adults only intervened with bullying acts one half of the time in elementary school and only one third of the time in a high school setting (Whitney & Smith, 1993). Such low rates of intervention may signify a lack of sympathy from teachers, especially teachers with lengthy school experience. After all, Boulton (1996; 1997) found that school personnel's sympathy for victims diminished as their years of service increased. Yet, this lack of intervention may also result because school personnel are not able to differentiate physical acts of bullying from playful fighting. In two separate studies, Boulton found that adults in general (1993) and lunchtime supervisors in particular (1996) often confused bullying with play fighting. This was especially true for adult males (Boulton, 1993).

Of course, bullying is often done covertly or secretly. The lack of intervention from school personnel may result then because personnel aren't aware of bullying that occurs. This position is supported by research demonstrating that bullying problems decrease as the level of adult supervision increases (Olweus, 1993; Espelage, Bosworth, & Simon, 2000).

Regardless, parents feel secure when they have confidence that their children are safe and that school staff know how to intervene when bullying problems occur (Garrity & Jens, 1997). Yet, teachers do not feel confident in their ability to deal with bullying and many teachers express a strong desire for more training on this topic (Boulton, 1997). In response, several studies have proposed comprehensive school-based interventions to address bullying (Garrity & Jens, 1997; Clarke & Kiselica, 1997; Garrett, 2001). These interventions usually include a training component for school personnel and a strong emphasis on engaging school personnel, parents, bullies, victims, and other students in open communication and discussions about bullying.

This involvement of parents and other adults is a critical component of any multisystemic intervention. Parent involvement in school education has been shown to have positive impacts on learning outcomes (Sammons, Hillman, & Mortimer, 1995; Pang and Watkins, 2000). Furthermore, a study conducted by Pang and Watkins (2000) indicated the importance of parent teacher communication to alleviate bullying among students. Communication allows both teachers and parents to exchange ideas and information about the development of students at home and at school.

According to Strom and Strom (2003), when teachers identify changes they believe are needed to ensure more appropriate behavior in class, the factor they mention most frequently is parent involvement (p. 165). When students misbehave at school, parental guidance is essential since they are responsible for teaching basic morals, civic behavior, and a healthy work ethic (Strom & Strom, 2003). Parents can help by asking their child if someone is bothering them in school, coaching them in assertiveness skills, and instructing them not to hit back as it often makes things worse for the victim (Saunders, 1997).

Garrett (2001) states that, "classroom teachers are the key to school efforts to reduce bullying" (p. 83). Teacher awareness and a desire to create a positive environment can result in an atmosphere where caring is the norm and bullying is not tolerated. Yet, if parents and teachers are not communicating, timely and well-reasoned responses to bullying cannot be offered. Without the combining efforts of parents and teachers, emotional and social needs of adolescents go unmet (McCarty, 2000; Strom & Strom, 2003).

To date, however, no known interventions have been designed specific to improving multisystemic communication in rural schools. This may result from a lack of knowledge about the existing lines of communication at these locations. With a better understanding of communication at rural school settings, interventions can be designed that build upon the strengths of rural schools while targeting areas that need improvement. As a first attempt to further the knowledge base on this topic, this study will explore communication issues in rural schools with special attention towards identifying areas that should be targeted for intervention and improvement.

METHODOLOGY

Study Design

This study utilized a survey research design to gather information from students, parents, and school personnel as to bullying occurring within the school setting between students. This article focuses on questions related to communication between students, parents, and school personnel related to behaviors of bullying occurring in the school. The IRB at a large research university in the Southeastern United States granted permission to conduct the research prior to the start of the project. Informed consent was obtained for all subjects whose participation was voluntary and confidential.

Study Sample

The sample consisted of students and their parents, as well as school personnel recruited from three rural public schools (an elementary school, a middle school, and a school that housed grades K-8) located within the same school district in a Southeastern rural region of the United States. School personnel were adult employees having contact with students in the school setting that included administrators, teachers, teacher's aides, ancillary professionals (e.g., nurses, librarians, social workers, counselors), secretaries, lunchroom workers, janitors, and bus drivers. The school district is located in a county characterized by high rates of poverty as evidenced by 43% to 61% of students receiving free or reduced lunches and 12% of the population still not having a telephone. The school district employees and students are 98% Caucasian and the dominate culture is Appalachian.

Ultimately, the convenience sample consisted of 192 students, 230 parents, and 72 school personnel. Data collection occurred in the fall of 2002. Since all subjects were measured at one point in time, no follow-up was necessary. Thus, attrition was not problematic.

Inclusion criteria for students were as follows: (a) subjects had to be students enrolled in the school where data collection occurred, and (b) subjects had to be in grades three through eight. Inclusion criteria for parents were as follows: (a) subjects had to be a parent of a student enrolled in the school where data collection occurred, and (b) subjects were parents of children in grades three through eight. Lastly, inclusion criteria for school personnel were: (a) subjects had to be an employee of the school district who had contact with students enrolled in the study schools, and/or (b) subjects had to be subcontracted by the school district to provide services to the student population in the study schools. Informed consent was obtained for each subject prior to their participating in the study. In addition, written parental consent was obtained for each student subject and all children completed an individual assent form.

Measures

Student subjects completed the Olweus Bully/Victim Questionnaire (Olweus, 1999). This 56-item, self-administered questionnaire, designed for grades 3 through 10, asks questions specific to student's victimization and/or participation in various aspects of bullying in the school setting during the previous three months. Each school personnel subject completed the Olweus School Personnel Observation and Awareness of Bullying Between Students at School Questionnaire (Olweus, 1999) that was further adapted for this study. This revised 71-item, self-administered questionnaire included questions specific to school personnel's perceptions and observations of student bullying in the school setting. Parent subjects completed an 11-item self-administered questionnaire designed specifically for this study that focused primarily on communication between parents, students, and school related to bullying in the school setting. All subjects were assured of the confidentiality of their responses throughout the study. There were minimal physical, psychological, legal, or social risks for participants. To ensure confidentiality and protection of subjects they were instructed not to put their names or any identifying information on the questionnaires.

For the purposes of this study and as per the Olweus questionnaire, we defined and explained bullying to all subjects as being when a student, or several other students do the following:

- completely ignore or exclude him or her from their group of friends or leave him or her out of thing on purpose
- hit, kick, push, shove around, or lock him or her inside a room
- tell lies or spread false rumors about him or her or send mean notes and try to make other students dislike him or her
- and other hurtful things like that

In addition, we explained that a student is being bullied when the above things happen over and over again, and it is difficult for the student being bullied to defend himself or herself. We further explained that bullying is when a student is teased over and over in a mean and hurtful way, but that bullying was not when teasing was done in a friendly or playful way.

Data Collection Procedures

Parents

A packet was sent home with students to give to their parents that included a letter with information about the study, a consent form for parents to complete for their and their child's participation in the study, as well as a parent questionnaire developed specifically for this study for completion. A stamped, addressed envelope was also included for parents to mail the consent form and completed questionnaire back to the principal investigator. As completed study materials were returned to the principal investigator via U.S. Postal Service, the signed informed consent form was separated from the questionnaire and stored separately.

Students

A team of researchers collected data in the school setting over a period of two days. Students whom parental consent had been obtained were called to the cafeteria during the school day to complete the assent form and questionnaire. Definition of bullying used for this study and directions for completion of the questionnaire were provided. Data collectors were trained to use appropriate and consistent responses to student questions and to utilize the study's definition of bullying. They also assisted students with the reading of questions as necessary. Upon completion of the questionnaires, students were given a pencil and key chain as a thank you gift and sent back to their classrooms.

School Personnel

School personnel were approached in the school setting and invited to participate in the study by a member of the research team. When approached, envelopes and a thank you gift of a coffee mug were handed to them. The envelopes included information about the study, an informed consent form for their signature, a questionnaire for them to complete that measured school personnel's perceptions and observations of bullying in the school setting, and a stamped addressed envelope to mail completed materials directly to the principal investigator. A definition of bullying used for this study and directions for completion of the questionnaire were also included in the envelope. All subjects were volunteers and were assured of the confidentiality of their responses. As completed study materials were returned to the principal investigator via U.S. Postal Service, the signed informed consent form was separated from the questionnaire and stored separately.

Data Analysis

All data were coded directly from respondent's answers to specific questions asked on the survey instruments. To better understand the flow of communication about bullying in schools, parents, school personnel and students were each asked about their involvement in discussions on bullying during the previous three months. Most of this data are presented in one figure. This figure is designed to visually depict the lines of communication between the four primary groups–parents, school personnel, children who are bullied, and children who bully others. Additional related information, not reported in the figure, is described in the Results section.

RESULTS

When all respondents are counted together, the total sample has 494 people. This includes 230 parents, 72 school personnel, and 192 students. Based on data obtained from the survey instruments, school bullying has been and continues to be a serious problem. Among 192 student respondents, 158 (82.3%) stated that they have been victimized by at least one bullying act in the previous three months. Similarly, 32 school personnel (44.4%) and 81 parents (35.2%) said that they were bullied as children. On the other hand, 70 students (36.5%) reported that they have bullied other students during the previous three months. Within this group, however, 68 students (97.1%) reported that they have also experienced being bullied.

As shown on Figure 1, many parents, school personnel and students have engaged in discussions of school bullying. For example, 71 students (37.0%) said that they have told a parent or guardian that they are being bullied at school and 59 parents (25.7%) responded that their child has complained to them about being bullied at school. Though not included on the figure, it is worth noting that 35 parents (15.2%) stated that their child has been afraid to go to school because they are being

FIGURE 1. Communication About Bullying

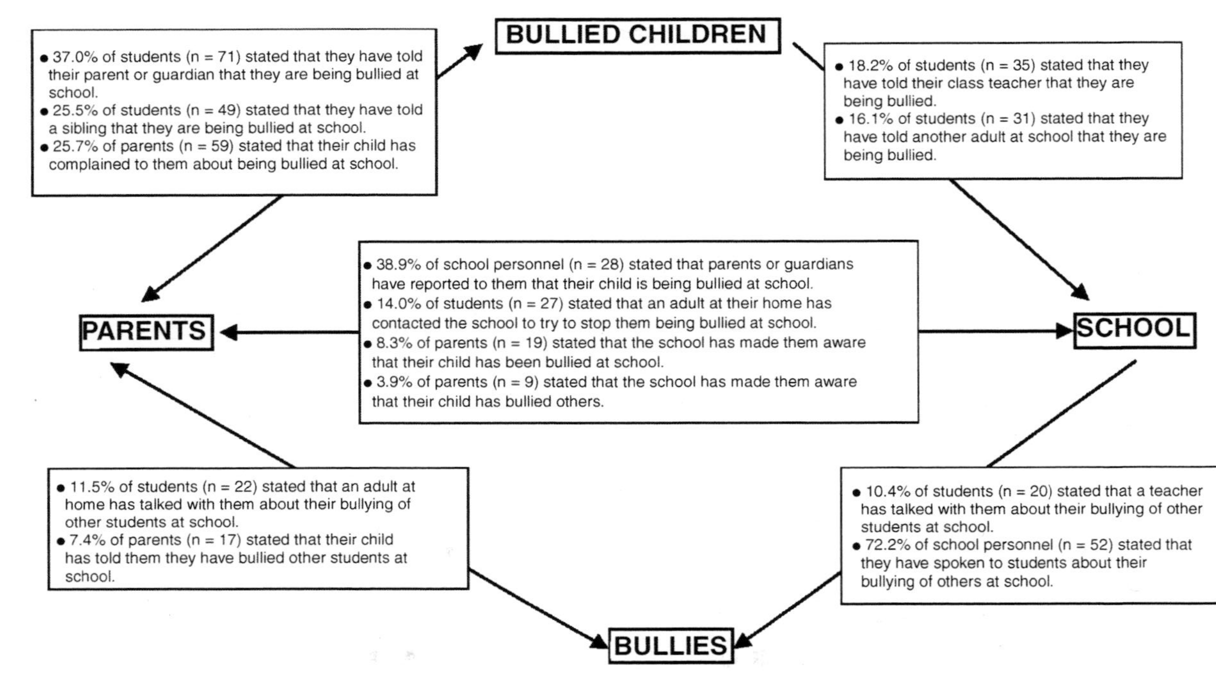

bullied there and 12 parents (5.2%) reported that their child has missed school because of fear that they would be bullied.

Many of these children who are being bullied also stated that they have spoken with school personnel about their experiences. Among the 192 children surveyed, 35 (18.2%) said that they have told a teacher about being bullied and 31 students (16.1%) said that they have told another adult at school. School personnel, in turn, reported that they communicate with bullying students. While 52 school personnel (72.2%) stated that they have spoken with bullying students about their behaviors, 20 students (10.4%) stated that a teacher has spoken with them about their bullying. Further regarding the children who commit bullying acts, 22 students (11.5%) said that an adult at their home has spoken with them about their bullying behaviors and 17 parents (7.4%) said that their child has talked with them about being a bully.

Finally, there also appears to be communication between parents and the school. These discussions flow both ways, especially regarding children being bullied. Among participating school personnel, 28 (38.9%) said that they have received reports from parents that their child is being bullied. Correspondingly, 27 students (14.0%) stated that an adult in their home has contacted the school to try and stop the bullying that they are experiencing and 19 parents (8.3%) said that the school has contacted them to report that their child is being bullied. Finally, nine parents (3.9%) stated that the school has notified them that their child is bullying other students at school.

DISCUSSION

Considering that 82.3% of students self-identified as victims of bullying, the relatively low percentages of people who reported talking in any way about bullying are strikingly low. With few exceptions, fewer than 40% of any group (and often fewer than 20%) said that they have talked with anyone about bullying. This would seem to speak volumes in support of implementing interventions to enhance communication across the various systems.

In conceptualizing such multisystemic interventions for rural schools, this study reveals discrepancies in communication that should be targeted for improvement. One such example is that 37% of all students (or 44.9% of students who reported being bullied) said they have talked with their parents about being bullied while only 25.7% of parents stated that their child has complained to them about bullying problems. This discrepancy may result from a difference in sample sizes, sibling groups, other factors, or genuine miscommunication. Regardless, given the large number of students who said that they have been bullied during a three-month period, the reported level of communication between parents and children is strikingly low. With better communication between parents and children, parents can be more aware of their child's bullying problems while helping them to learn assertiveness skills and non-violent conflict resolution (Saunders, 1997).

Along the same lines, many more school personnel (72.2%) stated that they have spoken with bullies compared to only a small number of bullies (28.6% of self-identified bullies). The sizable differences in these percentages may indicate that personnel are talking repeatedly with only a handful of the bullying population. Nonetheless, the implication is that many bullies are, indeed, not being punished (O'Connell, Pepler, & Craig, 1999).

Perhaps the most important area for intervention, though, concerns communication between parents and teachers. The foundation for such an intervention would seem to be firmly in place. As previously stated, teachers are the key to reducing bullying (Garrett, 2001) and, when teachers identify changes needed to improve classroom behavior, they most frequently want parent involvement (Strom & Strom, 2003). Considering also that parents feel most secure when they believe that school staff knows how to intervene when bullying occurs, all of these pieces support developing better lines of communication across the school and home settings. This may be an especially challenging and important task for rural schools in which school districts often cover larger geographic areas than their urban counterpart.

It is also important not to forget staff training and continuing education as a tool to combat bullying problems in schools. School personnel's low levels of communication about bullying may still stem from their lack of awareness about bullying problems or a difficulty in differentiating bullying acts from playful fighting. Thus, true to the design of multisystemic interventions described in this paper's opening section, efforts to improve communication should be complemented with efforts to educate staff and other adults about bullying.

FUTURE RESEARCH

This exploratory research is intended to provide beginning knowledge relating to communication about children's bullying in a rural school setting. The generalizability of this study is limited because study participants were recruited from only one region of the country. The school district also lacks significant diversity.

Future studies should seek to build upon this study and its limitations by gathering data from multiple sites. Other methods that will contribute to advancing the knowledge base on this topic would match students with parents. This will allow for a deeper understanding of the relationship between parenting and children's involvement in school bullying. It will also be important to gather data on the myriad of psychosocial factors that may be involved in bullying and communication about bullying. Lastly, the impact of minimal communication of school to home is problematic and needs further exploration. Such information will assist in the design and development of multisystemic interventions to increase communication between kids, parents and school personnel. It is essential that everyone talks and everyone listens if the serious problem of school bullying is to be successfully eliminated through prevention and intervention.

REFERENCES

Boulton, M. J. (1993). A comparison of adult's and children's abilities to distinguish between aggressive and playful fighting in middle school pupils. *Educational Studies, 19* (2), 193-204.

Boulton, M. J. (1996). Lunchtime supervisor's attitudes towards playful fighting, and ability to differentiate between playful and aggressive fighting: An intervention study. *British Journal of Educational Psychology, 66,* 367-381.

Boulton, M. J. (1997). Teacher's views on bullying: Definitions, attitudes and ability to cope. *British Journal of Educational Psychology, 67,* 223-233.

Clarke, E. A., & Kiselica, M. S. (1997). A systemic counseling approach to the problem of bullying. *Elementary School Guidance and Counseling, 31* (4).

Dulmus, C. N., Theriot, M. T., Sowers, K. M., & Blackburn, J. A. (in press). Student reports of peer bullying victimization in a rural school. *Stress, Trauma, and Crisis: An International Journal.*

Espelage, D. L., Bosworth, K., & Simon, T. R. (2000). Examining the social context of bullying behaviors in early adolescence. *Journal of Counseling and Development, 78,* 326-333.

Garrett, K. (2001). Reducing School-Based Bullying, *Journal of School Social Work,* 12 (1), 74-90.

Garrity, C., & Jens, K. (1997). Bully proofing your school: Creating a positive climate. *Intervention in School and Clinic, 32* (4), 235-244.

Hazler, R. J., Miller, D. L., Carney, J. V., Green, S. (2001). Adult recognition of school bullying situations. *Educational Research, 43* (2), 133-146.

Hoover, J. H., Oliver, R., & Hazler, R. J. (1992). Bullying: Perceptions of adolescent victims in the Midwestern USA. *School Psychology International, 13,* 5-16.

McCarty, S. (2000). Home-school connections: A review of literature, *Journal of Educational Research*, 93 (3), 145-153.

O'Connell, P., Pepler, D., & Craig W. (1999). Peer involvement in bullying: Insights and challenges for intervention. *Journal of Adolescence, 22* (4), 437-452.

Olweus, D. (1986). *The Olweus Bully/Victim Questionnaire.* Mimeo. Bergen, Norway: University of Bergen.

Olweus, D. (1993). *Bullying at school: What we know and what we can do.* Oxford, United Kingdom: Blackwell Publishers.

Pang, W., & Watkins, D. (2000). Toward a psychological model of teacher-parent communication in Hong Kong Primary School, *Educational Studies*, 26 (2), 141-163.

Roberts, W. & Coursol, D. (1996). Strategies for intervention with childhood and adolescent victims of bullying, teasing, and intimidation in school settings, *Elementary School Guidance and Counseling*, 30, 204-212.

Sammmons, P., Hillman, J., & Mortimer, P. (1995). Key characteristics of effective schools: A review of school effectiveness research. London, England: Office for Standards in Education.

Saunders, C. (1997). When push comes to shove: Dealing with bullies requires adult intervention, *Our Children*, 22, 34-35.

Strom, P. & Strom, R. (2003). Uniting Adolescent Support Systems for Safe Learning Environments, *The Educational Forum*, 67, 164-173.

Whitney, I. & Smith, P. (1993). A survey of the nature and extent of bullying in junior/middle and secondary schools. *Educational Research*, 35, 3-25.

Corporal Punishment: Another Form of School Violence

Carolyn Hilarski, PhD, CSW, ACSW

SUMMARY. It is vital to study and understand the underlying conditions that support and maintain the almost universal positive attitudes about the use of corporal punishment with children. Corporal punishment is a form of violence against children that affects child development and may possibly be a link to later violent behavior. Currently, the scientific community is in great debate regarding the use of corporal punishment with children and the adult or parental characteristics and milieu that produce these attitudes and behavior. This secondary analysis proposed to further examine the variables found significant in relation to favoring or using corporal punishment with children. The 207 participants, who answered all of the questions on the GSS93 subset survey, were studied with 15 independent variables, clustered into three categories–social system, demographic, and psychological. The hypothesis postulated that the social system variables, supported by the social interaction and systems model, would be the highest estimators of individuals favoring corporal punishment with children. The results from lo-

Carolyn Hilarski is Assistant Professor, Social Work Department, College of Liberal Arts, Rochester Institute of Technology, 18 Lomb Memorial Drive, Rochester, NY 14623 (E-mail: cxhgsw@rit.edu).

[Haworth co-indexing entry note]: "Corporal Punishment: Another Form of School Violence." Hilarski, Carolyn. Co-published simultaneously in *Journal of Evidence-Based Social Work* (The Haworth Social Work Practice Press, an imprint of The Haworth Press, Inc.) Vol. 1, No. 2/3, 2004, pp. 59-75; and: *Kids and Violence: The Invisible School Experience* (ed: Catherine N. Dulmus and Karen M. Sowers) The Haworth Social Work Practice Press, an imprint of The Haworth Press, Inc., 2004, pp. 59-75. Single or multiple copies of this article are available for a fee from The Haworth Document Delivery Service [1-800-HAWORTH, 9:00 a.m. - 5:00 p.m. (EST). E-mail address: docdelivery@haworthpress.com].

http://www.haworthpress.com/web/JEBSW

Digital Object Identifier: 10.1300/J394v1n02_05

gistic regression supported the hypothesis and agreed with previous study variables in the full and final models. The cultural norms that support corporal punishment in our schools and families need to be addressed. It has been suggested that the United States emulate Sweden's national policy where corporal punishment with children is seen as abuse. *[Article copies available for a fee from The Haworth Document Delivery Service: 1-800-HAWORTH. E-mail address: <docdelivery@haworthpress.com> Website: <http://www.HaworthPress.com> © 2004 by The Haworth Press, Inc. All rights reserved.]*

KEYWORDS. Corporal punishment, children, schools, violence

INTRODUCTION

Violence continues to be a prominent social issue (Astor et al., 1997). In truth, the consequences of violence overwhelms our nation in lost productivity and expense to the criminal justice and medical community, which has been estimated at more than $60 billion per year (Fraser, 1996).

Research on violence has offered innumerable markers for its existence, such as poverty, unemployment, mental disorder, and broken families (Conklin, 1992; McCaghy & Capron, 1994; Sampson & Laub, 1994). Eckersley (1993) argues that violent behavior in the United States is due to a nationally distorted value system that has profoundly affected our culture's consciousness.

Recently, crime indicators have suggested an overall decline in violent behavior. However, examination of these statistics shows a disturbing change regarding the age of violent offenders. Specifically, youth crime is rising (Blumstein, 1995; Stark, 1993). Interestingly, certain scientists (e.g., Straus & Mouradian, 1998; McCord, 1996) strongly suggest that there is a relationship between adult use of corporal punishment (i.e., "hard" spanking) and violent behavior in youth. The Center for Effective Discipline (2003) reports that in the United States, 22 states still allow use of corporal punishment within the school setting. The U.S. Department of Education (2000) further reports that in the year 2000, some 342,038 students were administered corporal punishment through paddling in the school setting. In light of the information, should corporal punishment be considered another form of school violence?

THE CORPORAL PUNISHMENT PERSPECTIVE

Hyman (1996) examined the legal and behavioral definitions of corporal punishment and paraphrases his results like this "(corporal punishment is) . . . a specific type of punishment intended to inflict pain" (p. 818). Graziano and Mills (1992) suggest that corporal punishment is fundamental to American culture through legal and religious attitudes. In fact, Straus (1996) presents evidence that over 90% of parents have used corporal punishment or spanked their children. Other studies using convenience samples of college students found that more than 90% reported being spanked (Graziano & Namaste, 1990). Graziano, Hamblen, and Plante (1996) describe violence against children as "everyday spanking, hitting, slapping" (p. 845)–behaviors that many adults accept as proper forms of discipline. In their study of 320 intact, middle-class, educated families, 83% reportedly used corporal punishment. Further, 35% of their children reported that objects were used in presenting the corporal punishment, such as sticks, paddles, whips, and cords, with 17% of the children reporting being hit with objects at least half the time (a few times a week) (Graziano, Hamblen, and Plante, 1996, p. 845).

Research over the past few decades has questioned the use of spanking or corporal punishment (Straus, 1996), as it has been linked to substance abuse and criminal activity (Straus & Lauer, 1992), low economic achievement (Straus & Gimpel, 1992), depression (Straus, 1996), and a positive attitude toward the use of physical aggression (Straus, 1996). Straus (1996) and Levinson (1989) agree that the greater the degree of approval for physical punishment, the higher the overall homicide rate.

However, the lack of empirical data relating to the negative results of corporal punishment is surprising (Cohen, 1996; Nelson, 1995; Trumbell, Ravenel, & Larson, 1995). Cohen (1996) relates that there is substantial literature supporting the premise that physical punishment is a serious risk for children, however, a multitude of methodological difficulties (i.e., contamination, lack of randomization, and delineation issues) cloud the results.

CHARACTERISTICS OF A PERSON WHO ENGAGES IN CORPORAL PUNISHMENT

Those who tend to use corporal punishment with children will generally have issues in seven different areas. The first four are personal and the remaining three are environmental. Although no one person may have all seven problems mentioned, most will be characterized by at least some of them.

The first is low self-esteem (see Larzelere, Klein, Schumm, & Alibrando, 1989). This finding is thought to be due to a lack of nurturing in childhood. The second is social isolation (Majonis, 1991) resulting from a fear of rejection–also thought to stem from childhood trauma. Further, there is a need to control and a demanding temperament (Garbarino, 1977; Sloan & Meier, 1983).

The environmental issues tend to be a lack of support systems, low socioeconomic status, and increased sensitivity to external life crisis (Zastrow & Kirst-Ashman, 1990; Elder, Nguyen, & Caspi, 1985). Gumaer (1984) describes a family where corporal punishment might be used as having a father with addictive attributes (i.e., works too much) and a mother with somatic problems (p. 304).

In some societies (i.e., Sweden), it is now considered abusive to spank a child. Yet, in England and in some regions of the United States it is legally acceptable to use corporal punishment with a child who misbehaves (Hyman, 1996). In a survey by Gelles (1978), 2,143 American families were examined regarding the use of corporal punishment. Eight percent of the parents interviewed reported having kicked, bitten, or hit their child with closed fists and that 3% had either threatened or actually used a gun or knife on their children (p. 580).

Interestingly, according to Starr (1979), parents who use corporal punishment do not have any greater psychiatric disorders than the population at large nor are they necessarily confined to the lowest social class. Many are well-educated middle-class adults (Starr, 1979).

REGIONAL DISTINCTIONS

State approval for corporal punishment is varied. In the educational arena, permission to use physical punishment ranges from only the principal to any school employee. Hurlbert (1989) examined the attitudes and beliefs of 11,982 White southerners. The significant results showed a propensity to use and approve of violence and force, a conservative political inclination, and a moral and religious orientation (p. 245).

Flynn (1996) examined regional differences in college students' experiences with corporal punishment. Northeastern students were less likely to have been hit than Southern students were. However, when controlling for religious affiliation, gender, and parents' education, the regional influences were diminished (p. 59).

RELIGION AND CORPORAL PUNISHMENT

Ellison and Sherkat (1993) evaluated the relationship between religiosity and corporal punishment and found three attitudes significant in those who espoused corporal punishment–an acceptance of the literal doctrine of the Bible, humans are inherently sinful, and sin needs to be punished (p. 131). However, Grasmick, Morgan, and Kennedy (1992) found that religion was significantly correlated with corporal punishment based on denominational affiliation, not personal religiosity (p.177).

CULTURAL DIFFERENCE REGARDING CORPORAL PUNISHMENT

A recent study (Deaterdeckard, Bates, Dodge, & Pettit, 1996) found clear ethnic differences in response to physical discipline. A sample of 466 European American and African-American boys and girls from a broad range of socioeconomic levels were followed from kindergarten through 3rd grade. Mothers reported their use of physical discipline in interviews and questionnaires, and mothers, teachers, and peers rated children's externalizing problems annually. The interaction between ethnic status and discipline was significant for teacher and peer rated externalizing scores (Deaterdeckard, Bates, Dodge, & Pettit, 1996, p. 1065).

We are told that the African American community is torn on the subject of corporal punishment (Comer, 1992; Kunjufu, 1986; & Wilson, 1978). Indeed, Polite (1996) asserts that in certain segments of African American society there are those who believe that many middle class parents are overly permissive with their children, which perpetuates general disrespect for humanity.

ATTITUDES ON CORPORAL PUNISHMENT

Hyman's (1996) review of corporal punishment suggested that American beliefs regarding corporal punishment relate to individual political orientation, religion, tradition, regional attitudes, and level of education (p. 818). Giles-Sims, Straus, and Sugarman (1995) described that adult spanking attitudes vary by age, sex, SES, marital status, ethnicity, religion, and community (p. 170). A logistic analysis examining a minority population by Sheline, Skipper, and Broadhead (1994) found that absent fathers, divorced parents, low SES, and numerous children were factors for corporal punishment in the home. Holden, Coleman, and Schmidt (1995) found in 39 college-educated mothers (age 22-41) that spanking occurred on average 2.5 times per week with no relationship to the child's gender, and that spanking attitudes were associated with a positive attitude towards physical punishment in addition to negative world views (p. 431). Straus and Kaufman's (1994) logistic analysis of 6,002 families found that poverty, alcohol, depression, and family violence were predictors of the use of corporal punishment in the home.

Yet, Kaplan (1995) sampled 1000 psychologists and found that age, race income, educational degree, and area of living were not related to attitudes and behavior regarding corporal punishment. Moreover, Morris' (1995) examination of the influence of others on mother's decision to use corporal punishment found similar results. Specifically, results showed that the choice to use corporal punishment did not depend on outside influence. It was more related to level of control. Furnham (1995) studied 136 persons (aged 18-38) regarding spanking attitudes and found that sex, age, and religious beliefs were not associated with corporal punishment, however, political beliefs were.

STATEMENT OF THE PROBLEM

Currently, there is great confusion regarding the use of physical punishment with children and the adult or parental characteristics and milieu that produce these behaviors or attitudes. Indeed, Larzelere's (1996) examination of two decades of relevant scientific research showed a lack of empirical studies documenting this phenomenon in any meaningful manner. Perhaps the ambiguity regarding this issue helps to perpetuate the powerful cultural norms that support its existence. Nevertheless, the question remains: what contingencies influence individual attitudes to engage in physical punishment?

OBJECTIVE OF THE STUDY

To determine, in this non-clinical sample, what specific variables or group of variables were significant probable estimators of a favorable attitude regarding the "hard" spanking of children.

CONCEPTUAL FRAMEWORK

Two theories help to explain how individuals develop and maintain their belief systems–the ecological and interactional theories.

The Ecological Theory

The ecological theory understands that behaviors and attitudes are shaped by the individual's interaction with his or her systems (Clancy, 1995). These systems are composed of family, neighborhood, community, spirituality, work, country and world. The ecological model describes the client as influencing and being influenced by many systems, through evolutionary and adaptive forces (Bartlett, 1970; Brower, 1988; Thyer & Myers, 1998). This model views coping behaviors as attempts by the individual and or systems to interact with the environment (Wodarski, 1987), in order to find a "goodness of fit", a "niche", or "life space" for survival or homeostasis sake (Brower, 1988, p.412-413). Hence, the ecological theory provides a framework for the social and structural experiences that form and maintain attitudes.

The Social Interactions Theory

This model focuses on the ramifications of daily social interactions. Specifically, that individual characteristics and beliefs are directly attributable to social interactions. Not necessarily a reaction to others but an interpretation of other's action in reference to the self. Thus, individuals are designed and forged by their environment.

RESEARCH QUESTION

Are variables related to an individual's social-system more likely to be probable estimators of a favorable attitude towards corporal punishment with children than demographic or psychological characteristics?

THE IMPORTANCE OF THE STUDY

It is vital to study and understand the underlying conditions that support and maintain attitudes about the use of corporal punishment with children for several reasons. First, the pervasiveness of its use–Buntain-Ricklefs, Kemper, Bell, and Baonis (1994) relate that corporal punishment is practiced and approved by 88% of American parents and supported by 67% of primary care physicians (McCormick, 1992). Second, the use of corporal punishment has been found to affect a child's development (Strassberg, Dodge, Pettit, & Bates, 1994). Indeed, Smith and Brooks-Gunn (1997) examined the incidence, predictors, and consequences of harsh discipline in a sample of children at 1 and 3 years of age and found that IQ scores for girls who received harsh discipline were 12 points lower than the IQ scores of girls who received very little punishment (p. 777). Third, there is a possible relationship between attitudes about the use of corporal punishment and child abuse (Graziano, 1994; Straus & Yodanis, 1996). McCord (1988) found that boys raised in and environment where physical punishment is condoned were more likely to become criminals than boys who were not. Moreover, Lefkowitz, Eron, Walder, and Huesmann (1977) showed an association between spanking and aggressive classroom behavior in kindergarten and elementary school children.

To date, there has been no specific empirical understanding of the particular variables that most support and maintain favorable attitudes regarding corporal punishment with children. This study examined a group of variables that had been previously cited by scholars as significant characteristics of those who favor corporal punishment with children in order to test the hypothesis that system characteristics are greater determinants of attitudes over demographic or psychological factors.

LIMITATIONS OF THE STUDY

This was a secondary analysis exploratory study. Therefore, it lacked random assignment, which inhibited generalizability. Moreover, the findings were based on self-reported data that may have been minimized or magnified by the respondents. Additionally, the research sample comprised only those participants who answered all of the GSS93 subset questions. One third of the original data set was lacking an answer for the dependent variable in this study. Finally, the probability sample limited the study's generalizability and conclusions to only this group of respondents.

METHODOLOGY

Research Design

This secondary analysis was completed to determine the variables most likely to predict, in this sample, the attitude prevalence rates regarding corporal punishment with children. Multiple logistic regression was employed, as the dependent variable was categorical and thus not amenable to multiple regression analysis. Moreover, logistic regression is less restrictive regarding assumptions. Effect coding was chosen for contrasting the categorical variables as the design did not include a control or reference group (see Pedhazur, 1982, p. 733).

Instrument and sample data

Data for this study was taken from the National Opinion Research Center's General Social Survey (GSS) subset from 1993. This survey is involved in social indicator research, replicating questionnaire items since 1972 in order to facilitate time trend studies. The survey source is a probability sample of personal interviews from non-institutionalized English-speaking persons 18 years of age and older, living in the United States. The data were collected in February, March, and April of 1993. The survey is funded by the National Science Foundation (Davis & Smith, 1992).

Dependent Variable

The dependent variable for this study was attitude regarding corporal punishment with children. This variable was measured using the following item:

> "Do you strongly agree, agree, disagree, or strongly disagree that it is sometimes necessary to discipline a child with a good, hard spanking?" Responses were originally coded from 1-4, with 4 being "strongly agree," so that a higher score indicated a more favorable attitude toward spanking or corporal punishment. However, in this study this question was dichotomized to 1-"agree" and 0-"disagree."

Independent Variables

The independent variables included demographic, psychological and social-system variables. The *demographic* variables were selected for their individual influences and were measured using the following items from the GSS93 survey:

1. "How old were you when you were first married?"
2. "How many children have you ever had?"

3. "In which of these groups did your total family income, from all sources, fall last year before taxes, that is? Just tell me the number."
4. "Are you currently married?" (yes-1 and no-0)
5. Interviewer coded sex (1 male and 2 female)(recorded as 1 male and 0 female)
6. Respondent's Age
7. "What is the highest grade in elementary school or high school that you finished and got credit for?"

The *psychological* variable was chosen for its overall measure of satisfaction and was measured with the following item from the GSS93 survey:

1. "In general, do you find life exciting, pretty routine, or dull?" (recoded as 1 = exciting/routine and 0 = dull)

The *social-system* variables were favored for their political, cultural, spiritual, economic, and family system influences and were measured with the following items from the GSS93 survey:

1. "What is your religious preference? Is it Protestant, Catholic, Jewish, some other religion, or no religion?" (recoded as Protestant-1 and all others-0). Not entered in full model as not significant on first run of 15 variables.
2. "Do you favor or oppose the death penalty for persons convicted of murder?" (1-favor and 0-oppose).
3. "We hear a lot of talk these days about liberals and conservatives. I'm going to show you a five-point scale on which the political views that people might hold are arranged from liberal-point 1 to conservative-5. Where would you place yourself on this scale? (Recoded 1 = Conservative; 0 = Liberal)
4. Race was interviewer coded 1 White, 2 Black, and 3 Other (recoded as 1 = White and 0 = Black and Other).
5. Region of interview
   1. New England–ME, VT, NH, MA, CT, RI
   2. Middle Atlantic–NY, NJ, PA
   3. E. Nor. Central–WI, IL, IN, MI, OH
   4. W. Nor. Central–MN, IA, MO, ND, SD, NE, KS
   5. South Atlantic–DE, MD, WV, VA, NC, SC, GA, FL, DC
   6. E. South Central–KY, TN, AL, MS
   7. South Central–AR, OK, LA, TX

8. Mountain–MT, ID, WY, NV, UT, CO, AZ, NM
9. Pacific–WA, OR, CA, AK, HA

6. Size of place of interview

1. City 250000 to 10 Open Country (1 largest-10 lowest)

7. "What is the highest grade that your mother finished and got credit for?" (recoded as 0-high school or less and 1-college).

DATA ANALYSIS

Missing data was a problem in this data set. For that reason, including, only those respondents who answered all of the questions solved the issue. However, this procedure left a sample of 207 respondents from a data set of 1500. In spite of that fact, the study's calculated power was .95 with a medium effect size (.50) and an alpha = . 05 (two-tail), which was a reasonable standard of power to detect a difference if one existed (Cohen, 1988).

Independent t-test and Pearson chi-square analysis was used to test any differences between the "missing data group" and the research group. In addition, bivariate analysis (Chi Square and Student t test) was conducted to measure the relationship between the independent and the dependent variables. Correlations were performed between independent variables to measure their relationship, and multiple logistic regression was utilized to test the hypothesis. Statistical Package for Social Sciences was the computer package used to run the research statistics.

RESULTS

This secondary analysis studied 207 participants who answered all of the questions on the GSS93 survey. Specifically, 15 independent variables were considered in order to explore, which, if any, made a significant contribution to the prediction of spanking attitudes with children.

HYPOTHESIS

The results from multiple logistic regression agreed with several previous study variables in the full and final models. Specifically, political affiliation (t (1) = 6.4, p = .01), community size (t (1) = 8.8, p = .003), and race (t (1) = 7.3, p = .007) showed significant probability for estimating favorable attitudes for corporal punishment with children (odds ratio = 3.27)–correctly classifying 72% of the cases. As these variables were defined in this examination as social system characteristics, the hypothesis was supported. Therefore, in this study, those who self reported being white, conservative, and living in a city were 58% more likely to favor corporal punishment with children. This outcome is supported by earlier evidence that social system variables, such as elitism, racism, conservative politics, and economic bias, are associated with the use of corporal punishment (Hyman, 1996; Hyman, Bongiovanni, Friedman, & McDowell, 1977).

IMPLICATIONS FOR PRACTICE AND POLICY

Longitudinal studies have discovered that criminal (Widom, 1989) and aggressive behaviors (i.e., Lefkowitz, Eron, Walder, & Huesmann, 1977) are associated with histories of corporal punishment in childhood. Yet, most Americans and many scientists believe that it is occasionally necessary and generally harmless to hit a child (Straus, 1996). Maintenance of this attitude is thought to be the result of institutional and cultural norms that legalize and require punishment for disobedience. This is justified by the need to maintain order, extinguish misbehavior, and promote obedience (Grasmick, Morgan, & Kenedy, 1992). It becomes obvious the extent and breadth of this conviction when looking at the results of a study of 500 school districts. Three hundred ninety four actually responded to the survey. The findings revealed that nearly half (43%) were legally allowed to use corporal punishment, but tried not to; one third actually used this measure, and another third reported that they were not allowed to use physical punishment, but did (Goldberg, 1993).

Eliminating the use of corporal punishment in our educational systems and instituting alternative disciplinary techniques, such as positive reinforcement, behavioral contracting, social skills training, and peer mediation, results in less incidents of misbehavior, suspension, and aggressive behavior (Hyman, 1996).

Violence is a social problem that must be addressed on a macro level. The cultural norms that support corporal punishment in our schools and families need to be addressed by our state and federal legislators. It has been suggested that the United States emulate Sweden's national policy where corporal punishment with children is seen as abuse (see Deley,

1988). Indeed, many countries across the globe agree that children need to be protected from physical abuse in schools and at home (Smith & Brooks-Gunn, 1997). I am not suggesting that ending all childhood corporal punishment would mean an end to violence. However, if it meant a reduction in crime, violence, victimization, and mental health issues, not to mention the cost for these consequences, then why not? Corporal punishment, at times, may appear to solve an immediate behavioral problem, however, its long-term effects can be deleterious health issues resulting from feelings of mistrust, anger, and resentment. Corporal punishment is seriously harming our nation's future generations and must be stopped.

REFERENCES

Astor, R. A., Behre, W. J., Fravil, K. A., & Wallace, J. M. Perceptions of School Violence as a Problem and Reports of Violence. *Journal of Social Workers*, 42 (1), 55-68

Bartlett, H. M. (1970). *The common base of social work.* New York: National Association of Social Workers.

Baumrind, D. (1973). The development of instrumental competence through socialization. In A. D. Pick (Ed.) *Minnesota symposia on child psychology* (pp. 7-36). Minneapolis, MN: University of Minnesota Press.

Bavolek, S. J. (1989). Assessing and treating high-risk parenting attitudes. *Early Child Development and care 42,* 99-112.

Blumstein, A. (1995). Violence by young people: Why the deadly nexus? *National Institute of Justice* pp. 2-9.

Brower, A. M. (1988). Can the ecological model guide social work practice? *Social Service Review, 62* (3), 411-429.

Brownie, K. (1995). Preventing child maltreatment through community nursing. *Journal of Advanced Nursing, 21 (1),* 57-63.

Buntain-Ricklefs, J. J., Kemper, K. J., Bell, M., & Baonis, T. (1994). Punishments: what predicts adult approval? *Child Abuse and Neglect, 18,* 945-956.

Center for Effective Discipline. (2003). Discipline and the law. Retrieved online December 4, 2003 from *www.stophitting.orrg/laws.stateLegislation.php*

Clancy, J. (1995). Ecological school social work: The reality and the vision. *Social Work in Education* 17 (1), 40-47.

Cohen, J. (1988). Statistical Power Analysis for the Behavioral Science (2nd ed.). Hillside, NJ: Erlbaum Publishers.

Cohen, P. (1996). How can generative theories of the effects of punishment be tested? *Pediatrics, 98 (4),* 834-836.

Coleman, J. W., & Cressey, D. R. (1984). *Social Problems* (2nd ed.). New York: Harper & Row.

Comer, J., & Poussaint, A. (1992). *Raising Black Children.* New York, NY: Plume Books.

Conklin, J. E. (1992). *Criminology* (4th ed.). New York: Macmillan.

Connelly, C.D., & Straus, M.A. (1992). Mother's age and risk for physical abuse. *Child Abuse & Neglect, 16 (5),* 709-718.

Davis, J., & Smith, T. W. (1992). *The NORC [National Opinion Research Center] General Social Survey: A user's guide.* Newbury Park, CA: Sage. Zastrow, C., & Kirst-Ashman, K.K. (1990). *Understanding human behavior and the social environment* 2nd ed.). Chicago: Nelson-Hall Publishers.

Deley, W. (1988). Physical punishment of children: Sweden and the USA. *Journal of Comparative Family Studies, 19 (3),* 419-431.

Deaterdeckard, K., Bates, J. E., Dodge, K. A., & Pettit, G. S. (1996). Physical discipline among African American and European American mother: Links to children's externalizing behaviors. *Development Psychology, 32 (6),* 1065-1072.

Eckersley, R. (1993). The west's deepening cultural crisis. *The Futurist,* 8-12.

Elder, G. H. Jr., Nguyen, T. V., & Caspi, A. (1985). Linking family hardship to children's lives. *Child Development 56,* 361-375.

Ellison, C. G., & Sherkat, D. E.(1993). Conservative Protestantism and support for corporal punishment. *American Sociological Review, 58 (1),* 131-144.

Furnham, A. (1995). Attitudes to spanking children. *Personality & Individual Differences, 19 (3),* 397-398.

Flynn, C. P. (1996). Regional differences in spanking experiences and attitudes: A comparison of northeastern and southern college students. *Journal of Family Violence, 11 (1),* 59-80.

Garbarino, J. (1977). The human ecology of child maltreatment: A conceptual model for research. *Journal of Marriage and the Family, 39,* 721-735.

Gelles, R. J. (1978). Violence toward children in the United States. *American Journal of Orthopsychiatry, 48,* 580-592.

Giles-Sims, J., Straus, M. A., & sugarman, D. B. (1995). Child, maternal, and family caracteristics associated with spanking. *Journal of Applied Family & Child Studies, 44 (2),* 170-176.

Grasmick, H. G., Morgan, C. S., & Kennedy, M. B. (1992). Support for corporal punishment in the schools: A comparison of the effects of socioeconomic status and religion. *Social Science quarterly, 73 (1),* 177-187.

Graziano, A. M., & Namaste, K. A. (1990). Parental use of physical force in child discipline: A survey of 679 college students. *Journal of Interpersonal Violence, 5,* 449-463.

Graziano, A. M. (1994). Why we should study subabusive violence against children. *Journal of Interpersonal Violence, 9 (3),* 412-419.

Graziano, A. M., & Hamblen, J. L., & Plante, W. A. (1996). Presentation: Subabusive violence in child rearing in middle class American families. *Pediatrics, 98 (4),* 845-848.

Graziano, A. M., Mills, J. R.(1992). Treatment for abused children: When is a partial solution acceptable? *Child Abuse and Neglect, 16 (2),* 217-228.

Greven, P. (1990). *Spare the child: The religious roots of punishment and the psychological impact of physical abuse.* New York, NY: Alfred A. Knopf, Inc.

Gumaer, J. (1984). *Counseling and therapy for children. New York: The Free Press.*

Holden, G. W., Coleman, S. M., Schmidt, K. L. (1995). Why 3-year old children get spanked: Parent and child determinants as reported by college-educated mothers. *Merrill-Palmer Quarterly, 41 (4),* 431-452.

Hurlbert, J. S. (1989). The southern region: A test of the hypothesis of cultural distinctiveness. *Sociological Quarterly, 41 (4),* 245-266.

Hyman, I. A. (1996). Using research to change public policy: Reflections on 20 years of effort to eliminate corporal punishment in schools. *Pediatrics, 98 (4),* 818-821.

Jackson, A. P., Gyamfi, P., Brooks-Gunn, J. & Blake, M. (1998). Employment status, psychological well-being, social support, and physical discipline practices of single Black. *Journal of Marriage and the Family, 60 (4),* 894-902.

Kaplan, J. P. (1995). Psychologist's attitudes towards corporal punishment. *Dissertation Abstracts Internaltion, 56-09, B,* 5151.

Kunjufu, J. (1986). *Countering the conspiracy to destroy black boys* (2nd ed.). Chicago, Il: African American Images.

Larzelere, R. E. (1996). A review of the outcomes of parental use of nonabusive or customary physical punishment. *Pediatrics, 98 (4),* 824-827.

Larzelere, R. E., Klein, M., Schumm, W. R., & Alibrando, S. A. (1989). The effects of spanking and other parenting characteristics on self-esteem and perceived fairness of parental discipline. *Psychol Rep,* 64, 1140-1142.

Lefkowitz, M. M., Eron, L. D., Walder, L. O., & Huesmann, L. R. (1977). *Growing up to be violent: A longitudinal study of the development of aggression.* New York, NY: Pergamon Press.

Levinson, D. (1989). *Family violence in cross-cultural perspective.* Newbury Park, CA: Sage Publications.

Majonis, J. (1991). Discipline and socialization of children in abusive and nonabusive families. *Child and Adolescent Social work Journal, 8 (3),* 203-224.

McCaghy, C. H., & Capron, T. A. (1994). McCord, J. (1988). Parental behavior in the cycle of aggression. *Deviant behavior (3rd ed.). New York: Macmillan.* 14-23.

McCord, J. (1988). Parental behavior in the cycle of aggression. *Psychiatry, 51,* 14-23.

McCord, J. (1996). Unintended consequences of punishment. *Pediatrics, 98* (4), 832-834.

McCormick, K. (1992). Attitudes of primary care physicians toward corporal punishment. *JAMA, 267,* 3161-3165.

Morris, J. D. (1995). The normative influence of social network members on mother's attitudes toward corporal punishment. *Dissertation Abstract International, 57-01, B,* 0765.

Nelson, F. P. (1995). Corporal Punishment. *Pediatrics, 96 (4),* 793-794.

Olds, D. L., Eckenrode, J., Henderson, C. R., Kitzman, H., Powers, J., Cole, R. et al. Long term effects of home visitation on maternal life course and child abuse and neglect: fifteen-year follow-up of a randomized trial. *JAMA, 278,* 637-643.

Pedhazur, E. J. (1982). *Multiple regression in behavioral research: Explanation and prediction.* New York: Holt, Rinehart and Winston.

Polite, K. (1996). The medium/the message: Corporal punishment, an empirical critique. *Pediatrics, 98 (4),* 849-851.

Sampson, R. J., & Laub, J. H. (1994). Urban poverty and the family context of delinquency: A new look at structure and process in a classic study. *Child Development, 65*, 523-540.

Sheline, J. L., Skipper, B. J., & Broadhead, W. E. (1994). Risk factors for violent behavior in elementary school boys: Have you hugged your child today? *American Journal of Public Health, 64 (4)*, 661-663.

Sloan, M. P., & Meier, J. H. (1983). Typology for parents of abused children. *Child Abuse and Neglect, 7 (4)*, 443-450.

Smith, J. R., Brooks-Gunn (1997). Correlates and consequences of harsh discipline for young children. *Archives of Pediatrics & Adolescent Medicine, 151 (8)*, 777-786.

Stark, Evan (1993), The Myth of Black Violence. *Journal of the National Association of Social Workers*, V 38, Number 4, 485-490.

Starr, R. J. (1979). Child Abuse. *American Psychologist, 34*, 872-878.

Strassberg, Z., Dodge, K. A., Pettit, G. S., & Bates, J. E. (1994). Spanking in the home and children's subsequent aggression toward kindergarten peers. *Developmental Psychopathology*, 445-461.

Straus, M. A., & Mouradian, V. E. (1998). Impulsive corporal punishment by mothers and antisocial behavior and impulsiveness children. *Behavioral Sciences and the Law, 16 (3)*, 353-374.

Straus, M. A. (1996). Spanking and the making of a violent society. *Pediatrics, 98 (4)*, 837-842.

Straus, M. A. (1992). Background and goals of the task force on the effects of corporal punishment on children. *Quarterly, The Child, Youth, and Family Services, Division* 37 (p. 4) Washington, DD: American Psychological Association.

Straus, M. A. & Kantor, G. K. (1994). Corporal punishment of adolescents by parents: A risk factor in the epidemiology of depression, suicide, alcohol abuse, child abuse, and wife beating. *Adolescence, 29 (115)*, 543-561.

Straus, M. A., & Yodanis, C. L. (1996). Corporal punishment in adolescence and physical assaults on spouses in later life: What accounts for the link? *Journal of Marriage & Family, 58 (4)*, 825-841.

Thyer, B. A., & Myers, L. L. (1998). Social learning theory: An empirically based approach to understanding human behavior in the social environment. *Journal of Human Behavior in the Social Environment, 1* (1), 33-52.

Trumbull, D. A., Ravenel, D., & Larson, D. (1995). Corporal punishment. *Pediatrics, 96 (4)*, 792-793.

U. S. Department of Education (2000). 2000 Elementary and Secondary School Civil Rights Report. Retrieved online December 4, 2003. (*http://www.ed.gov/about/offices/list/orc/reports2000/index.html*).

Vicente, K. J., & Wang, J. H. (1998). An ecological theory of expertise effects in memory recall. *Psychological Review, 105 (1)*, 33-57.

Weir, I. K., & Dinnick, S. (1988). Behavior modification in the treatment of sleep problems in young children: A controlled trial using visitors as therapists. *Child Care, Health and Development, 14*, 355-368.

Widom, C. S. (1989). Child abuse, neglect, and adult behavior: Research design and findings on criminality, violence, and child abuse. *American Journal of Orthopsychiatry, 59 (3)*, 355-367.

Wiehe, V.R. (1990). Religious influence on parental attitudes toward the use of corporal punishment. *Journal of Family Violence, 5 (2),* 173-186.

Wilson, A. (1978). *The development psychology of the black child.* New York, NY: African Research Publications.

Wodarski, J. S. (1987). *Social work practice with children and adolescents.* Springfield, Illinois: Charles C. Thomas.

Wolfe, D. A. (1991). *Preventing physical and emotional abuse of children.* New York: Guildford Press.

Zastrow, C., & Kirst-Ashman, K. K. (1990). *Understanding human behavior and the social environment* 2nd ed.). Chicago: Nelson-Hall Publishers.

The Criminal Bully–Linking Criminal Peer Bullying Behavior in Schools to a Continuum of Delinquency

Matthew T. Theriot, PhD
Catherine N. Dulmus, PhD
Karen M. Sowers, PhD
Stan L. Bowie, PhD

SUMMARY. In light of a recent wave of anti-bullying legislation following several high-profile incidents of school violence, this study explores the criminality that is inherent in certain acts of school bullying. These acts include physical aggression, theft of property or money, and damage to property, among others. As research continues to link school bullying and childhood aggression to later delinquency and adult criminal offending, "criminal bullies" may be an especially vulnerable population

---

Matthew T. Theriot is Assistant Professor, Catherine N. Dulmus is Associate Professor, Karen M. Sowers is Dean and Professor, and Stan L. Bowie is Assistant Professor, with the College of Social Work, The University of Tennessee.

Address correspondence to: Matthew T. Theriot, The University of Tennessee, College of Social Work, 1618 Cumberland Avenue, 322 Henson Hall, Knoxville, TN 37996-3333 (E-mail: mtheriot@utk.edu).

The authors would like to gratefully acknowledge the contributions of Pamela Jinks and David Dupper to the project.

[Haworth co-indexing entry note]: "The Criminal Bully–Linking Criminal Peer Bullying Behavior in Schools to a Continuum of Delinquency." Theriot, Matthew T. et al. Co-published simultaneously in *Journal of Evidence-Based Social Work* (The Haworth Social Work Practice Press, an imprint of The Haworth Press, Inc.) Vol. 1, No. 2/3, 2004, pp. 77-92; and: *Kids and Violence: The Invisible School Experience* (ed: Catherine N. Dulmus and Karen M. Sowers) The Haworth Social Work Practice Press, an imprint of The Haworth Press, Inc., 2004, pp. 77-92. Single or multiple copies of this article are available for a fee from The Haworth Document Delivery Service [1-800-HAWORTH, 9:00 a.m. - 5:00 p.m. (EST). E-mail address: docdelivery@haworthpress.com].

http://www.haworthpress.com/web/JEBSW

Digital Object Identifier: 10.1300/J394v1n02_06

for subsequent criminal justice system complications. Consequently, early identification and intervention with these children may yield better long-term outcomes. In this study of 192 students at rural elementary and middle schools, 34 children reported committing a criminal bullying act during a three-month period. This equates to 17.7% of the total sample or 48.6% of all self-identified bullies. The authors discuss the significance of these findings as well as the proposed utility of "criminal bully" as a new typology of school bullying.

KEYWORDS. Bullying, victimization, violence in schools, criminal offending, and juvenile delinquency

The belief that criminal violence is a recent phenomenon in American schools is a striking misconception. Certainly, there has been a rise in lethal school violence during the past fifteen years. From Littleton, Colorado to Springfield, Oregon to Jonesboro, Arkansas, the American educational landscape is increasingly spotted with highly-publicized school shootings. Yet, despite this recent wave of media and public attention, criminal violence has existed in schools for decades. In fact, thousands of students are victims of crimes at school each day (MacNeil, 2002). These children are the victims of bullying, much of which is criminal in nature.

Bullying is a global phenomenon–perpetrated in schoolyards, classrooms, hallways, and bathrooms around the world. In studies done outside of the United States, the prevalence of being a bully ranges from 4.1% to 49.7% (Dake, Price, & Telljohann, 2003). Dan Olweus (1993; 1994), a pioneer in bullying research, found that, in his extensive studies of students in Norway, 7% of the children were bullies and 1.6% of children are both victims and bullies. American studies have likewise placed the prevalence of bullying students consistently between 13% and 20% (Pellegrini, Bartini, & Brooks, 1999; Nansel et al., 2001). Bullying is believed to occur at almost all American schools (Furlong & Morrison, 2000).

Though there are variations in the definition of school bullying, most definitions derive from that originated by Olweus (1993; 1994). According to his definition, "a student is being bullied or victimized when he or she is exposed, repeatedly and over time, to negative actions on the part of one or more other students" (p. 1173; Olweus, 1994). These *negative actions* include actual or threatened physical contact or harm, verbal abuse, teasing or inappropriate gestures, theft or destruction of property or money, and relational bullying (such as intentionally excluding one from a peer group, spreading rumors and false lies, and so on). A key concept for these negative actions to be "bullying" is the requisite imbalance of strength (or an *asymmetric power relationship*; Olweus, 1994). Specifically, the student being harassed must be in a position of less power or strength than the harassing student(s). As a result, conflicts between students of nearly equal physical or mental strength cannot be considered bullying (Dake, Price, & Telljohann, 2003).

Clearly, many different behaviors meet the definitional criteria for bullying. However, it must be noted that a handful of these acts are technically criminal. That is, if students engaged in these behaviors outside of the school setting, the juvenile or criminal justice system would be expected to intervene. This includes physically assaulting a peer, threatening such harm, forcing others to do things against their will, and the theft or destruction of money and property.

This paper will examine the prevalence of this "criminal bullying" and define such bullies as a new typology of bullying. Since bullying in American schools has only begun to receive adequate research attention during the past 20 years, researchers in this field are still struggling to define and assess bullying behaviors (Espelage & Swearer, 2003). To this end, several different bullying typologies have been proposed. For example, bullies may be differentiated by type of aggression. This includes *proactive*, *reactive, direct*, *indirect*, or *relational* aggression (Espelage & Swearer, 2003). Previous research has also identified the *bully/victim*, or those children who are both a bully and a victim. Still another type of bully is the *passive bully*. This is the henchman or follower–a child who bullies others but does not take the initiative (Olweus, 1993). Undoubtedly, these varied typologies provide useful insight for understanding bullies and their behavior. Nevertheless, recent shifts in public and legislative attitudes towards bullying would seem to necessitate a new typology of bullying–*the criminal bully*. This typology would highlight those children who bully others by employment of criminal behaviors, such as those listed above.

Historically, school bullying has been seen as a disciplinary matter and not a criminal one (Furniss, 2000). Bullying has often been excused or ignored within schools as a normal part of growing up, as a rite of passage in childhood, or as an example of "boys being boys" and "kids being kids" (Will & Neufeld, 2003; Limber & Smalls, 2003). Now, however, and partly in response to many of the same high profile incidents of school violence mentioned in this paper's opening paragraph, fifteen states have passed legislation that addresses bullying in schools (Limber & Small, 2003). The actual benefit of this new wave of legislation remains to be determined, yet these legislative actions may signify the beginning of a very real shift in the way that bullying is viewed by American society and the way that bullying is handled in schools. While most legislation still leaves the disciplining of bullies in the hands of the school or the school district, such emerging policies may mark the beginning of a formal criminalization of school bullying.

The recognition of a relationship between bullying and criminality is neither novel nor new. Instead, research has clearly connected childhood bullying to later delinquency and criminal offending. Olweus (1993; 1994) found that, in his follow-up studies with former bullies, approximately 60% of males who bullied others during grades 6-9 had at least one criminal conviction by the age of 24 years. Moreover, 35-40% of these former bullies had three or more convictions by this same age compared to only 10% of males in a non-bullying control group. Along the same lines, former bullies are also more likely than their peers to violently abuse their spouses and to utilize harsher discipline with their own children (MacNeil, 2002). As an interesting side note, there is little evidence that bullies commit other, non-bullying forms of delinquent behavior while still in school (Rigby & Cox, 1996).

Not surprisingly, there are also striking similarities in the characteristics of bullies and criminal offenders. For example, Dake, Price and Telljohann (2003) reviewed the professional literature on characteristics of bullies. They found that, among other characteristics, bullies are likely to engage in substance abuse, fighting or violent behavior, and minor academic or criminal misconduct. Bullies are also likely to have inadequate adult role models, to suffer child abuse, to have lower academic achievement, and to have psychiatric problems. Comparably, in a review of the literature on factors that predict criminal arrest and recidivism, Farrington (1987) found that an early age of onset for offending, early antisocial behavior, convicted parents, low family income, school failure, and drug use were all among recurring predictors of criminal justice system involvement.

Moreover, in yet another example of the relationship between bullying and criminology, classic criminological theories, such as Sutherland's (1924) differential association theory, Cloward and Ohlin's

(1960) theory on the development of delinquent subcultures, and Akers' (1973) differential association-reinforcement theory, are frequently reflected in discussions of bullying. For instance, Pellegrini and associates (1999), in their description of the rejection often experienced by bullies, draw quite heavily on each of these theoretical orientations. In their scenario, a bully's aggressive values and behavior place the child at odds with the majority of other students and school personnel. This rejection by peers and teachers leads the bully to increasing school failures and stronger affiliations with other aggressive children. The bully may eventually reject all school connections by dropping out of school.

Despite this complex relationship of bullying and delinquency, the conceptualization of bullying itself as a criminal act (and not simply a school disciplinary matter) is a relatively recent phenomenon. In this emerging era of anti-bullying legislation and in light of the demonstrated relationship between bullying and future criminality, the typology of the criminal bully may have its greatest utility as a mechanism for identifying those children most at risk for future legal and criminal justice complications. While the criminal labeling of children may be distasteful to some, this paper is not intended to promote the criminal processing of bullies. The detrimental impact of such actions and the lasting stigma associated with such adjudication would yield only long-term negative consequences. Instead, this new proposed typology is suggested as a research tool for advancing the knowledge base about bullies and bullying. The typology acknowledges the role that certain forms of bullying may have on a continuum of evolving criminality. Studies have shown that a younger onset of serious delinquency may pose an increased risk for serious offending later (Farrington, 1987). For example, in one study of juvenile offenders, it was determined that approximately half of all males who become serious juvenile offenders had an onset of delinquent behavior before the age of 12 years (Stouthamer-Loeber & Loeber, 2002). Young children already perpetrating criminal bullying behaviors while still in elementary or middle school may be among those most likely to become juvenile or adult offenders. Thus, this group may be among those most needing immediate intervention.

A first step in understanding criminal bullying requires an assessment of the prevalence of such bullying in schools. Utilizing descriptive statistics, this paper will evaluate the prevalence of such bullying in a sample of rural elementary and middle school children. Further analyses will also seek to elaborate on the spectrum of bullying behaviors that a criminal bullying group engages in.

METHODS

Study Design

This study utilized a survey research design to gather information from students as to their experiences and observations of bullying among students in their school. The questionnaire also solicited responses from students as to their own bullying behaviors, which is the focus of the results reported in this article. The IRB at a large research university in the Southeastern United States granted permission to conduct the research prior to the start of the project. Parental consent was obtained for all student subjects whose participation was voluntary and confidential.

Study Sample

Letters to parents were sent home with students to recruit subjects. Subjects were recruited from three rural public schools (an elementary school, a middle school, and a school that housed grades K-8) located within the same school district in a Southeastern rural region of the United States. The school district is located in a county characterized by high rates of poverty as evidenced by 43% to 61% of students receiving free or reduced lunches and 12% of the population still not having a telephone. The school district's students are 98% Caucasian and the dominant culture is Appalachian.

The letter sent home to parents included information related to the study and a consent form for parents to complete to allow their child to participate in the study. A self-addressed stamped envelope was provided for parents to mail the consent form back to the principal investigator at the university. Ultimately, the convenience sample consisted of 192 students in grades three through eight, representing an 18.4% response rate. Data collection occurred in the fall of 2002. A team of researchers conducted data collection in the school setting for all children who met inclusion criteria and for whom written parental consent was obtained. Since all subjects were measured at one point in time, no follow-up was necessary. Thus, attrition was not problematic.

Inclusion criteria were as follows: (a) subjects had to be students enrolled in the school where data collection occurred, and (b) subjects had to be in grades three through eight. Written parental consent was obtained for each subject prior to their participating in the study. In addition, all children completed an individual assent form.

Measure

Each subject completed the Olweus Bully/Victim Questionnaire (Olweus, 1986). This 56-item, self-administered questionnaire, designed for grades 3 through 10, asks questions specific to student's perceptions, observations, and participation in various aspects of bullying in the school setting.

For the purposes of this study and as per the Olweus questionnaire, we defined and explained bullying to the students as being when another student, or several other students do the following:

- completely ignore or exclude him or her from their group of friends or leave him or her out of things on purpose
- hit, kick, push, shove around, or lock him or her inside a room
- tell lies or spread false rumors about him or her or send mean notes and try to make other students dislike him or her
- and other hurtful things like that.

In addition, we explained that a student is being bullied when the above things happen over and over again, and it is difficult for the student being bullied to defend himself or herself. We further explained that bullying is when a student is teased over and over in a mean and hurtful way, but that bullying was not when teasing was done in a friendly or playful way.

Data Collection Procedures

A team of researchers collected data in the school setting over a period of two days. Students whom parental consent had been obtained were called to the cafeteria during the school day to complete the assent form and questionnaire. Definition of bullying used for this study and directions for completion of the questionnaire were provided. Data collectors were trained to use appropriate and consistent responses to student questions and to utilize the study's definition of bullying. They also assisted students with the reading of questions as necessary. Upon completion of the questionnaires, students were given a pencil and key chain as a thank you gift and sent back to their classrooms. All subjects were assured of the confidentiality of their responses throughout the study. There were minimal physical, psychological, legal, or social risks for participants. To ensure confidentiality and protection of subjects they were instructed not to put their names or any identifying information on the questionnaire.

Data Analysis

All data were coded directly from respondent's answers to specific questions asked on the survey instrument. The primary group to be analyzed is the "criminal bullying" group, or those students reporting the perpetration of a bullying behavior that is criminal in nature. These behaviors include hitting, kicking, or otherwise physically assaulting another student, taking or damaging another student's money or property, and/or threatening or forcing other students to do something that they do not want to do. While racist name-calling and comments about another student's race, ethnicity, or skin color may be a criminal violation under broad definitions of a hate crime, these acts were not included in the definition of "criminal bullying" utilized in this study. Likewise, names, comments, or gestures of a sexual nature, while technically forms of sexual harassment, were also excluded so that this study may focus more specifically on other criminal aspects of bullying.

The data are displayed on four tables. Table 1 compares demographic and attitudinal characteristics for three groups–students who reported perpetrating bullying of a criminal nature, students perpetrating bullying of a non-criminal nature, and students who responded that they have not bullied others and they have not done any of the nine types of bullying listed in the survey at any time during the previous three months. Tables 2, 3, and 4 show information for only those students committing the aforementioned criminal acts of bullying. Specifically, Table 2 describes the types of bullying committed by each gender, Table 3 differentiates these types of bullying by student's grade level, and Table 4 shows bullying by both gender and grade level. Consistent with the structure of the school district, students in grades 3, 4, and 5 are elementary school students while those in grades 6, 7, and 8 are middle school students. Furthermore, one child in the "criminal behavior" group failed to identify their gender on the survey instrument and, as a result, is excluded from analyses when necessary. On all 4 tables, categorical variables are presented in frequencies and percentages while continuous variables are reported as means (± standard deviations).

RESULTS

Only 40 students responded that they have bullied other students when asked directly in one survey question, yet 70 students responded positively to perpetrating some form of bullying when asked about specific types of bullying behaviors or actions. Within this bullying group, 34 students (48.6%) reported that they have bullied a peer within the previous three months with a behavior that is technically a criminal offense. This group, the *criminal bullies*, forms one comparison group while non-criminal bullies and non-bullying students form the others. As detailed on Table 1, there does not appear to be substantial differences between the three groups on the limited demographic and attitudinal measures included here. The one exception, however, is student's feeling towards school. On this measure, although a vast majority of students in all three groups report liking school, a larger percentage of the students who have engaged in criminal bullying behaviors stated that they dislike school (11.8% compared to 8.3% and 7.4% in the other two groups, respectively). Accordingly, across the three groups, the "criminal bullying" group has the lowest percentage of students reporting that they like school.

Moving now to a focus only on those students who reported acts of criminal bullying, Table 2 shows that the most common criminal behavior for both genders is bullying of a physically abusive nature. The least common is the taking or damaging of money or property. More males reported threatening or forcing others to do things than females did (64.7% of males versus 37.5% of females). In fact, most males have engaged in multiple criminal behaviors while physical assault was the only behavior that involved a majority of females. Furthermore, males in this group participated in a wider variety of bullying behaviors, both criminal and otherwise, than females did. Specifically, a majority of males reported engaging in five of the nine bullying behaviors whereas a majority of females engaged in only three of these behaviors.

Table 3 shifts the focus from gender to student's grade level. In general, elementary school students engaged in almost all of the different types of bullying at a higher percentage than middle school students in the sub-sample did. The only exceptions were physical assault (86.7%

TABLE 1. Demographic and Attitudinal Characteristics (N = 192)

Characteristic	**Have Bullied Peers with Criminal Behavior in Past Three Months (n = 34)** Frequency (%) or Mean ± SD	**Have Bullied Peers with Non-Criminal Behavior in Past Three Months (n = 36)** Frequency (%) or Mean ± SD	**Have Not Bullied Peers in Past Three Months (n = 122)** Frequency (%) or Mean ± SD
Gender (n = 191)			
Male	17 (51.5)	17 (47.2)	58 (47.5)
Female	16 (48.5)	19 (52.8)	64 (52.5)
Current School Grade Level			
3rd Grade	6 (17.6)	7 (19.4)	32 (26.2)
4th Grade	4 (11.8)	6 (16.7)	14 (11.5)
5th Grade	9 (26.5)	5 (13.9)	22 (18.0)
6th Grade	2 (5.9)	6 (16.7)	22 (18.0)
7th Grade	5 (14.7)	6 (16.7)	17 (13.9)
8th Grade	8 (23.5)	6 (16.7)	15 (12.3)
Age	10.85 ± 1.79	10.78 ± 1.88	10.47 ± 1.83
Do you like school?			
I dislike school.	4 (11.8)	3 (8.3)	9 (7.4)
Neutral	8 (23.5)	9 (25.0)	22 (18.0)
I like school.	22 (64.7)	24 (66.7)	91 (74.6)
How many good friends do you have?			
None	0 (0.0)	0 (0.0)	1 (0.8)
1	3 (8.8)	3 (8.3)	6 (4.9)
2-3	7 (20.6)	4 (11.1)	27 (22.1)
4 or more	24 (70.6)	29 (80.6)	88 (72.1)

Column percentages may not total 100% because of rounding, SD = standard deviation

TABLE 2. Types of Bullying Committed in the Past Three Months by Gender (N = 33)

Type of Bullying	Males (n = 17) Frequency (%)	Females (n = 16) Frequency (%)
Criminal Behaviors		
Hit, Kicked, Shoved, or Assaulted Others	13 (76.5)	12 (75.0)
Took or Damaged Money or Items	6 (35.3)	5 (31.3)
Threatened or Forced Others to Do Things	11 (64.7)	6 (37.5)
Non-Criminal Behaviors		
Called Others Mean Names, Made Fun of, or Teased Them	10 (58.8)	12 (75.0)
Intentionally Excluded or Ignored Others	9 (52.9)	8 (50.0)
Spread Lies or False Rumors About Others	5 (29.4)	7 (43.8)
Said Comments or Called Others Names Based on Race or Color	6 (35.3)	2 (12.5)
Bullied Others with Sexual Comments, Names, or Gestures	10 (58.8)	5 (31.3)
Bullied Peers in Other Ways	7 (41.2)	3 (18.8)

TABLE 3. Types of Bullying Committed in the Past Three Months by Grade Level (N = 34)

Type of Bullying	Elementary School Students (n = 19) Frequency (%)	Middle School Students (n = 15) Frequency (%)
Criminal Behaviors		
Hit, Kicked, Shoved, or Assaulted Others	12 (63.2)	13 (86.7)
Took or Damaged Money or Items	8 (42.1)	3 (20.0)
Threatened or Forced Others to Do Things	11 (57.9)	7 (46.7)
Non-Criminal Behaviors		
Called Others Mean Names, Made Fun of, or Teased Them	13 (68.4)	10 (66.7)
Intentionally Excluded or Ignored Others	10 (52.6)	8 (53.3)
Spread Lies or False Rumors about Others	8 (42.1)	4 (26.7)
Said Comments or Called Others Names Based on Race or Color	5 (26.3)	3 (20.0)
Bullied Others with Sexual Comments, Names, or Gestures	10 (52.6)	6 (40.0)
Bullied Peers in Other Ways	10 (52.6)	1 (6.7)

of middle school students versus 63.2% of elementary school students) and the intentional exclusion of others (53.3% versus 52.6%).

Finally, Table 4 combines gender and grade level. Unfortunately, though this table allows for a greater depth of analysis, making such a combination yields smaller sample sizes for each column. As a result, the reduction in cell counts makes comparisons difficult and suspect. Nonetheless, it is important to note that there does not appear to be any glaring differences across the four groups.

DISCUSSION

Perhaps the most important finding to be extracted from the data is the overall prevalence of criminal bullying within this sample. Explicitly, 17.7% of the total sample (or 48.6% of bullies) reported engaging in these specific behaviors at some point in the previous three months. It is also interesting to note the differences in attitudes towards school, with the criminal bullying group reporting higher levels of dislike and neutrality for school. While this group is more extreme in their negativity than the non-criminal bullying group, the finding is consistent with other studies that describe bullies as being in opposition to peers and teachers and, eventually, less interested in school affiliations (Pellegrini, Bartini, & Brooks, 1999).

The remaining three tables (Tables 2-4) provide deeper descriptive analyses of the criminal bullying subgroup. Beyond this purpose, however, the utility of these tables is limited. This may be due to the relatively small sample size or the lack of a relevant comparison group. In any case, the general pattern that males are more involved in bullying is consistent with the existing literature (Nansel et al., 2001; Dake, Price, & Telljohann, 2003). The finding on Table 3, however, that elementary school bullies were more involved in a variety of bullying behaviors than their middle school counterparts, deviates somewhat from the conclusions of other studies that show a rise in bullying problems during early adolescence (which usually coincides with the end of middle school and beginning of high school; Pellegrini, Bartini, & Brooks, 1999). One explanation for this finding, though, may be that this study measured variety in bullying behaviors and not frequency.

Implications for Service Delivery

The recognition of the criminality inherent in specific bullying behaviors has real implications for social work intervention and service

TABLE 4. Types of Bullying Committed in Past Three Months by Gender and Grade Level (N = 33)

Type of Bullying	Elementary School Students		Middle School Students	
	Males (n = 13) Frequency (%)	**Females (n = 5)** Frequency (%)	**Males (n = 4)** Frequency (%)	**Females (n = 11)** Frequency (%)
Criminal Behaviors				
Hit, Kicked, Shoved, or Assaulted Others	9 (69.2)	3 (60.0)	4 (100.0)	9 (81.8)
Took or Damaged Money or Items	6 (46.2)	2 (40.0)	0 (0.0)	3 (27.3)
Threatened or Forced Others to Do Things	9 (69.2)	1 (20.0)	2 (50.0)	5 (45.5)
Non-Criminal Behaviors				
Called Others Mean Names, Made Fun of, or Teased Them	8 (61.5)	4 (80.0)	2 (50.0)	8 (72.7)
Intentionally Excluded or Ignored Others	6 (46.2)	3 (60.0)	3 (75.0)	5 (45.5)
Spread Lies or False Rumors About Others	4 (30.8)	4 (80.0)	1 (25.0)	3 (27.3)
Said Comments or Called Others Names Based on Race or Color	4 (30.8)	1 (20.0)	2 (50.0)	1 (9.1)
Bullied Others with Sexual Comments, Names, or Gestures	7 (53.8)	2 (40.0)	3 (75.0)	3 (27.3)
Bullied Peers in Other Ways	7 (53.8)	2 (40.0)	0 (0.0)	1 (9.1)

delivery. Previous research has established the link between childhood or juvenile delinquency and an increased likelihood of offending in adulthood (Wolfgang, Thornberry, & Figlio, 1987; Sampson & Laub, 1993). This relationship has also been clearly demonstrated for bullies. As outlined in the introductory section, Olweus (1993; 1994) and others (see MacNeil, 2002) have shown that, as young adults, males with a history of school bullying have as much as a fourfold increase in their level of serious, recidivist criminality when compared to a control group of males who have not engaged in bullying. These former bullies are also more likely to violently abuse their spouses and to utilize harsher discipline with their own children (MacNeil, 2002).

The findings of these previous research studies combined with the main finding of this study that many students have indeed engaged in criminal bullying would seem to clearly place bullying into a continuum of criminal offending. In fact, given the young age of the students in this study, these children may be an even more problematic group than most, especially since studies have shown that approximately half of all males who become serious juvenile offenders have an onset of delinquent behavior before the age of 12 years (Stouthamer-Loeber & Loeber, 2002).

Of course, many school bullies and young offenders do not continue their criminal careers into adulthood and curbing future criminal involvement should be a very real goal of any interventions intended for a criminal bullying population. Before the development of such interventions, however, more research is needed to further develop and expand upon the notion of the "criminal bully" as a unique type of school bully. Similarly, it is also imperative not to ignore the influence of childhood developmental stages on perceptions of bullying. For example, fighting, especially among very young children, may signify age-appropriate conflict resolution skills or the child's level of emotional maturity. It will be important, therefore, to incorporate developmental theory into these research endeavors aimed at characterizing and conceptualizing the "criminal bully."

This study should be viewed as a first step in this direction. The data reported here are descriptive and not without limitations. Specifically, this study did not use random assignment or a control group and subjects were impaneled from only one region of the country. Besides utilizing a more rigorous study design, the next step in this line of research should evaluate the myriad of psychosocial factors that may differentiate those students engaging in criminal bullying from other bullies as well as from other students. Future studies seeking to advance knowledge on this topic should consider using a longitudinal study design and a variety of data collection tools, instruments, and standardized measures.

CONCLUSION

At this point, the "criminal bully" typology is conceptual. It is a hypothesis–a proposal or a suggestion–inviting further investigation, rigorous evaluation, discussion, and debate. The research done here is exploratory and done with the intention of stimulating deeper exploration. The data suggest that the scope of criminal bullying in schools is sizable, with approximately one-fifth of all study respondents (and 50% of all bullies) engaging in such behavior. The development of evidence-based interventions designed to serve this group will, therefore, not only help to deter these individuals from later deviance, but will also make schools safer and more comfortable for all children.

Regardless of bullying typologies, the seriousness of criminal bullying should be appreciated. The behaviors contained within a "criminal bully" label are among the most serious and threatening acts confronting children in schools today. The inclusion of such behaviors on a continuum of aggression, juvenile delinquency, and later adult offending is natural and appropriate. While progression along such a continuum is far from inevitable, the similarities between bullies and criminal offenders and the current trend towards criminalizing school bullying suggests that criminal bullying should, at the very least, be recognized as a marker for the development of more serious problems later.

REFERENCES

Akers, R. (1973). *Deviant behavior: A social learning approach.* Belmont, CA: Wadsworth.

Cloward, R. A., & Ohlin, L. E. (1960). *Delinquency and opportunity: A theory of delinquent gangs* (3rd ed.). Glencoe, IL: The Free Press of Glencoe.

Dake, J. A., Price, J. H., & Telljohann, S. K. (2003). The nature and extent of bullying at school. *Journal of School Health, 73* (5), 173-181.

Espelage, D. L., & Swearer, S. M. (2003). Research on school bullying and victimization: What have we learned and where do we go from here? *School Psychology Review, 32* (3), 365-383.

Farrington, D. (1987). Predicting individual crime rates. In D. Gottfredson & M. Tonry (Eds.), *Prediction and classification: Criminal justice decision making* (pp. 53-102). Chicago, IL: University of Chicago Press.

Furlong, M., & Morrison, G. (2000). The school in school violence: Definitions and facts. *Journal of Emotional and Behavioral Disorders, 8* (2), 71-85.

Furniss, C. (2000). Bullying in schools: It's not a crime–is it? *Education and the Law, 12* (1), 10-29.

Limber, S. P., & Small, M. A. (2003). State laws and policies to address bullying in schools. *School Psychology Review, 32* (3), 445-455.

MacNeil, G. (2002). School bullying: An overview. In L. A. Rapp-Paglicci, A. R. Roberts, & J. S. Wodarski (Eds.), *Handbook of violence* (pp. 247-261). New York, NY: John Wiley & Sons, Inc.

Nansel, T. R., Overpeck, M., Pilla, R. S., Ruan, W. J., Simons-Morton, B., & Scheidt, P. (2001). Bullying behaviors among US youth: Prevalence and association with psychosocial adjustment. *Journal of the American Medical Association, 285* (16), 2094-2100.

Olweus, D. (1993). *Bullying at school: What we know and what we can do.* Oxford, United Kingdom: Blackwell Publishers.

Olweus, D. (1994). Annotation: Bullying at school: Basic facts and effects of a school based intervention program. *Journal of Child Psychology and Psychiatry, 35* (7), 1171-1190.

Olweus, D. (1986). *The Olweus Bully/Victim Questionnaire.* Mimeo. Bergen, Norway: University of Bergen.

Pellegrini, A. D., Bartini, M., & Brooks, F. (1999). School bullies, victims, and aggressive victims: Factors relating to group affiliation and victimization in early adolescence. *Journal of Educational Psychology, 91* (2), 216-224.

Rigby, K., & Cox, I. (1996). The contribution of bullying at school and low self-esteem to acts of delinquency among Australian teenagers. *Personality and individual differences, 21* (4), 609-612.

Sampson, R. J., & Laub, J. H. (1993). *Crime in the making: Pathways and turning points through life.* Cambridge, MA: Harvard University Press.

Stouthamer-Loeber, M., & Loeber, R. (2002). Lost opportunities for intervention: Undetected markers for the development of serious juvenile delinquency. *Criminal behavior and mental health, 12,* 69-82.

Sutherland, E. (1924). *Criminology.* Philadelphia, PA: J.B. Lippincott.

Will, J. D., & Neufeld, P. J. (2003). Keep bullying from growing into greater violence. *Education Digest, 68* (6), 32-37.

Wolfgang, M. E., Thornberry, T. P., & Figlio, R. M. (1987). *From boy to man, from delinquency to crime.* Chicago, IL: University of Chicago Press.

A Solution-Focused Approach to Crisis Intervention with Adolescents

Laura M. Hopson, MSSW
Johnny S. Kim, MSW

SUMMARY. The article provides a description of a solution-focused approach to crisis intervention with adolescents. A description of common developmental and environmental factors that may result in crises for adolescents is presented, followed by an overview of solution-focused therapy. Similarities between solution-focused therapy and strength's-based crisis intervention and intervention with adolescents are discussed. The assumptions and techniques of solution focused therapy that meet the particular needs of adolescents in crisis are presented along with a typical solution-focused session adapted for use with adolescents in crisis. An overview of efficacy research on solution-focused therapy with adolescents is also presented. *[Article copies available for a fee from The Haworth Document Delivery Service: 1-800-HAWORTH. E-mail address: <docdelivery@haworthpress.com> Website: <http://www.HaworthPress.com> © 2004 by The Haworth Press, Inc. All rights reserved.]*

Laura M. Hopson (Email: laurahopson@mail.utexas.edu) and Johnny S. Kim are affiliated with The University of Texas at Austin, School of Social Work, 1925 San Jacinto Boulevard, Austin, TX 78712-1203.

[Haworth co-indexing entry note]: "A Solution-Focused Approach to Crisis Intervention with Adolescents." Hopson, Laura M. and Johnny S. Kim. Co-published simultaneously in *Journal of Evidence-Based Social Work* (The Haworth Social Work Practice Press, an imprint of The Haworth Press, Inc.) Vol. 1, No. 2/3, 2004, pp. 93-110; and: *Kids and Violence: The Invisible School Experience* (ed: Catherine N. Dulmus and Karen M. Sowers) The Haworth Social Work Practice Press, an imprint of The Haworth Press, Inc., 2004, pp. 93-110. Single or multiple copies of this article are available for a fee from The Haworth Document Delivery Service [1-800-HAWORTH, 9:00 a.m. - 5:00 p.m. (EST). E-mail address: docdelivery@haworthpress.com].

http://www.haworthpress.com/web/JEBSW

Digital Object Identifier: 10.1300/J394v1n02_07

KEYWORDS. Adolescence, crisis, crisis intervention, solution-focused therapy, suicide

ADOLESCENTS IN CRISIS

Adolescents may be at greater risk than adults for experiencing a crisis because the developmental tasks associated with adolescence and daily environmental stressors can require sophisticated coping strategies. An adolescent does not have control over many aspects of daily life and may be more susceptible than an adult to experiencing a situation as a crisis (O'Halloran and Copeland, 2000). Teens may have strained relationships with family members because they are struggling with a desire for more autonomy while continuing to want guidance from adults. Sexual development can result in dissatisfaction with appearance, low self-esteem, and a concern that developmental changes are not normal (Aguilera, 1990). A typical adolescent may experience conflicts with parents and peers, fluctuation in mood, and experimentation with risky behaviors (Arnett, 1999, as cited in O'Halloran and Copeland, 2000). Because adolescents are already engaged in rapid change and, at times, disequilibrium, they are more vulnerable in crisis situations in which they are thrown into a state of further disequilibrium (O'Halloran and Copeland, 2000).

In addition to being more vulnerable to crises because of their stage in development, adolescents are also likely to be exposed to many stressors in their environment that can precipitate a crisis. Such stressors include exposure to violence in schools and gang activity, experiencing the loss of a parent due to divorce, and consequences of alcohol and drug use and unprotected sexual intercourse (Jobes, Berman, and Martin, 2000; O'Halloran and Copeland, 2000; Putnam, 1995).

In a 1997 survey conducted by the National Institute on Alcohol Abuse and Alcoholism, 16% of eighth graders, 25% of 10th graders and 30% of 12th graders reported binge drinking (defined as five or more drinks in a row) at least once in the two weeks prior to completing the survey. These teens are vulnerable to experiencing a crisis because alcohol use is associated with considering and attempting suicide, deaths due to drinking and driving, and risky sexual behavior (National Institute on Alcohol Abuse and Alcoholism, 1997). Drug use among teens may result in similar consequences. Despite decreases in drug use among teens in the past few years, 24.5% of 8th graders, 44.6% of 10th graders, and 53% of 12th graders reported using some kind of illicit drug in a 2002 survey (National Institutes on Drug Abuse, 2003). Unprotected intercourse also continues to put adolescents at risk for crisis. In 1999, three million teens were diagnosed with a sexually transmitted disease, and 10% of girls between the ages of 15 and 19 became pregnant. Twenty percent of abortions involved teens 19 years old or younger (Alan Guttmacher Instititute, 1999).

Situations at home and at school can precipitate crises for adolescents. High divorce rates mean that more than half of parents' marriages will end in divorce, which can be a source of great stress for adolescents (O'Halloran and Copeland, 2000). They may also experience many stressors while at school. According to survey data collected by the National Center for Educational Statistics in 1999, 8% of students in grades six through twelve reported criminal victimization at school, 8% of students in grades nine through twelve reported being threatened or injured with a weapon on school property, and 5% of students age twelve through eighteen reported that they had been afraid of being attacked or harmed on school property during the past six months (Kaufman, Chen, Choi, Peter, Ruddy, Miller, Fleury, Chandler, Planty, and Rand, 2001).

Determining when a teen is experiencing a crisis is important because of the potential for suicidal ideation. Suicide is the third leading cause of death among teenagers and results in the death of 8 of every 100,000 teens between the ages of 15 and 19. Nineteen percent of teens in grades one through twelve reported that they had considered suicide, and 8.8% reported that they had attempted suicide in 2001 (National Center for Health Statistics, 2002).

DEFINING CRISIS

Defining crisis is difficult because it is the individual's perception of an event that determines whether it is a crisis (Roberts, 2000). The same situation may be called stress for one person, a trauma for another, and a crisis for a third. Many factors, such as stage of development, personality, life experience, and coping strategies, may determine whether an event causes a crisis for an individual (Dulmus and Hilarski, 2003). In order to reduce ambiguity about the meaning of crisis, Roberts (2000) has created a definition of crisis and a model for crisis intervention that represents a synthesis of ideas expressed by Gerald Caplan, Naomi Golan, Howard Parad, and Albert Roberts, and Sophia Dziegielewski. He defines a crisis as a state of psychological disequilibium caused by an event perceived as hazardous and an inability to use existing coping skills to resolve the crisis (Roberts, 2000). Three criteria must exist in order for an individual to experience a crisis: the individual must have been exposed to a stressful or hazardous event; the individual's perception of that event leads to considerable upset or disruption; the individual is unable to resolve the disruption with previously used coping mechanisms (Parad, 1971, as cited in Roberts, 2000).

Determining when an adolescent is in crisis can be especially challenging. Whether stressors precipitate a crisis for adolescents depends on many factors, such as the teen's resiliency, maturity, and protective factors. Adolescents of the same age may vary widely in their maturity level and their ability to cope with daily stressors. Because adolescents may be more vulnerable to experiencing a crisis than an adult, practitioners working with adolescents cannot assume that their perception accurately reflects an adolescent's perspective (O'Halloran and Copeland, 2000).

A STRENGTHS-BASED APPROACH TO CRISIS INTERVENTION

There are numerous approaches to crisis intervention that differ in style, length of treatment, and the parameters of treatment (Roberts, 2000). Despite the variation among approaches, there are commonalities between the different models. Many approaches emphasize the need for intervening quickly with brief treatment, obtaining a detailed description of the crisis situation and the client's emotional state, and defining clear, specific goals (Roberts, 2000; Berg, 2002; Aguilera, 1990; Golan, 1978). Many traditional approaches to crisis intervention define an intervention as successful if it returns a client to their pre-crisis state of functioning. A strengths-based approach to crisis intervention goes beyond this definition by viewing crisis intervention as an opportunity to develop new coping skills and leave the client with more strengths and resources after the crisis is resolved (Greene, Lee, Trask, and Rheinsheld, 2000). A strengths-based approach to crisis intervention emphasizes active listening, building on inner strengths, and developing new coping skills. During crisis intervention, it is important to maintain a strengths-focused approach that emphasizes joining and active listening in order to adequately understand the crisis from the client's perspective, since the client's perspective defines whether a situation is a crisis (Roberts, 2000; Greene et al., 2000). Examining inner strengths is important because it helps the therapist understand the strengths on which the therapist can encourage the client to draw in managing the crisis. It is important to develop new coping skills in order to ensure that clients emerge from the crisis with more strengths than they had before. These characteristics are also central to solution-focused therapy and contribute to its potential as an effective model for crisis intervention (Roberts, 2000; Greene et. al., 2000).

The solution-focused approach goes beyond returning a client to their pre-crisis state of functioning. Solution-focused therapy views a crisis as an opportunity for clients to develop new coping skills, which can result in increased resiliency in dealing with future crisis situations. It is appropriate for crisis intervention because it is a brief therapy model that can produce quick change in clients, and it focuses on the client's present situation instead of the history of the problem. Solution-focused therapy aims to use empathy and active listening to understand the client's view of the problem, which is critical in understanding whether a client is experiencing a crisis (Greene et al., 2000). A crisis for one individual may not be a crisis for another (Dulmus and Hilarski, 2003; Roberts, 2000). The solution-focused therapist also works with clients to define concrete, specific goals as quickly as possible and moves quickly toward discussing solutions. This is critical in effective crisis intervention, when clients often feel too overwhelmed to define goals but need to do so quickly to ensure their safety and well-being (Green et al., 2000).

A strength's-based approach has also been described as useful for work with adolescents in crisis. (O'Halloran and Copeland, 2000; Yeager and Gregoire, 2000). Solution-focused therapy is well-suited for work with adolescents in crisis because their stage in development may cause them to feel resentful of a more directive or problem-focused approach to therapy. Adolescents in crisis are likely to view themselves as responsible for negative outcomes in their lives and the therapist may need to help them reduce feelings of self-blame (O'Halloran and Copeland, 2000). Solution-focused therapy minimizes these feelings by emphasizing strengths and helping the adolescent see that their problems exist outside of themselves (Corcoran, 1998). Working with adolescents can also present many challenges in therapy because they may be distrustful of adults. While they still need to feel protected by their families, they want to separate from their parents and gain more independence. Because of these developmental tasks, adolescents are likely to be resistant to engaging in treatment (O'Halloran and Copeland, 2000). Solution-focused therapy communicates a great deal of respect for the client from the beginning and view the client as the expert on the problem. This can reduce feelings of resistance while helping the adolescent feel that they may already have some of the resources needed to address their problems (Corcoran, 1998).

AN OVERVIEW OF SOLUTION-FOCUSED THERAPY

Solution-focused therapists work to demonstrate great respect for the client and belief that the client is the expert in resolving their problem. They assume that clients have the knowledge, strength, skills, and insights to solve their own problems (Berg, 1994). Four underlying assumptions guide solution-focused therapy sessions:

1. Every client is unique;
2. Clients have the inherent strength and resources to help themselves;
3. Change is constant and inevitable, and small change can lead to bigger changes;
4. Since it is not possible to change the past, the session should concentrate on the present and future (Lipchik, 2002). A review of the main techniques of solution-focused therapy and description of sessions provides an understanding of how the approach draws on client strengths to achieve goals quickly.

Franklin and Biever (1997, as cited in Franklin and Moore, 1999) outline the following steps of a typical first session in solution-focused therapy:

- A conversation between the therapist and client to find out about the client's life
- Gathering a brief description of the problem and the context of the problem
- Asking relationship questions
- Tracking exceptions to the problem
- Scaling the problem
- Using coping questions
- Asking the miracle question to develop solutions
- Negotiating the goal for change
- Taking a session break
- Delivering compliments and tasks or homework assignments

Throughout the intervention, the therapist defines the problem and potential helpful solutions in terms of the client's perceptions. There is continuous reinforcing of clients' strengths and complimenting them for every success in their attempts to cope.

SOLUTION-FOCUSED THERAPY WITH ADOLESCENTS IN CRISIS

Some modifications to the typical solution-focused therapy session may be necessary to make it appropriate for crisis intervention with adolescents. The following represents a description of the steps outlined by Franklin and Biever (1997, as cited in Franklin and Moore, 1999) and suggests some modifications for use with adolescents in crisis:

A Conversation Between the Therapist and Client to Find Out About the Client's Life

This conversation begins the process of joining with the client by understanding the things that are important to the client, the problem-solving strategies the client has used, the client's successes and failures around the presenting problem, motivation level, and the client's resources (Berg, 1994). The therapist takes the position of "not knowing" by laying aside all preconceptions about the problem and its potential solutions (Berg, 2002). Since adolescents of the same age group may vary on each of these factors, the solution-focused approach of laying aside all preconceived notions about the client and the problem can be valuable.

This conversation is helpful for work with adolescents in crisis, because it is important to join with them immediately to begin assessing the potential lethality of their situation, their existing coping skills and resiliency (Greene et al., 2000). The solution-focused approach may be better suited for adolescents than other approaches because of the distrust they often feel for adults (O'Halloran and Copeland, 2000). A respectful, not-knowing approach may decrease such feelings of distrust. It is especially important to establish a supportive working relationship between the adolescent and therapist quickly when the adolescent may be suicidal because it may help them feel more comfortable discussing their desire to harm themselves (Jobes, Berman, and Martin, 2000; Sharry, Darmody, and Madden, 2002).

Gather a Description of the Problem and the Context of the Problem

Joining with the client continues during this step in the intervention. The therapist allows the client to define the problem and does not impose his or her own ideas about the problem and its potential solutions. The therapist typically works to change the focus of the discussion from the problem to potential solutions. Through the technique of externalizing the problem, the therapist encourages clients to view their problems as separate from themselves and develop confidence that they can overcome the problem (Franklin and Moore, 1999).

Affirming the client's definition of the problem demonstrates the therapist's commitment to understanding the client's perspective (Berg, 2002). This can continue to decrease any resistance an adolescent might feel towards the therapist. While a solution-focused therapist typically works quickly to shift the client's pattern of talking about the problem to talking about solutions, the solution-focused approach to crisis intervention devotes more time to gathering a detailed description of the problem. Because clients are so overwhelmed, they are likely to devote much of the first session to discussing the problem. In a crisis situation, giving the client space to talk about their feelings surrounding the problem and can help the client feel less overwhelmed and help the therapist gain a more complete understanding of the client's perception of the problem and how it has become a crisis for the client (Berg, 2002; Greene et al., 2000). However, the detailed problem description should not take the place of solution-building, because solution-focused therapy assumes that talking about strengths and coping successes can provide a more thorough client assessment than simply asking for a description of the problem (Berg, 2002).

Adolescents who are vulnerable to crises are likely to view themselves as responsible for negative outcomes in their lives (O'Halloran and Copeland, 2000). The solution-focused therapist's reliance on the client's understanding of the crisis can help reveal when an adolescent blames him or herself for the crisis event (O'Halloran and Copeland, 2000). The technique of externalizing the problem may help reduce feelings of self-blame because the problem is viewed as existing separately from the individual (Corcoran, 1998).

If an adolescent expresses suicidal ideation, the therapist will need to ask questions that specifically address the lethality of their intentions. This may require a more direct questioning approach than that usually taken in solution-focused therapy. If the adolescent is actively suicidal and has a plan for suicide, the therapist may need to hospitalize the client instead of proceeding with solution-focused therapy. However, the techniques used in therapy to join with the clients and obtain a definition of the problem from the client's perspective can ensure that the therapist is assessing the lethality of the situation as accurately as possible (Berg, 2002).

Asking Relationship Questions

Relationship questions ask the client how others, such as parents or teachers, would perceive the presenting problem. They help determine what the client believes are others' perceptions of the problem. These questions are helpful in understanding who is involved in the problem and who are potential resources for the client. Relationship questions are helpful in working with adolescents in crisis because they give the therapist information about who is involved in the teen's definition of the crisis situation. The teen's answers to these questions also help the practitioner know who to consult during the treatment and whom to include in sessions (Franklin and Biever, 1997). These questions can also assess for resiliency since spending more time with peers and social skills are associated with resiliency (O'Halloran and Copeland, 2000).

Tracking Exceptions to the Problem

In order to shift client's focus away from the problem to times when the problem was not present, the therapist asks about times when the presenting problem could have happened but did not. In finding examples of times when the problem was absent and how they accomplished this absence, clients may feel that they already have the skills and knowledge to succeed (de Shazer, 1988; Berg, 1994). When a client is having difficulty in thinking of exceptions to the problem, the therapist can ask for times when the problem was less severe or less frequent (Berg, 1994).

As with any other client, practitioners can ask adolescents in crisis about exceptions to the problem to engender a sense of hope that things will get better. This can be helpful in crisis situations, since clients who are overwhelmed and are currently unable to use coping skills to resolve the crisis (Roberts, 2000). With adolescents, this can be especially problematic because they have difficulty seeing beyond the present situation and believing that things will improve (Jobes et al., 2000). Finding exceptions to the problem encourages clients to see that they have been able to cope with similar problems in the past, that the problem could possibly be worse, and that they can imagine a future without the problem. This technique can help adolescents think of ways they may be able to cope with the current crisis (O'Halloran and Copeland, 2000).

Scaling the Problem

Scaling questions are used for assessment in many areas, such as self-esteem, prioritizing problems, perceptions of hopelessness, and progress towards achieving goals. Typically, scaling questions ask clients to rate where they are on a scale from 0 to 10 with 0 being the worst/lowest and 10 being the best/highest. Scaling is a versatile technique that most clients easily understand and can be especially helpful when clients are having a difficult time seeing their progress (Sklare, 1997; Berg, 1994).

Scaling questions are useful in gathering many different kind of information throughout solution-focused therapy sessions (Berg, 1994). They can be very helpful with children and adolescents because even young children can relate to the idea of rating something on a scale from one to ten (Berg, 1994). They are also helpful in identifying potential solutions to a problem. If a client ranks the situation as less problematic in successive sessions, the therapist asks the client about the reasons for the improvement (Greene et al., 2000; Berg, 2002). This technique also places the responsibility for evaluating progress toward achieving goals on the adolescent (Corcoran, 1998).

Scaling questions are helpful in assessing an adolescent's safety, feelings of depression or suicidality, and perceived coping ability. Asking how seriously an adolescent is considering suicide on a scale from 1 to 10 can help the solution-focused therapist assess the lethality of the crisis situation and how well the adolescent perceives their own coping ability (O'Halloran and Copeland, 2000; Sharry, Darmody, and Madden, 2002).

Using Coping and Motivation Questions

In asking coping questions, the practitioner begins with the client's definition of the problem and asks how they have been able to cope with this problem until now. The practitioner listens for any strengths in the client's explanation and directs coping questions based on the strengths and resources the client has used (Berg, 1994). Coping questions can be helpful when an adolescent in crisis has difficulty identifying exceptions to the problem or past successes in dealing with a similar problem (Greene et al., 2000). The therapist asks how the client has managed to function as well as they have given the presence of the crisis situation. Asking a coping question such as, "What have you found helpful so far?" demonstrates that the therapist thinks the client has already learned some coping skills. This further emphasizes the client's strengths and can instill hope and motivation in clients (Berg, 2002).

Coping questions can be helpful with suicidal adolescents in determining the appropriate treatment. Therapists working with clients in crisis are often quick to consider medication and hospitalization. If they ask coping questions first, they can make a better determination of how well the client is coping and whether more extreme measures are needed to ensure the client's safety (Berg, 2002).

Asking the Miracle Question to Develop Solutions

The miracle question is used to help the client formulate a well-defined and achievable goal. The therapist asks the client to imagine what their lives would be like if the problem were suddenly solved. In shifting client's focus away from the presenting problem so they can envision their lives after their problems are resolved, the miracle question engenders hope and defines the desired outcome in the client's terms. In addition, the therapist also uses the miracle question to help clients identify ways that the solution may already be occurring in their lives (Berg, 1994).

The miracle question may not be appropriate in working with adolescents in crisis. In order for the miracle question to be helpful, the client must be able to consider the possibility that the problem can be solved (Berg, 2002). Clients in crisis and especially adolescents who have difficulty seeing beyond the present situation may be too overwhelmed to begin considering what life would be like if the problem were suddenly and magically solved (Berg, 2002). If the client is able to consider what life would be like after the crisis is resolved, the miracle question can be helpful in defining concrete, specific goals (Greene et al., 2000). It may be helpful to ask a miracle question about a small aspect of the crisis situation instead of asking what it would be like if the crisis were solved altogether (Berg, 2002).

Negotiating the Goal for Change

The therapist and client work together to develop goals. Goals need to be specific, attainable, and important to the clients so that they will be motivated to accomplish them. Occasionally, clients will state harmful or unlawful goals, which the therapist cannot support. In this case, the therapist asks questions about the desired outcome of the goal instead of the harmful goal itself and helps the client formulate a positive goal that can achieve the desired result. If, for example, the client is a teenager who wants to run away from home, the therapist could ask questions to help identify why the client wants to run away from home and then co-construct healthier goals that the client can attain (Sklare, 1997).

Solution-focused therapy emphasizes the importance of setting small, specific, achievable goals. This is especially helpful for adolescents in crisis because they feel that the problem is beyond their control and may need to work toward small goals (Roberts, 2000). Adolescents often define their problem in vague, ambiguous terms and may need help creating manageable goals (Corcoran, 1998). Solution-focused goals are based on the client's ideas about potential solutions and are expressed in their own words. Such goals are important in crisis situations, because a client is more likely to work toward a goal in which they feel personally invested (Greene et al., 2000). Goals are articulated in positive terms indicating what clients want to be present in their lives instead of what they want to be absent. This is important in engendering hope and creating goals that define concretely actions the client can take to improve their situation (Berg, 1994) and can be especially important when working with a suicidal adolescent (Sharry et al., 2002).

With a suicidal adolescent, the session goals will need to include removing any means for self-harm, such as pills or weapons, making a contract with the adolescent that they will not harm him or herself, scheduling the next session and phone contacts between sessions, if necessary, referring the adolescent for an assessment to determine whether medication is needed, decreasing isolation by mobilizing friends and family to be available to the adolescent, considering hospitalization if the adolescent cannot negotiate his or her safety (Jobes et al., 2000). While these techniques are not part of a traditional solution-focused therapy session, the approach is flexible in incorporating other techniques as long as they are used because the client sees them as helpful.

At this stage in the session, after exploring coping questions and scaling questions, the client may be too overwhelmed to identify any means of coping with the crisis. If this is the case, the therapist may need to consider alternatives such as medication or hospitalization. The solution-focused approach remains helpful because clients may be willing to consider such alternatives after forming a close, supporting relationship with the therapist (Berg, 2002).

Taking a Session Break

Solution-focused therapy sessions typically include a break near the end of the session. The break is important in allowing the therapist time to formulate feedback and genuine compliments for the client as well as generating ideas for appropriate homework tasks.

Delivering Compliments and Tasks or Homework Assignments

The therapist delivers genuine compliments based on the client's strengths, such as those elicited through exception questions or the miracle question. Delivering compliments is another step in the process of helping clients see their own strengths and increase their awareness that they have the ability to solve their problems. With an adolescent in crisis, genuine compliments can continue the process of identifying client strengths and resources that they already have and can use to resolve the crisis. The therapist should be only use genuine compliments based on session content and should not overcompliment adolescents because they are likely to view this behavior as insincere.

The therapist and client also set a behavioral task for the client to complete before the next session. Tasks are often defined by behaviors the client has indicated as helpful through exception questions or coping questions. The therapist will give the client the talk of "Doing more of the same" for behaviors that clients have describes as helpful in coping. Clients will be directed to "do something different" when they indicate that they have tried one way of coping numerous times with no success (Berg, 1994; Berg, 2002). Such strategies result in concrete tasks that the adolescent may be likely to complete, because they are based on strategies that the client has defined as helpful or not helpful.

IMPORTANCE OF CRISIS INTERVENTION IN A SCHOOL SETTING

Any approach to crisis intervention with adolescents must be useful in a school setting. Many precipitating events of a crisis for adolescents may take place while they are at school. Because depressed or suicidal adolescents may express suicidal ideation at school, schools should be prepared for how to thoroughly assess students and respond quickly with appropriate treatments. Addressing crisis situations in a school setting requires great collaboration to ensure that the students' needs are met. Teachers, counselors, social workers, and other staff may have different understandings about the best approach for the student, which can lead to a situation in which no one addresses the crisis situation appropriately (Kline, Schonfeld, and Lichenstein, 1995; Poland, 1994).

Solution-focused therapy can be applied well to situations that arise in a school setting because of its emphasis on active listening and focusing on strengths, which can facilitate collaboration with others involved with the client. Solution-focused therapy allows for the use of tools from other models as long as they are used thoughtfully to accommodate the client's goals instead of attempting to fit the client's situation into a predetermined mold defined by that approach. Therefore, solution-focused therapists in a school setting collaborate with students, parents and teachers in developing interventions. The therapist adopts the stance that there are many approaches that may result in solutions and respects the unique ideas, beliefs, and styles of students, parents, and teachers (Murphy, 2000). A collaborative approach to crisis intervention in which all staff members involved with a student work together can develop an atmosphere promoting sharing and more personal and positive relationships between students and staff that can last after the crisis is resolved (Kline et al., 1995). The solution-focused practice of defining small, concrete goals is also more realistic is a school situation in which those involved have limited time and resources (Murphy, 1996).

EFFICACY OF SOLUTION-FOCUSED THERAPY WITH ADOLESCENTS

While much more research is needed on the efficacy of solution-focused therapy, there are a few existing studies that demonstrate its effectiveness with adolescents. Many of these studies were conducted in a school setting as well. Findings suggest that solution-focused therapy results in positive outcomes for students on self-esteem measures and coping measures (Lafountain and Garner, 1996), a reduction in acting-out behaviors and other behavior problems (Franklin, Biever, Moore, Clemons, and Scamardo, 2001; Franklin, Corcoran, Nowicki, and Streeter, 1997; Corcoran and Stephenson, 2000; Newsome, 2002), reaching goals (Newsome, 2002; LaFountain and Garner, 1996; Littrell,

Malia, and Vanderwood, 1995), and improved social skills (Newsome, 2002).

Not all findings conclusively support the efficacy of solution-focused intervention. Littrell et al. (1995) found that each of three brief-therapy approaches were equally in adolescents reaching their goals in many areas, even though participants in solution-focused therapy achieved their goals more quickly than did adolescents in the other two conditions. Springer, Lynch, and Rubin (2000) found no significant treatment effects on children's self-esteem in their study evaluating the effectiveness of a solution-focused approach with Hispanic children of incarcerated parents.

While some of the studies have well-controlled designs or moderately controlled designs, many of the studies have design limitations. Some of the studies lack a comparison group (Newsome, 2002; Corcoran and Stephenson, 2000) or had a comparison group but did not use random assignment (Springer et al., 2000). Others used single case designs which may have limited external validity (Franklin et al., 2001; Franklin et al., 1997), or used subjective measures in evaluating progress (LaFountain and Garner, 1996; Corcoran and Stephenson, 2000), and limited monitoring of treatment fidelity (Corcoran and Stephenson, 2000). Despite such limitations, the findings of most of the outcome studies evaluating solution-focused therapy with adolescents demonstrate that solution-focused therapy is a promising model and warrants further research on its effectiveness. Research is needed to specifically investigate whether solution-focused therapy is effective when applied to adolescents in crisis.

SUMMARY AND CONCLUSION

Many basic solution-focused techniques are consistent with practices recommended by those advocating a strengths-based approach to crisis intervention. Roberts (2000) emphasizes establishing rapport and communication and identifying major problems quickly in crisis intervention, which is consistent with the solution-focused approach of immediately joining with the client and understanding the client's definition of the problem. Dealing with feelings and providing support, which is consistent throughout the solution-focused therapy session, is also important in crisis intervention (Roberts, 2000; Berg, 2002; Greene et al., 2000). Exception questions, coping questions, and the miracle question allow the therapist to explore coping skills and strengths clients already have which can be helpful in resolving the crisis. The solution-focused practice of defining specific, achievable goals quickly is consistent with the need in crisis intervention to define concrete goals that will ensure the client's safety and a resolution to the crisis that will result in increased strengths and coping skills (Greene et al., 2000).

While a crisis represents a painful disruption in individuals' lives, it also has the potential to promote growth and new coping skills (Dulmus and Hilarski, 2003; Roberts, 2000; Berg, 2002). Crisis intervention presents an opportunity for those working with adolescents to strengthen their skills and their self-esteem at a time when they may be the most vulnerable (O'Halloran and Copeland, 2000). The solution-focused approach is well-suited for work with adolescents because of its emphasis on moving clients beyond a resolution of the crisis situation to developing an increased awareness of their strengths and a belief that they have the resources to cope with their problems. Learning solution-focused strategies during adolescence can promote a sense of strength and efficacy. It is the strategy of the solution-focused therapist to "leave no footprint." In other words, the client should feel that they alone are responsible for their successes (Berg, 1994). Leaving adolescents with this sense of self-confidence can help them cope more effectively with the many stressors they may face in the future.

REFERENCES

Aguilera, D. C. (1990). Crisis Intervention: Theory and Methodology (7th ed.). St. Louis. MO: Mosby.

Alan Guttmacher Institute (1999). Teen sex and pregnancy. Facts in Brief. New York: Alan Guttmacher Institute. Available at http://www.agi-usa.org.

Berg, I.K. (2002). Interviewing for Solutions (2nd ed.). Pacific Grove, CA: Brooks/Cole.

Berg, I.K. (1994). Family-Based Services: A Solution-Focused Approach. New York: W. W. Norton and Company, Inc.

Berg, I. K. and Kelly, S. (2000). Building Solutions in Child Protective Services. New York: W. W. Norton and Company.

Corcoran, J. (1998). Solution-focused practice with middle and high school at-risk youths. Social Work in Education, 20 (4), 232-244.

Corcoran, J., and Stephenson, M. (2000). The effectiveness of solution-focused therapy with child behavior problems: A preliminary report. *Families in Society: The Journal of Contemporary Human Services, 81* (5), 468-474.

de Shazer, S. (1985). *Keys to Solution in Brief Therapy.* (pp. 3-17). New York: W. W. Norton.

Dulmus, C. N., and Hilarski, C. (2003). When stress constitutes trauma and trauma constitutes crisis: The stress-trauma-crisis continuum. *Brief Treatment and Crisis Intervention, 3* (1), 27-35.

Franklin, C., Biever, J., Moore, K., Clemons, D., and Scamardo, M. (2001). The effectiveness of solution-focused therapy with children in a school setting. *Research on Social Work Practice, 11* (4), 411-434.

Franklin, C., Corcoran, J., Nowicki, J., and Streeter, C. (1997). Using self-anchored scales to measure outcomes in solution-focused therapy. *Journal of Systemic Therapies, 16* (3), 246-265.

Franklin, C., Moore, K. C. (1999). Solution-focused brief family therapy. In C. Franklin & C. Jordan, *Family Practice: Brief systems methods for social work* (pp. 105-142). Pacific Grove, CA: Brooks/Cole.

Golan, N. (1978). Treatment in Crisis Situations. New York: Free Press.

Greene, G. J., Lee, M., Trask, R., Rheinsheld, J. (2000). How to work with client's strengths in crisis intervention: A solution-focused approach. In A. R. Roberts (Ed.), Crisis Intervention Handbook: Assessment, Treatment, and Research (2nd ed.) (pp. 31-55). New York: Oxford University Press.

Jobes, D. A., Berman, A. L., and Martin, C. E. (2000). Adolescent suicidality and crisis intervention. In A. R. Roberts (Ed.), Crisis Intervention Handbook: Assessment, Treatment, and Research (2nd ed.) (pp. 131-151). New York: Oxford University Press.

Kaufman, P., Chen, X., Choi, S. P., Peter, K., Ruddy, S. A., Miller, A.K., Fleury, J. K., Chandler, K. A., Planty, M. G., and Rand, M. R. (2001) Indicators of school crime and safety: 2001. Washington DC: US Departments of Education and Justice. Available at http://nces.ed.gov.

Kline, M., Schonfeld, D. J., and Lichtenstein, R. (1995). Benefits and challenges of a school-based crisis response teams. *Journal of School Health,* 65 (7), 245-250.

LaFountain, R. M., and Garner, N. E. (1996). Solution-focused counseling groups: The results are in. *The Journal for Specialists in Group Work, 21* (2), 128-143.

Littrell, J. M., Malia, J. A., and Vanderwood, M. (1995). Single-session brief counseling in a high school. Journal of Counseling and Development, 73, 451-458.

Lipchik, E. (2002). *Beyond Techniques in Solution-Focused Therapy* (pp. 3-23). New York, NY: Guildford Press.

Murphy, J. J. (1996). Solution-focused brief therapy in the school. In S. D. Miller, M. A. Hubble, and B. L. Duncan (Eds.) Handbook of Solution-Focused Brief Therapy (pp. 184-204). San Francisco, CA: Jossey-Bass Publishers.

National Center for Health Statistics. (2002). Vital Statistics of the United States. Washington, DC: U.S. Government Printing Office.

National Institute on Alcohol Abuse and Alcoholism. (1997). Alcohol alert, Number 37. Washington, DC: National Institutes of Health. Available at www.niaaa-nih.gov.

National Institute on Drug Abuse. (2003). NIDA info facts: High school and youth trends. Washington, DC: National Institutes of Health. Available at www.drugabuse.gov.

Newsome, S. (2002). The impact of solution-focused brief therapy with at-risk junior high school students. Unpublished doctoral dissertation, Ohio State University, Columbus, Ohio.

O'Halloran, M. S., and Copeland, E. P. (2000). Crisis intervention with early adolescents who have suffered a significant loss. In A. R. Roberts (Ed.), Crisis Intervention Handbook: Assessment, Treatment, and Research (2nd ed.) (pp. 101-130). New York: Oxford University Press.

Poland, S. (1994). The role of school crisis intervention teams to prevent and reduce school violence and trauma. *School Psychology Review, 23* (2), 175-190.

Roberts, A. (2000). An overview of crisis theory and crisis intervention. In A. R. Roberts (Ed.), Crisis Intervention Handbook: Assessment, Treatment, and Research (2nd ed.) (pp. 3-30). New York: Oxford University Press.

Sharry, J., Darmony, M., and Madden, B. (2002). A solution-focused approach to working with clients who are suicidal. *British Journal of Guidance and Counseling, 30* (4), 383-399.

Sklare, G. (1997). *Brief Counseling that Works: A Solution-Focused Approach for School Counselors.* (pp. 43-64). Thousand Oaks, California: Corwin Press, Inc., Sage Publications.

Springer, D. W., Lynch, C., and Rubin, A. (2000). Effects of a solution-focused mutual aid group for Hispanic children of incarcerated parents. *Child and Adolescent Social Work Journal, 17* (6), 431-442.

Abuse of Power: When School Personnel Bully Students

Richard Edwards, PhD
Paul Smokowski, PhD
Karen M. Sowers, PhD
Catherine N. Dulmus, PhD
Matthew T. Theriot, PhD

SUMMARY. Bullying is a serious concern in our schools. Some estimates suggest that a high proportion of U.S. children have been victimized by bullying, with much of the bullying occurring in schools. This article examines the particular issue of bullying of children by school personnel. Data were gathered from a sample of school personnel in three rural public schools located within the same school district. Of the seventy school personnel who responded to the survey, twenty-five

---

Richard Edwards is Alumni Distinguished Professor, and Paul Smokowski is Assistant Professor, The University of Chapel Hill, School of Social Work, Chapel Hill.

Karen M. Sowers is Dean and Professor, Catherine N. Dulmus is Associate Professor, and Matthew T. Theriot is Assistant Professor, The University of Tennessee, College of Social Work.

Address correspondence to: Richard Edwards, PhD, The University of Chapel Hill, School of Social Work, Tate-Turner-Kurault Building, Chapel Hill, NC 27599 (E-mail: redwards@unc.edu).

The authors would like to gratefully acknowledge the contributions of Pamela Jinks and David Dupper to the project.

[Haworth co-indexing entry note]: "Abuse of Power: When School Personnel Bully Students." Edwards, Richard et al. Co-published simultaneously in *Journal of Evidence-Based Social Work* (The Haworth Social Work Practice Press, an imprint of The Haworth Press, Inc.) Vol. 1, No. 2/3, 2004, pp. 111-129; and: *Kids and Violence: The Invisible School Experience* (ed: Catherine N. Dulmus and Karen M. Sowers) The Haworth Social Work Practice Press, an imprint of The Haworth Press, Inc., 2004, pp. 111-129. Single or multiple copies of this article are available for a fee from The Haworth Document Delivery Service [1-800-HAWORTH, 9:00 a.m. - 5:00 p.m. (EST). E-mail address: docdelivery@haworthpress.com].

http://www.haworthpress.com/web/JEBSW

Digital Object Identifier: 10.1300/J394v1n02_08

(36%) indicated they had observed other school personnel bullying students during the previous three-month period. The implications of bullying by school personnel are discussed, along with the implications for social work practice in the schools.

KEYWORDS. Bullying, rural schools, school personnel, students, abuse of power

BULLYING BY SCHOOL PERSONNEL: PERCEPTIONS OF BULLYING INCIDENTS THAT OCCUR BETWEEN STAFF AND STUDENTS

Introduction

During the academic year, students spend a large portion of their working hours in school. Because of the amount of time they spend there, our schools play a "... critical role in the lives of developing children and adolescents" and a great deal of "... educational research has sought to identify school characteristics that are most conducive to positive student outcomes" (Bowen, Bowen, & Richman, 2000: p. 69). On the other hand, recent incidences of violence in schools, such as the shootings in Columbine, Colorado and other places, have raised concerns about what is taking place in the school environment that may be contributing to negative student outcomes which may result in students engaging in violent acts. In this context, the potential negative effect on students of bullying increasingly has been a matter of concern to students, parents, educators and researchers. While a substantial amount of research has focused on the effects of bullying of students by other students, little research has been conducted on bullying of students by school personnel. This article examines bullying in general and then reports the findings of research aimed specifically at the issue of bullying of students by school personnel.

Bullying: Prevalence and Characteristics

Bullying is a serious concern and is considered by some researchers to be the most enduring and underrated problem in U. S. schools (Beale,

2001). Although few investigations have been conducted to estimate the prevalence of bullying, estimates that are available suggest that approximately 10% of children in the United States have experienced extreme victimization by bullying (Perry, Kusel, & Perry, 1988). In a recent nationally representative sample, nearly 30% of 15,686 students surveyed reported being involved in bullying in the current term, either as a perpetrator or a victim (Nansel, Overpeck, Pilla, Ruan, Simons-Morton & Scheidt, 2001). This generalizes to a nationwide estimate of 3,708,284 students reporting bullying and 3,245,904 students reporting victimization (Nansel et al., 2001). In a smaller survey of 4,263 students in one Maryland high school, Haynie and her colleagues (2001) reported that nearly 31% of students reported being victimized three or more times in the past year and 7.4% reported bullying others three or more times in the past year. Generalization of these percentages provides national estimates of approximately two million bullies and three million victims-rates striking similar to those reported by the Namsel study (2001). These estimates clearly show that schools in the United States have serious problems related to bullying and victimization.

The bullying dynamic is usually characterized as a form of aggression in which one or more individuals intend to harm, disturb, or harass another individual, the target or victim, who is perceived as being unable to defend himself or herself (Glew, Rivara, & Feudtner, 2000). A major feature of the bullying dynamic is a power imbalance between the bully and the victim. Bullies are almost always physically, psychologically, or socially more powerful (Nansel et al., 2001; Smokowski & Holland, 2003). Bullies use this physically or emotionally abusive behavior to establish dominance or maintain status (Pellegrini, Bartini, & Brooks, 1999; Roberts, 2000). Bullying behaviors tend to occur repeatedly over time (Nansel et al., 2001) and commonly include using sarcasm, making demeaning or disrespectful comments, slandering, excluding, taunting, threatening, or actually using physical force against another person (Beale, 2001; Smokowski & Holland, 2003). Most importantly, bullying is marked by an intimidating physical or verbal attack that creates a pattern of humiliation, abuse, and fear for the victim (Roberts, 2000). Bullying behaviors are more negative, intense, and frequent than actions that would be considered teasing. The victim's reaction dictates whether a behavior is considered teasing or bullying (Roberts, 2000). Unwanted teasing may be considered bullying if the victim finds the behaviors to be aversive or humiliating, and if there is an imbalance of power between the two parties.

The Impact of Bullying

Over the past thirty years, clinicians and researchers have found bullying to be a serious threat to healthy child development and a potential cause of school violence (Olweus, 1978; Spivak & Prothrow-Stith, 2001). Much of this research on bullying has focused on children bullying each other. Overviews of this body of research are available elsewhere (Banks, 1999; Carney & Merrell, 2001; Glew, Rivara, & Feudtner, 2000; Smokowski & Holland, 2003). These studies and literature reviews show that bullying is a problem with both serious and long-term consequences for both perpetrators and victims. Perpetrators, victims, and individuals who both bully and who are bullied by others (i.e., bully/victims) show poorer psychosocial adjustment than peers who do not bully and have not been victimized (Namsel et al., 2001; Olweus, 1978).

Research studies suggest that nearly one-third of bullies have attention-deficit disorder, 12.5% suffer from depression, and 12.5% have oppositional/conduct disorder (Kumpulainen, Rasanen, & Puura, 2001; see also Kaltiala-Heino, Rimpela, Rantanen, & Rimpela, 2000; Salmon et al., 1996). Bullies have been found to possess positive attitudes towards physical aggression (Andreou, 2001; Olweus, 1978), and, later in life, to engage in frequent, excessive drinking and other substance use more often than victims or bully/victims (Kaltiala-Heino et al., 2000). As adults, research has found that bullies often display externalizing behaviors, hyperactivity, and antisocial development (Hamalainen & Pulkkinen, 1995; Kaltiala-Heino et al., 2000; Kumpulainen & Rasanen, 2000; Olweus, 1993; Pulkkinen & Pitkanen, 1993). According to the National School Safety Center, a disproportionately high number of bullies underachieve in school and later perform below potential in employment settings (NSSC, 1995; Carney & Merrell, 2001). These adults who were bullies are more likely to display aggression towards their spouses and to use severe physical punishment on their own children (Roberts, 2000).

Victims also experience detrimental short- and long-term effects as a result of being bullied (Smokowski & Holland, 2003). Victims may gradually see themselves as outcasts and failures (McNamara & McNamara, 1997). Studies suggest that victimization has a significant positive correlation with several internalizing disorders such as anxiety and depression (Brockenbrough et al., 2002; Kaltiala-Heino et al., 2000). This link between victimization and internalizing disorders is particularly strong for adolescent girls and may contribute to the development of eating disorders (Bond, Carlin, Thomas, Rubin, & Patton, 2001). One recent study found that attention deficit disorder was common among victims (Kumpulainen et al., 2001), perhaps because these children feel the need to constantly monitor their environment in anticipation of the next victimization episode. Academic achievement often decreases after victimization (Olweus, 1993) and may lead to school disengagement. Victims of bullying often suffer from one or more of the following; chronic absenteeism, reduced academic performance, increased apprehension, loneliness, feelings of abandonment from peers, and suicidal ideation (Beale, 2001; Roberts & Coursol, 1996; Smokowski & Holland, 2003). At age 23, former victims report more depression and lower self-esteem than non-victimized young adults (Olweus, 1993), illustrating the long-lasting impact that victimization can have.

Bullying as Abuse of Power

The bullying dynamic has been applied to victimization in non-school settings and in interactions other than child-to-child transactions. Investigating damaging experiences in adult therapy groups, Lieberman, Yalom, and Miles (1973 cited in Yalom, 1985/1995) estimated that 12% (16 out of 133) of group participants suffered enduring psychological deterioration from their group experience and were considered to be group casualties. Another 10% (13/133) of participants who completed the groups displayed negative psychological changes that were not severe or enduring enough to classify them as group casualties. These psychological deterioration and negative changes were attributed to attacks or rejection by the leader or the group. Further, some leaders had little ability to identify damaging group experiences, even after they were told that casualties occurred in their own groups (Galinsky & Schopler, 1977; Lieberman et al., 1973)

Smokowski and his colleagues (Smokowski, Rose, & Bacallao, 2001; Smokowski, Rose, Todar, & Reardon, 1999) also investigated the occurrence of bullying behaviors in small group settings. Analyzing interviews from 83 individuals who had damaging experiences in a variety of small group settings (e.g., therapy groups, psycho-educational groups, educational classes), these authors found that leader behavior or inactivity was at the heart of humiliating group experiences. Group members who were humiliated by group leaders in front of the group commonly experienced intense emotional reactions that had long-lasting effects on their self-esteem. Group members also felt victimized when other members attacked them and the group leader did nothing to intervene. These acts of commission or omission were seen as an abuse of the group leader's power and prestige. Many of these experiences were so troubling that victims reported that they still had vivid memories of the damaging event years later and never again wanted to be a part of a small group.

Considering the severity and long-term effects of bullying both in child-to-child and in leader-to-participant interactions, it is important for researchers and practitioners to understand all aspects of this important problem. Having established the importance and wide applicability of the bullying dynamic, we now turn our attention to a new context for bullying research, i.e., applying the bullying dynamic to situations where school personnel misuse their power to bully students.

School Personnel as Bullies

Schools are clearly critical developmental contexts for most children. School environments have a strong influence on child development and learning due to the amount of time children spend in school and the nature of the atmosphere that characterizes the school. The school's atmosphere, created primarily by school personnel such as teachers and administrators, may contribute to a sense of achievement and community (Baker, Terry, Bridger, & Winsor, 1997) or it may be a factor in student violence and dropping out (Baker, 1998; Baker, Derrer, Davis, Dinklage-Travis, Linder, & Nicholson, 2001). The atmosphere created in individual classrooms and the school as a whole is crucial because student learning and participation in education is rooted in this social milieu (Vygotsky, 1978) and is dependent upon interactions with others in this setting. When the nature of social interactions between school personnel and students is negative and abusive, not only are students victimized, but also important opportunities for education and development are placed in jeopardy.

Unfortunately, we know very little about the nature of staff-to-student bullying in U.S. schools. Recent school shootings of students and teachers, such as the Columbine massacre, have thrust the problem of school violence into the media spotlight. This has led to intense scrutiny of student and familial correlates of youth violence (US DHHS, 2001), but little attention has been paid to ways in which school atmosphere and staff behaviors might contribute to this problem (Baker, 1998). While the occurrence of physical and verbal abuse in school has been reported to be problematic in other countries such as Poland (Piekarska, 2000) or Zimbabwe (Shumba, 2002), and principal maltreatment of teachers has been delineated in the U.S. (Blasé & Blasé, 2003), little data is available on staff-to-student bullying in U.S. schools. What is available leads us to believe that bullying by school personnel is an important problem.

In the United States, 23 states still allow corporal punishment and almost 500,000 children received corporal punishment during the 1996-1997 school year (United States Department of Education, Office for Civil Rights, 1997). Nearly 11 percent of children in Arkansas and over 12 percent of schoolchildren in Mississippi have been punished in this way (United States Department of Education, Office for Civil Rights, 1997).

Shidler (1995 reported in Shidler, 2001) asked nearly 600 teachers to label certain behaviors violent or nonviolent. She found that 65 percent of teachers surveyed considered pulling a child by the arm and/or paddling/spanking a child in school to be nonviolent. Twenty-eight percent of the teachers surveyed considered it nonviolent when another individual was verbally assaulting a child. She concluded that, "Violence is not only schoolmates bringing in weapons, but also teacher behavior that explicitly and implicitly contributes to a sense of general hostility" (Shidler, 2001, p. 168). This hostile atmosphere has strong potential to influence student well-being. Curwin and Mendler (1988), for example, reported that the percentage of students reporting high self-esteem drops from 80% in first grade to 20% by fifth grade. Similarly, the percentage of students with a high sense of dignity drops from 80% in first grade to 5% in high school (Curwin & Mendler, 1988). While many factors influence child well-being during these formative years, a significant portion of this decline in self-esteem and dignity may be due to negative interactions children have at school.

Hyman and Zelikoff (1987) conducted a retrospective study of psychological trauma in school settings. One hundred and eighty-one college students, school teachers, and special educators completed a survey about teacher abuse in school. Sixty to 86 percent of respondents reported having a traumatic experience in school. Traumatic school experiences were associated with teacher's use of sarcasm, ridicule, criticism for low achievement, unjustified punishment, and being restricted from nonacademic activities. For victims, experiencing abuse was associated with subsequent personality changes, painful recollection of the damaging event, concentration difficulties, avoidant reactions, physical problems (e.g., head and stomach aches), and psychological numbing (Hyman & Zelikoff, 1987). Reduction in self-esteem was reported to be the longest lasting consequence of the traumatic event.

These traumatic school events perpetrated by teachers, and the impact they have on victims, are similar to damaging small group experiences caused by group leaders (Smokowski, Rose, & Bacallao, 2001; Smokowski, Rose, Todar, & Reardon, 1999). Inappropriate behavior by an individual with power and prestige, like a teacher or group leader, can be humiliating and traumatic enough to have a lasting impact on victim's psychological well-being.

The research reported in this article contributes to our knowledge of bullying by investigating the occurrence of bullying of students by school personnel. Little research has been conducted in this area. In laying the groundwork for future research in this area, we posed four critical research questions. How often do school personnel bully students? In what ways do school personnel bully students? Where does this happen? And, finally, do teachers and administrators engage in this bullying behavior more than other members of school staff?

METHODOLOGY

Design

This study utilized a survey research design to gather information from school personnel about their observations (or awareness of) bullying of students by other school personnel. The survey was conducted in a rural school setting. The IRB at a large research university in the Southeastern United States granted permission to conduct the research prior to the start of the project. Participation was voluntary and confidential, and informed consent was obtained from all participants. Data collection occurred in the fall of 2002.

Sample

The sample consisted of school personnel recruited from three rural public schools (an elementary school, a middle school, and a school that housed grades K-8) located within the same school district in a Southeastern rural region of the United States. School personnel were adult employees having contact with students. This included administrators, teachers, teacher's aides, nurses, librarians, social workers, counselors, secretaries, lunchroom workers, janitors, and bus drivers. All participants had to be employees or subcontractors of the school district who had contact with students enrolled in the study schools. The school district where the three study schools are located is situated in a county characterized by high rates of poverty. Between 43 and 61% of students received free or reduced lunches and 12% of the population did not have a telephone. Ninety-eight percent of the school district employees and students were Caucasian.

The sample characteristics are presented in Table 1. Seventy employees from the three rural schools responded to the survey. This represents a 33.7% response rate.

Measures

The School Personnel Observation and Awareness of Bullying Between Students at School Questionnaire (Solberg & Olweus, 2003) was adapted to include questions related to treatment of students by school personnel. Each participant completed fifteen questions that were added to the original questionnaire to assess school personnel's awareness of bullying of students by other school personnel. This paper focuses on responses to these fifteen questions. These questions related to school personnel using their positions of power to intimidate students with sarcasm, demeaning or disrespectful comments, or physical force. For the purposes of this paper, these behaviors are collectively labeled as bullying. Additional questions examined specific locations within the school setting where these behaviors occurred, the frequency of these behaviors, and reporting of such actions to administration. The questionnaire was self-administered.

Data Collection Procedures

School personnel were approached in the school setting and invited to participate in the study by a member of the research team. When approached, envelopes were handed to participants with information about the study, an informed consent form, the questionnaire described above, and a stamped addressed envelope to mail completed materials directly to the research team. Directions for completion of the questionnaire and a request that materials be returned within a 2-week period were also included in the envelope. A coffee mug was given to each participant as a thank you gift.

The following week, a flyer emphasizing the importance of the study and encouraging questionnaire completion was placed in the mailboxes of all school personnel. All participants were volunteers and were assured of the confidentiality of their responses. As completed study materials were returned via U.S. Mail, the signed informed consent form was separated from the questionnaire and stored separately. To ensure confidentiality and protection of subjects, participants were instructed not to put their names or any identifying information on the questionnaire. There were minimal physical, psychological, legal, or social risks for participants.

Data Analysis

All data were coded directly from respondent's answers to specific questions asked on the survey instrument. The data are presented in three tables. Table 1 shows demographic and attitudinal characteristics for the sample. On this table, the school personnel have been divided into four groups. These groups are teachers and administrators who have observed the bullying of students by other personnel, teachers and administrators who have not, other school staff who have observed this bullying of students, and other school staff who have not. For the purposes of this table, *other school staff* includes counselors, secretaries, janitors, bus drivers, lunchroom workers, aides, and all other school employees except teachers and administrators.

Comparatively, Table 2 and Table 3 include only those respondents who have observed (or are aware of) the bullying of students by school personnel. Table 2 presents information on the type and frequency of the observed bullying while Table 3 displays the data on the location of this bullying. Since not all study participants answered each question on bullying location, variations in the response frequencies for each question are reported on Table 3.

RESULTS

As shown on Table 1, seventy participants from the three rural schools completed the questionnaire. School personnel were asked if they had observed (or if they were aware of) other school personnel bullying students during the previous 3-month period. Of the 70 people completing the survey instrument, 25 (36%) reported that they had witnessed such behavior by school personnel against students. Thirty-four percent (14 of 41) of teachers and administrators who responded and 38% (11 of 29) of other school staff who responded observed or were aware of school personnel bullying students. Half of the study respondents were female teachers or administrators. For teachers and adminis-

TABLE 1. Demographic and Attitudinal Characteristics of School Personnel (N = 70)

Characteristic	Teachers and Administrators (n = 41)		Other School Staff (n = 29)	
	Have observed school personnel bullying students (n = 14) Freq. (%) or Mean ± SD	**Have not observed school personnel bullying students (n = 27)** Freq. (%) or Mean ± SD	**Have observed school personnel bullying students (n =11)** Freq. (%) or Mean ± SD	**Have not observed school personnel bullying students (n = 18)** Freq. (%) or Mean ± SD
Gender				
Male	0 (0.0)	6 (22.2)	4 (36.4)	3 (16.7)
Female	14 (100.0)	21 (77.8)	7 (63.6)	15 (83.3)
Age	39.1 ± 9.5	39.7 ± 11.2	39.6 ± 8.1	47.1 ± 11.6
Years working in an educational setting	11.7 ± 8.4	13.1 ± 9.1	9.6 ± 10.6	14.1 ± 10.5
I was bullied in school when I was child.	4 (28.6)	10 (37.0)	7 (63.6)	11 (61.1)

Column percentages may not total 100% because of rounding. SD = standard deviation trators, 40% (14/35) of female respondents reported having observed school personnel bullying students while 60% (21/35) did not. No male teachers and administrators reported observing or being aware of other school personnel bullying students. For other school staff, 32% (7/22) of females and 57% (4/7) of males reported observing this bullying behavior.

The reported age of each group is remarkably similar for three of the four groups, with the staff group that has not observed bullying being the exception. This group, on average, is approximately eight years older than the other groups. Likewise, this group also has the highest mean number of years worked in an educational setting (14.1 years ± 10.5). Comparatively, school staff who have observed bullying have the fewest years worked in an educational setting (9.6 years ± 10.6). Finally, it is interesting to note that while the minority of teachers and administrators reported being bullied as a child (34.1%), the majority of the school staff reported such victimization during their childhood (62.1%).

Table 2 shows types and frequencies of bullying by school personnel. Among the school personnel who reported that they have observed (or been made aware of) school employees bullying students, the most common and frequently occurring form of bullying is the use of sarcasm and demeaning or disrespectful comments. All 25 participants who observed or were aware of bullying responded that they have observed this type of behavior from other school personnel. Furthermore, 6 people across both groups (24% or 6/25) reported that this behavior occurs several times weekly. Physical attacks were the least frequent type of bullying, with only 2 people reporting such actions (8.0%). Twenty-eight (7/25) percent of respondents also reported that school personnel abuse their position of power with students in other ways, though they did provide specific examples of such.

Though not presented on Table 2, it is important to recognize that when asked about how many school personnel were involved in these incidents of bullying, most study participants reported that one person was involved (52.0%). Ten respondents (40.0%) reported that these incidents involved 2 or more people and 2 people did not respond (8.0%). Along similar lines, 15 people (60.0%), state that despite observing bullying incidents, they have not spoken to anyone about it. Four people (16.0%) state that they have reported these incidents to a school administrator and one person (4.0%) says that they have talked with the bully about the incident.

TABLE 2. Frequency and Type of Bullying by School Personnel Against Students (N = 25)

Types of Bullying	**Teachers or School Administrators (n = 14)**					**Other School Staff (n = 11)**				
	Has Not Observed this in Past 3 Months Freq. (%)	**Observed Only Once or Twice** Freq. (%)	**Observed 2-3 Times a Month** Freq. (%)	**Observed About Once a Week** Freq. (%)	**Observed Several Times a Week** Freq. (%)	**Has Not Observed this in Past 3 Months** Freq. (%)	**Observed Only Once or Twice** Freq. (%)	**Observed 2-3 Times a Month** Freq. (%)	**Observed About Once a Week** Freq. (%)	**Observed Several Times a Week** Freq. (%)
I have observed or been made aware of school personnel using their position of power to intimidate students by use of **sarcasm and/or demeaning or disrespectful comments.**	0 (0.0)	9 (64.3)	0 (0.0)	2 (14.3)	3 (21.4)	0 (0.0)	7 (63.6)	1 (9.1)	0 (0.0)	3 (27.3)
I am aware of students **being hit, kicked, pushed, or shoved around** by school personnel.	12 (85.7)	1 (7.1)	1 (7.1)	0 (0.0)	0 (0.0)	11 (100.0)	0 (0.0)	0 (0.0)	0 (0.0)	0 (0.0)
I have observed or been made aware of school personnel abusing their position of power with students in **another way.**	11 (78.6)	1 (7.1)	0 (0.0)	1 (7.1)	1 (7.1)	7 (63.6)	3 (27.3)	1 (9.1)	0 (0.0)	0 (0.0)

Column percentages may not total 100% because of rounding.

It is important to address where the bullying occurred. Out of the 14 teachers and administrators who reported that they observed or had been made aware of bullying by school personnel, 10 (10/14 or 71%) said this behavior happened in the classroom. Nine participants (64%) said it happened in hallways or stairwells. Four participants (29%) said it happened on the playground/athletic field, in the bathroom, and/or in the lunchroom. Three participants (21%) said that it happened in gym class, in the locker room, or in the shower. And two participants (14%) said it happened somewhere else in school.

Out of the 11 other school staff members who reported that they observed or had been made aware of bullying by school personnel, 5 (5/11 or 45%) said it happened in the classroom and/or in the lunchroom, 4 (36%) said in the hallways or stairwells, and 1 (9%) said it happened on the playground. Neither group observed school personnel bullying students on the school bus; however, few teachers, administrators, or school staff members other than drivers ride the bus with students.

LIMITATIONS

This exploratory research provides beginning knowledge as to the actions of school personnel who bully students by use of sarcasm, demeaning or disrespectful comments, or physical force. However, the generalizability of the findings is limited by several factors. These include the small sample size and the fact that the participants came from only one region of the country, which was a rural area that lacks ethnic and racial diversity. Further, the results do not provide specific information as to the exact number of adults who are bullying students. While the data indicate that more than one third of the respondents are aware that bullying of students by school personnel is occurring, the study does not provide specific information about perpetrators and victims. Finally, while the small sample size limited statistical analysis of the data, the study nonetheless provides a beginning estimate of the nature of the problem, thus providing a starting point for future research.

DISCUSSION AND RECOMMENDATIONS

As noted earlier, while a substantial amount of research has demonstrated that bullying behavior is a serious problem in U.S. schools, very little research has focused on bullying of students by school personnel.

The study reported in this article suggests that bullying of students by school personnel occurs far too frequently. More than one-third of the teachers, administrators, and other school staff members who responded to the survey instrument indicated they either had observed or were aware of bullying of students by school personnel. While the degree of generalizability of the study results is limited, the results nonetheless clearly provide beginning evidence that bullying by school personnel is a serious problem that merits further investigation.

Despite the limitations of this study, there were a number of findings that are worth considering. One very troubling finding is that while one-third of the respondents stated they were aware of school personnel bullying students, sixty percent of those respondents indicated they had not spoken to anyone about the bullying they observed. While this is a matter of concern, it is not really surprising, given that in other bullying situations there is frequently a substantial pool of spectators who are aware of the bullying but do not intervene. Nevertheless, it might be expected that school personnel would be more proactive about protecting students from detrimental behaviors like bullying. It may be that many of those observing bullying of students by school personnel fear personal repercussions if they intervene. This might be the case, for instance, if the perpetrator is an individual in a higher position or with more seniority than the observer. Further research may shed more light on why school personnel who observe bullying do nothing about it, and such information may lead to formulating recommendations for corrective actions.

In this study, the respondents indicated that most of the bullying by school personnel occurred in classrooms. This is understandable because the classroom is where teachers, who comprised the largest portion of respondents, most feel a need to exert their power and maintain control. Yet, the fact that such bullying behavior is occurring in the classroom is troubling because it may be a significant impediment to student learning.

The type of bullying most frequently observed by respondents was in the form of sarcasm and demeaning comments. Far fewer respondents reported observing or hearing about bullying by school personnel that involved physical force. Clearly, both physical and emotional abuses violate laws and, in most school districts, formal school policies. However, it often is easier to substantiate physical abuse than emotional abuse, which tends to be more subtle and harder to substantiate. Nonetheless, as Smokowski et al. (2001) and Hyman and Zelikoff (1987) have pointed out, the impact of emotional abuse can be quite devastat-

TABLE 3. Location of Bullying by School Personnel Against Students

Location of Bullying	**Teachers and Administrators** Frequency (%; n)	**Other School Staff** Frequency (%; n)
On the playground/athletic field (during recess or break times)	4 (40.0; n = 10)	1 (11.1; n = 9)
In the hallways/stairwells	9 (75.0; n = 12)	4 (50.0; n = 8)
In the classroom	10 (83.3; n = 12)	5 (62.5; n = 8)
In the bathroom	4 (33.3; n = 12)	0 (0.0; n = 8)
In gym class or in the gym locker room/shower	3 (27.3; n = 11)	0 (0.0; n = 7)
In the lunchroom	4 (33.3; n = 12)	5 (55.6; n = 9)
On the school bus	0 (0.0; n = 12)	0 (0.0; n = 8)
Somewhere else in school	2 (18.2; n = 11)	0 (0.0; n = 8)

Column percentages may not total 100% because of rounding.

ing and long lasting. It may be that some school personnel are not aware that their sarcasm and demeaning comments are really abusive and that they can have serious long term consequences on their victims. Further research may shed light on this issue.

It is interesting to note that no male teachers or administrators reported observing or being aware of other school personnel bullying students. While the data do not provide answers as to why there was this gender difference, there are several possibilities that merit further exploration. It may be that males were in higher positions of power and didn't let themselves acknowledge this problem, or perhaps male respondents were less likely to be in the classrooms, which was where most of the reported bullying behavior occurred. Or it may be that males were the primary perpetrators of the bullying behavior. Certainly more research is needed to draw any definitive conclusions about the nature of this gender difference.

Another interesting finding is that, while only a little over a third (34.1%) of the respondents who are teachers and administrators reported being bullied as a child, nearly two-thirds (62.1%) of the school staff reported being bullied during their childhoods. Again, while it is not possible to draw definitive conclusions about this from the data obtained in this study, it is something that should be explored further in future research.

Despite the limitations of this study, there are some implications for social work practitioners. First, school social workers, as well as social workers employed outside of the schools, need to be aware of the impact of bullying on children and alert to indicators that children may be victims of bullying. Second, in exploring whether a child is being bullied, it is incumbent on the social worker to attempt to identify and intervene with the perpetrator of the bullying, whether the perpetrator is another student or a school employee. Third, social workers should be proactive in attempting to prevent bullying from occurring. One way to do this is to advocate for regular, ongoing in-service training for all school personnel, as well as parents, that addresses bullying and its impacts. If everyone involved with school children is knowledgeable about the detrimental effects of all forms of bullying and committed to doing everything possible to prevent it from occurring, our schools may become safer places that are more conducive to learning.

REFERENCES

Andreou, E. (2001). Bully/victim problems and their association with coping behaviour in conflictual peer interactions among school-age children. *Educational Psychology, 21,* 59-66.

Baker, J., A. (1998). Are we missing the forest from the trees? Considering the social context of youth violence. *Journal of School Psychology, 36* (1), 29-44.

Baker, J., A., Derrer, R. D., Davis, S. M., Dinklage-Travis, H. E., Linder, D. S., & Nicholson, M. D. (2001). The flip side of the coin: Understanding the school's contribution to dropout and completion. *School Psychology Quarterly, 16* (4), 406-426.

Baker, J. A., Terry, T., Bridger, R., & Winsor, A. (1997). Schools as caring communities: A relational approach to school reform. *School Psychology Review, 26,* 586-602.

Banks, R. (1999). *Bullying in school.* Moravia, NY: Chronicle Guidance Publications.

Beale, A. V. (2001). Bullybusters: Using drama to empower students to take a stand against bullying behavior. *Professional School Counseling, 4,* 300-306.

Blasé, J. & Blasé, J. (2003). *Breaking the silence: Overcoming the problem of principal maltreatment of teachers.* Thousand Oaks, CA: Sage.

Bond, L., Carlin, J. B., Thomas, L., Rubin, K., & Patton, G. (2001). Does bullying cause emotional problems: A prospective study of young teenagers. *British Medical Journal, 323,* 480-483.

Bowen, G. L., Bowen, N. K., & Richman, J. M. (2000). School size and middle school student's perceptions of the school environment. *Social Work in Education, 22 (2),* 69-82.

Brockenbrough, K. K., Cornell, D. G., & Loper, A. B (2002). Aggressive attitudes among victims of violence at school. *Education & Treatment of Children, 25* (3), 273-287.

Carney, A. G., & Merrell, K. W. (2001). Bullying in schools: Perspectives on understanding and preventing an international problem. *School Psychology International, 22,* 364-382.

Curwin, R., & Mendler, A. (1988). *Discipline with dignity.* Alexandria, VA: Association for Supervision and Curriculum Development.

Galinsky, M. & Schopler, J. (1977). Warning: Groups may be dangerous for your health. *Social Work, 22*, 89-93.

Hamalainen, M., & Pulkkinen, L. (1995). Aggressive and non-prosocial behavior as precursors of criminality. *Studies on Crime and Crime Prevention, 4*, 6-21.

Haynie, D. L., Nansel, D., Eitel, P., Crump, A. D., Saylor, K., Yu, K., & Simons-Morton, B. (2001). Bullies, victims, and bully/victims: Distinct groups of at-risk youth. *Journal of Early Adolescence, 21* (1), 29-49.

Hyman, I., A., & Zellikoff, W. L. (1984). *Psychological trauma in the schools: A retrospective study.* Paper presented at the annual meeting of the National Association of School Psychologists, New Orlean, LA, March 4-8, 1987, ERIC Clearinghouse No. EA020040.

Kaltiala-Heino, R., Rimpela, P. R., & Rimpela, A. (2000). Bullying at school: An indicator of adolescents at risk for mental disorders. *Journal of Adolescence, 23*, 661-674.

Kumpulainen, K., & Rasanen, E. (2000). Children involved in bullying at elementary and school age: Their psychiatric symptoms and deviance in adolescence. *Child Abuse and Neglect, 24*, 1567-1577.

Kumpulainen, K., Rasanen, E., & Puura, K. (2001). Psychiatric disorders and the use of mental health services among children involved in bullying. *Aggressive Behavior, 27,* 102-110.

Lieberman, M., Yalom, I. & Miles, M. (1973). *Encounter Groups: First Facts.* San Francisco, CA: Basic Books.

McNamara, B. E., & McNamara, F. J. (1997). *Keys to dealing with bullies.* Hauppauge, NY: Barron's.

Nansel, T. R., Overpeck, M., Pilla, R. S., Ruan, W. J., Simons-Morton, B., & Scheidt, P. (2001). Bullying behaviors among US youth: Prevalence and association with psychosocial adjustment. *Journal of the American Medical Association, 285,* 2094-2110.

National School Safety Center. (NSSC, 1995). *School Bullying and Victimization NSSC Resource Paper.* Malibu: Author.

Olweus, D. (1978). *Aggression in the schools: Bullies and whipping boys.* London: Hemisphere Publishing Corporation.

Olweus, D. (1993). *Bullying at school: What we know and what we can do.* Cambridge, MA: Blackwell Publishers.

Olweus, D. (1995). Bullying or peer abuse in school: Fact and intervention. *Current Directions in Psychological Science, 4*, 196-200.

Pellegrini, A. D., Bartini, M., & Brooks, F. (1999). School bullies, victims, and aggressive victims: Factors relating to group affiliation and victimization in early adolescence. *Journal of Educational Psychology, 91*, 216-224.

Perry, D., Kusel, S., & Perry, L. (1988). Victims of peer aggression. *Developmental Psychology, 24,* 807-814.

Piekarska, A. (2000). School stress, teacher's abusive behaviors, and children's coping strategies. *Child Abuse & Neglect: The International Journal, 24* (11), 1443-1449.

Pulkkinen, L., & Pitkanen, T. (1993). Continuities in aggressive behavior from childhood to adulthood. *Aggressive Behavior, 19*, 249-264.

Roberts, W. B. (2000). The bully as victim. *Professional School Counseling, 4,* 148-156.

Roberts, W., & Coursol, D. (1996). Strategies for intervention with childhood and adolescent victims of bullying, teasing, and intimidation in school setting. *Elementary School Guidance and Counseling, 30*, 204-212.

Shidler, L. (2001). Teacher-sanctioned violence. *Childhood Education (Spring)*, 167-168.

Shumba, A. (2002). The nature, extent, and effects of emotional abuse on primary school pupils by teachers in Zimbabwe. *Child Abuse & Neglect: The International Journal, 26* (8), 783-791.

Smokowski, P. R. & Holland, K. (2003). *Bullying in School: Correlates, Consequences, and Intervention Strategies for School Social Workers.* Manuscript submitted for publication.

Smokowski, P. R., Rose, S. D. & Bacallao, M. (2001). Damaging experiences in therapeutic groups: How vulnerable consumers become group casualties. *Small Group Research, 32* (2), 223-251.

Smokowski, P., Rose, S., Todar, K. & Reardon, K. (1999). Post-group casualty status, group events and leader behavior: An early look into the dynamics of damaging group experiences. *Research on Social Work Practice, 9* (5), 555-574.

Solberg, M. E., Olweus, D. (2003). Prevalence estimation of school bullying with the Olweus Bully/Victim Questionnaire. *Aggressive Behavior*, 29 (3), 239-268.

Spivak, H., & Prothrow-Stith, D. (2001). The need to address bullying–An important component of violence prevention. *Journal of the American Medical Association, 285* (16), 2131-2132.

United States Department of Education, Office for Civil Rights (1997). *Elementary and secondary school civil rights compliance report.* Washington, DC: Author.

United States Department of Health and Human Services (US DHHS) (2001). Youth violence: A report of the Surgeon General. Rockville, MD: US DHHS.

Vygotsky, L. (1978). *Mind in society: The development of higher psychological processes.* Cambridge, MA: Harvard University Press.

Yalom (1985). *The theory and practice of group psychotherapy, Third Edition.* San Francisco, CA: Basic Books.

"Hotspots" for Bullying: Exploring the Role of Environment in School Violence

Lisa Rapp-Paglicci, PhD
Catherine N. Dulmus, PhD
Karen M. Sowers, PhD
Matthew T. Theriot, PhD

SUMMARY. Bullying is a chronic and ubiquitous problem that has ignited concern about children's safety at school. Most studies completed thus far have focused on the interpersonal psychological characteristics of bully and victim, but little has been examined regarding common locations or hotspots for bullying. This study found location to be of import in that hotspots can be identified at each school and differ with regard to gender and grade. Schools can prevent and intercede more effectively with bullying if they can identify their particular hotspots, target those specific locations, and educate school personnel. Our full

---

Lisa Rapp-Paglicci is Associate Professor, University of South Florida-Lakeland.

Catherine N. Dulmus is Associate Professor, Karen M. Sowers is Dean and Professor, Matthew T. Theriot is Assistant Professor, The University of Tennessee, College of Social Work.

Address correspondence to: Lisa Rapp-Paglicci, University of South Florida-Lakeland, Lakeland, FL 33803.

The authors would like to gratefully acknowledge the contributions of Pamela Jinks and David Dupper to the project.

[Haworth co-indexing entry note]: "'Hotspots' for Bullying: Exploring the Role of Environment in School Violence." Rapp-Paglicci, Lisa et al. Co-published simultaneously in *Journal of Evidence-Based Social Work* (The Haworth Social Work Practice Press, an imprint of The Haworth Press, Inc.) Vol. 1, No. 2/3, 2004, pp. 131-141; and: *Kids and Violence: The Invisible School Experience* (ed: Catherine N. Dulmus and Karen M. Sowers) The Haworth Social Work Practice Press, an imprint of The Haworth Press, Inc., 2004, pp. 131-141. Single or multiple copies of this article are available for a fee from The Haworth Document Delivery Service [1-800-HAWORTH, 9:00 a.m. - 5:00 p.m. (EST). E-mail address: docdelivery@haworthpress.com].

http://www.haworthpress.com/web/JEBSW

Digital Object Identifier: 10.1300/J394v1n02_09

development of this area has yet to be achieved. Research is critically needed, in order to further understand hotspots, their relation to types of bullying behaviors, and their implication for prevention of bullying.

KEYWORDS. Bullying, schools, location, environment, students

The longstanding problem of bullying has finally been acknowledged as a serious concern in U.S. schools. Unfortunately this occurred after several lethal school shootings magnified the problem in a way that would never allow Americans to ignore this issue again. It's surprising that the problem of bullying was unrecognized for so long since most American adults can recount being either the perpetrator or victim of bullying during their childhood (Espelage & Asidao, 2001).

Recent studies suggest that one in seven children is bullied in or around school resulting in approximately five million elementary and middle school victims per year (Beane, 1999). Bullying encompasses a variety of negative acts carried out repeatedly over time, and can include physical (hitting), verbal (taunting, teasing), and psychological (exclusion, extortion) forms (Erickson, 2001). Although most attention is drawn to dramatic forms of school violence, like shootings and rape; bullying behavior has been found to be more pervasive, chronic, and perhaps more debilitating to more students in the long-term.

Many studies have explored the individual characteristics of bully and victim and although interpersonal psychological considerations of bullying are important, the linkage between this and the location of bullying provides a more comprehensive framework for understanding and subsequently addressing bullying within schools. Regrettably, research has yet to be fully developed regarding the relationship between bullying and location.

Very few studies have thoroughly explored dangerous locations at schools, but those that have found hallways, cafeterias, bathrooms, classrooms, playgrounds, and locker rooms to be dangerous areas or "hot spots" where bullying tends to occur (Arnette & Walsleban, 1998; Astor, Meyer, & Behre, 1999; Craig, Pepler, & Atlas, 2000; Reiff, 2003). Most research suggests that bullying occurs wherever teachers/adults are not present and students are readily able to identify these dangerous locations.

Beginning research has also suggested that bullying occurs in different locations for male and female students. A study conducted by Astor and Meyer (1999) found differences between male and female students, in that females were more aware of violent events which happened in their school and could identify particular hallways where bullying was more likely to occur. In addition, Astor et al. (1999) found that hallways unsupervised by adults were the most common hotspot where female high school students were bullied.

Bulach, Fulbright, and Williams (2003) found that bullying behavior usually begins in elementary school, increases in middle school, and drops off in High school. Playgrounds and classrooms seem to be frequent sites for bullying in elementary schools, but much less is known about where bullying occurs in middle schools (Espelage & Asidao, 2001).

Clearly, there is still little information about the location of bullying, especially differences pertaining to gender and grade. The intent of this study is to advance the knowledge base regarding bullying and location and to specifically identify the location of bullying in a rural, southeast elementary and middle school. In addition, the location of bullying was identified via the gender and grade of students.

METHODOLOGY

Study Design

This study utilized a survey research design to gather information from students as to their self-reported bullying victimization during the three month period prior to data collection. The questionnaire also included questions related to types of bullying and locations in the school setting where bullying behaviors take place. The IRB at a large research university in the Southeastern United States granted permission to conduct the research prior to the start of the project. Parental consent was obtained for all student subjects whose participation was voluntary and confidential.

Study Sample

Letters to parents were sent home with students to recruit subjects. Subjects were recruited from three rural public schools (an elementary school, a middle school, and a school that housed grades K-8) located within the same school district in a Southeastern rural region of the United States. The school district is located in a county characterized by high rates of poverty as evidenced by 43% to 61% of students receiving free or reduced lunches and 12% of the population still not having a telephone. The school district students are 98% Caucasian and the dominate culture is Appalachian.

The letter sent home to parents included information related to the study and a consent form for parents to complete to allow their child to participate in the study. A self-addressed stamped envelope was provided for parents to mail the consent form back to the principal investigator at the university. Ultimately, the convenience sample consisted of 192 students in grades three through eight, representing an 18.4% response rate. Data collection occurred in the fall of 2002. A team of researchers conducted data collection in the school setting for all children who met inclusion criteria and for whom written parental consent was obtained. Since all subjects were measured at one point in time, no follow-up was necessary. Thus, attrition was not problematic.

Inclusion criteria were as follows: (a) subjects had to be students enrolled in the school where data collection occurred, and (b) subjects had to be in grades three through eight. Written parental consent was obtained for each subject prior to their participating in the study. In addition, all children completed an individual assent form.

Measure

Each subject completed the Olweus Bully/Victim Questionnaire (Olweus, 1986). This 56-item, self-administered questionnaire, designed for grades 3 through 10, asks questions specific to student's experiences and participation in various aspects of bullying in the school setting. The questions from the survey focused on in this article are those related to the locations in the school where bullying behaviors occur and the differences in location between males/females and grade level.

For the purposes of this study and as per the Olweus questionnaire, we defined and explained bullying to the students as being when another student or several other students do the following:

- completely ignore or exclude him or her from their group of friends or leave him or her out of things on purpose
- hit, kick, push, shove around, or lock him or her inside a room

- tell lies or spread false rumors about him or her or send mean notes and try to make other students dislike him or her
- and other hurtful things like that.

In addition, we explained that a student is being bullied when the above things happen over and over again, and it is difficult for the student being bullied to defend himself or herself. We further explained that bullying is when a student is teased over and over in a mean and hurtful way, but that bullying was not when teasing was done in a friendly or playful way.

Data Collection Procedures

A team of researchers collected data in the school setting over a period of two days. Students whom parental consent had been obtained were called to the cafeteria during the school day to complete the assent form and questionnaire. Definition of bullying used for this study and directions for completion of the questionnaire were provided. Data collectors were trained to use appropriate and consistent responses to student questions and to utilize the study's definition of bullying. They also assisted students with the reading of questions as necessary. Upon completion of the questionnaires, students were given a pencil and key chain as a thank you gift and sent back to their classrooms. All subjects were assured of the confidentiality of their responses throughout the study. There were minimal physical, psychological, legal, or social risks for participants. To ensure confidentiality and protection of subjects they were instructed not to put their names or any identifying information on the questionnaire.

Data Analysis

All data were coded directly from respondent's answers to specific questions asked on the survey instrument. In addition to answering questions about being bullied in the past three months, students also identified the locations at which such bullying occurred. Any student not responding to all relevant survey questions was excluded from the analyses presented here.

The data for these students are displayed on three tables. Table 1 reveals the location of bullying for the entire bullied sample. Table 2 and Table 3 explore this information further by considering gender and then student's grade level, respectively. Consistent with the structure of the school district, students in grades 3, 4, and 5 are elementary school students while those in grades 6, 7, and 8 are middle school students. On all 3 tables, data are presented in frequencies and percentages.

RESULTS

Regarding the experience of being bullied, 158 students responded that they have been victimized at least once in the previous three months. After excluding those students who did not answer all relevant survey questions, the final sample included 153 students who have experienced being bullied in the previous three months. As shown on Table 1, the most common locations for school bullying are on the playground and in the classroom during times when the teacher is not present (both locations were identified by 34.8% of the sample). Among other specified locales, popular locations included the lunchroom (29.7%), in the hallways (25.3%), and in the bathroom (25.3%). The least common location was at the school bus stop (5.7%).

Regarding the interaction between gender and bullying location (see Table 2), there does appear to be differences between the male and female students. Among males, the most common place to experience bullying is on the playground (32.4%) followed by bullying in the classroom (without a teacher's presence; 29.7%). This ordering is reversed for females. It should be recognized, however, that the percentage of females exceeds that of males at both locations. Once again, the school bus stop is the least common location of bullying for males and females.

It is also interesting to note differences in the frequencies between the two groups. Specifically, among the ten locations, only one site was shared by more than 30% of the male sample. Conversely, four sites were shared by more than 30% of females. Likewise, all but two locales were shared by 20% or more of the female sample while this is only true for half of the sites among males.

Finally, concerning the role of grade level on location as displayed in Table 3, more elementary school students report being bullied on the playground than middle school students (42.0% compared to 27.7%). This is also true for the bathroom (29.5% versus 21.5%) and traveling to and from school (18.2% versus 7.7%). The opposite relationship holds regarding hallways, where middle school students (32.3%) are bullied more than elementary school students (21.6%). Beyond these sites, there does not appear to be further substantial differences between the two groups.

TABLE 1. Location of Bullying (N = 153)

Locations	**Have Been Bullied at this Location** Frequency (%)
On the Playground/Athletic Field (during recess or break time)	55 (34.8)
In the Hallways/Stairwells	40 (25.3)
In Class (with Teacher Present)	31 (19.6)
In Class (with Teacher Absent)	55 (34.8)
In the Bathroom	40 (25.3)
In Gym Class or Locker Room/Shower	30 (19.0)
In the Lunchroom	47 (29.7)
On the Way to and from School	21 (13.3)
At the School Bus Stop	9 (5.7)
Somewhere Else in School	41 (25.9)

TABLE 2. Location of Bullying by Gender (N = 153)

Locations	**Have Been Bullied at this Location**	
	Males (n = 74) Frequency (%)	**Females (n = 79)** Frequency (%)
On the Playground/Athletic Field (during recess or break time)	24 (32.4)	31 (39.2)
In the Hallways/Stairwells	12 (16.2)	27 (34.2)
In Class (with Teacher Present)	10 (13.5)	20 (25.3)
In Class (with Teacher Absent)	22 (29.7)	33 (41.8)
In the Bathroom	20 (27.0)	19 (24.1)
In Gym Class or Locker Room/Shower	10 (13.5)	19 (24.1)
In the Lunchroom	18 (24.3)	28 (35.4)
On the Way to and from School	13 (17.6)	8 (10.1)
At the School Bus Stop	2 (2.7)	7 (8.9)
Somewhere Else in School	18 (24.3)	22 (27.8)

DISCUSSION

The intent of this study was to explore the dynamics of bullying in a rural elementary and middle school and to specifically increase our understanding of locations where bullying occurs. The results indicate that most bullying takes place on the playground and in the classroom while the teacher is not present. In this study, students were less likely to be

TABLE 3. Location of Bullying by Grade Level (N = 153)

Locations	Have Been Bullied at this Location	
	Elementary School Students (n = 88) Frequency (%)	**Middle School Students (n = 65)** Frequency (%)
On the Playground/Athletic Field (during recess or break time)	37 (42.0)	18 (27.7)
In the Hallways/Stairwells	19 (21.6)	21 (32.3)
In Class (with Teacher Present)	18 (20.5)	13 (20.0)
In Class (with Teacher Absent)	31 (35.2)	24 (36.9)
In the Bathroom	26 (29.5)	14 (21.5)
In Gym Class or Locker Room/Shower	17 (19.3)	13 (20.0)
In the Lunchroom	28 (31.8)	19 (29.2)
On the Way to and from School	16 (18.2)	5 (7.7)
At the School Bus Stop	8 (9.1)	1 (1.5)
Somewhere Else in School	26 (29.5)	15 (23.1)

bullied in the lunchroom, hallways, bathrooms, and bus stops, which is similar to what past studies have found.

There were differences between male and female students regarding where they were bullied. Males were bullied most often on the playground, while females were bullied more often in the classroom without a teacher present. This makes sense since most males are physically bullied (hit, pushed), while females are more often bullied verbally (teasing) and psychologically (excluded). These respective locations facilitate male's and female's respective forms of bullying. However, previous studies on High School students found females to be bullied more often in the hallways. Our findings suggest that there may be differences in where younger females versus older females are bullied.

The results also posited some differences between where elementary and middle school students were bullied. Elementary students were bullied most often on the playground, followed by the classroom and lunchroom, while middle school students were bullied most frequently in the classroom, hallways, and lunchroom, respectively. These differences may actually be insignificant since middle school students do not go on the playground during school hours and elementary students are rarely in the hallways because they do not yet change classes. With these two areas removed from the analysis, these two age groups appear to be bullied in very similar locations.

One interesting finding was that some students were bullied in the classroom with the teacher present. This occurred more often for females than males. Although this was a relatively small percent, it behooves further exploration.

LIMITATIONS

This exploratory research provides beginning knowledge as to the location in rural schools where students are being victimized by bullying. Generalizability is limited by the lack of random assignment, low response rate, no control group, subjects coming from only one region of the country, and the lack of diversity among students in the school district. The questionnaire used in this study also limited statistical analysis. The purpose of this study was exploratory and did not examine the myriad of psychosocial factors that may be involved in bullying and being bullied.

IMPLICATIONS

There are several important implications which can be drawn from this study. Many prevention and intervention programs for bullying have focused solely on the interpersonal psychological aspects of bullying and have failed to address the environmental variables necessary to make substantial changes in the problem. Likewise, other schools have taken the approach of instituting metal detectors and security guards, with little knowledge of the location of particular hot spots at their school. Neither approach has shown much success. This data supports the premise that a comprehensive approach including interpersonal interventions as well as specific environmental modifications would be better served. Schools interested in curbing bullying need to assess the location of bullying particular to their own property, and address those areas specifically. The most cost-effective and efficient method would require educating school personnel on the hotspots for bullying and then implementing a plan and training personnel to intervene at those locations. It soon becomes clear that locating security guards at the front door is futile when bullying is occurring in the playground or classroom. It's also not cost-efficient or practical to attempt to have adults monitor every area of school property, when there may be only 2-3 hotspots of bullying behavior.

The location of bullying has been too often forgotten in bullying research and needs to be addressed in a more in-depth approach in the future. Information such as the types of bullying that occurs in different locations would be helpful for schools looking to prevent or reduce this critical problem. In addition, bullying which occurs directly under the supervision of teachers or school personnel is also concerning and requires further inquiry. Are teachers unaware, fearful of their own safety, or do they believe like many adults that bullying is a "rite of passage" for childhood?

CONCLUSIONS

Bullying is a chronic and ubiquitous problem that has ignited concern about children's safety at school. Most studies completed thus far have focused on the interpersonal psychological characteristics of bully and victim, but have ignored the relevance of location. This study found location to be of import, in that, hotspots can be identified at each school and differ with regard to gender and grade. Schools can prevent and intercede more effectively with bullying if they can identify their particular hotspots and provide a comprehensive intervention that includes targeting specific locations, educating school personnel, as well as providing interpersonal treatment to bully and victim. Further research is desperately needed in this area to expand our knowledge of hotspots and the types of bullying behaviors that occur at each location.

REFERENCES

Arnette, J. & Walseben, M. (1998). *Combating fear and restoring safety in schools* (NCJ-167888). Washington, DC: Office of Juvenile Justice and Delinquency Prevention.

Astor, R., and Meyer, H. (1999). Where girls and women won't go: Female students', teachers', and social workers' views of school safety. *Social Work in Education, 21,* 201-219.

Astor, R., Meyer, H., & Behre, W. (1999). Unowned places and times: Maps and interviews about violence in High schools. *American Educational Research Journal, 36,* 1, 3-42.

Beane, A. (1999). *The Bully Free Classroom.* Minneapolis, MN: Free Spirit Publishing Co.

Bulach, C., Fulbright, J., & Williams, R. (2003). Bullying behavior: What is the potential for violence at your school? *Journal of Instructional Psychology, 30,* 2, 156-164.

Craig, W., Pepler, D., & Atlas, R. (2000). Observations of bullying in the playground and in the classroom. *School Psychology International, 21,* 22-36.

Erickson, N. (2001). Addressing the problem of juvenile bullying. *OJJDP Fact Sheet # 27.* Washington, DC: U.S. Department of Justice.

Espelage, D. & Asidao, C. (2001). Conversations with middle school students about bullying and victimization: Should we be concerned? *Journal of Emotional Abuse, 2,* 2/3, 49-62.

Olweus, D. (1986). The Olweus Bully/Victim Questionnaire. Mimeo. Bergen, Norway: University of Bergen.

Reiff, M. (2003). Bullying and Violence. *Journal of Developmental & Behavioral Pediatrics, 24,* 4, 296-310.

Adolescent Dating Violence on School Campuses

Gretchen Ely, PhD

SUMMARY. This paper reviews the adolescent dating violence literature in order to synthesize the risk factors that are associated with dating violence in school-aged adolescents. A review of the adolescent dating violence literature indicates that risk factors occur in three domains: individual, familial and societal. Research has shown that up to 43% of students report dating violence occurring on school grounds. School social workers and other school personnel must develop intervention programs based on empirical evidence to prevent adolescent dating violence on school campuses. In addition, schools must implement policies to protect victims from such violence. *[Article copies available for a fee from The Haworth Document Delivery Service: 1-800-HAWORTH. E-mail address: <docdelivery@haworthpress.com> Website: <http://www.HaworthPress.com> © 2004 by The Haworth Press, Inc. All rights reserved.]*

KEYWORDS. Adolescents, dating violence, schools, prevention

Gretchen Ely is Assistant Professor, University of Kentucky, College of Social Work, 619 Patterson Office Tower, Lexington, KY 40506 (gretchen.ely@uky.edu).

[Haworth co-indexing entry note]: "Adolescent Dating Violence on School Campuses." Ely, Gretchen. Co-published simultaneously in *Journal of Evidence-Based Social Work* (The Haworth Social Work Practice Press, an imprint of The Haworth Press, Inc.) Vol. 1, No. 2/3, 2004, pp. 143-157; and: *Kids and Violence: The Invisible School Experience* (ed: Catherine N. Dulmus and Karen M. Sowers) The Haworth Social Work Practice Press, an imprint of The Haworth Press, Inc., 2004, pp. 143-157. Single or multiple copies of this article are available for a fee from The Haworth Document Delivery Service [1-800-HAWORTH, 9:00 a.m. - 5:00 p.m. (EST). E-mail address: docdelivery@haworthpress.com].

http://www.haworthpress.com/web/JEBSW

Digital Object Identifier: 10.1300/J394v1n02_10

INTRODUCTION

This paper examines the literature related to risk factors and adolescent dating violence. A review of the adolescent dating violence literature indicates that risk factors occur in three domains: individual, familial and societal. This information is of vital importance to school social workers and other school professionals who are working to prevent dating violence on school campuses. Awareness of the risk factors associated with dating violence is important for school social workers who wish to develop school based interventions aimed at reducing violence (Astor, Behre, Fravil & Wallace, 1997).

Even though most dating violence studies take place in school, school policies generally do not address dating violence. Schools must implement policies to protect victims from such violence (Molidor & Tolman, 1998). Schools need to take some responsibility for controlling dating violent behavior on campus, especially in lieu of findings from one study indicating that 43% of students reported experiencing dating violence on school grounds (Molidor & Tolman, 1998).

Acts of intimidation and fear may often occur on campus, yet professionals are overlooking this type of violence within the school setting. Dating violence is another form of school violence that must be dealt with. Thus, it is vitally important that school social workers and other professionals become familiar with the risk factors related to dating violence so that incidences of dating violence that occur on campus can be reduced.

Intervention programs that target violence in the schools are often limited due to lack of resources and funding. Thus, school social workers are forced to limit their interventions to groups of children who are identified to be "at risk" for a certain problem. The purpose of this paper is to synthesize the literature in such a way that school social workers and other school professionals can gain an understanding of the potential risk factors related to adolescent dating violence so that students who may be at risk for the problem can be identified and placed in interventions aimed at preventing dating violence before it actually occurs.

Dating violence is a serious problem for modern adolescents. Researchers have found that between 32% and 60% of females reported that they had been victims of dating violence, and around 40% to 50% of boys and girls report perpetration of dating violence (Bergman, 1992; Foshee, 1996; Jezl, Molidor & Wright, 1996; Molidor & Tolman, 1998; Schwartz, O'Leary & Kendziora, 1997). Forty-five percent of female and 43% of male high school students have reported involvement in at least one dating violent incident (O'Keefe & Treister, 1998). Alarmingly, 82% of girls and 76% of boys in a high school sample reported recently being involved in dating violence that was defined as monopolization, degradation and isolation (Jackson, Cram & Seymour, 2000).

If many of these dating violent events take place on school grounds, school social workers are likely to encounter referrals related to dating violence on a regular basis. School personnel have begun to take a proactive approach to bullying, gun violence and fighting. Knowing the risk factors related to dating violence will allow personnel to take a proactive approach with on campus dating violence, as well. If school social workers are to take a proactive approach toward preventing on campus dating violence, the risk factors related to dating violence must be outlined and understood.

The author reviewed three multidisciplinary search engines (PSYCH INFO, Social Science Abstracts and Social Work Abstracts) and two electronic databases (InfoTrac and ProQuest) in January 2003, and pulled all the articles related to adolescent dating violence in those databases to examine for this literature review. The following section is a review of those studies, which have demonstrated that, to date, risk factors related to adolescent dating violence can be grouped into three domains: individual risk factors, familial risk factors and societal risk factors.

INDIVIDUAL RISK FACTORS

Conflict Resolution and Aggressiveness

Dysfunctional conflict approaches, personal aggressiveness, and tendency towards aggressive acts have been associated with male propensity to use dating violence as a control tactic. Researchers report that dysfunctional conflict negotiation approaches in males, which include: being disagreeable, being insulting, and using inflammatory language, are associated with increased likelihood of involvement in dating violence (Bird, Stith & Schladale, 1991; Riggs & O'Leary, 1996). This is not surprising considering that Billingham and Sack (1986) reported that courtship violence should be viewed as a breakdown in attempted conflict resolution rather than a phenomenon in and of itself. Because studies of adolescents in this area are limited, it is important to include the work of Ryan (1995), who conducted three studies designed to examine the presence of battering personalities in courtship violent men. He found that previous use of threats, verbal abuse and aggression were most predictive of the use of courtship violence. Later, Ryan (1998) reported that, in men, dating aggressiveness in one category, such as verbal aggression, was associated with higher levels of other types of aggression, such as sexual or physical aggression towards a dating partner. His results support findings from another study of males indicating that aggression in one category was related to aggression in another category (Riggs & Caulfield, 1997). Male engagement in hostile talk about women with peers has also been associated with male dating aggression towards women (Capaldi, et al., 2001).

Perceived Benefits and Acceptance of Dating Violence

Perceived beneficial outcomes have been associated with the use of dating violence in boys (O'Keefe, 1998; Williams & Martinez, 1999). Results indicate that adolescents who were involved in dating violence were more accepting of it and respondents who reported being involved in premarital dating violence also reported more positive attitudes towards marital violence (Foshee, Bauman & Fletcher, 1999; Henton et al., 1983). Others report that the need to gain control in a dating relationship, and dissatisfaction with relationship power predict subject involvement in physical and psychological dating abuse (Ronfeldt, Kimerling & Arias, 1998). O'Keefe (1997) found that girls were more likely to be violent to a dating partner when they believed that female to male violence was acceptable and male to female violence was not acceptable. Bethke and DeJoy (1993) reported that relationship status affected the acceptability of violence, and affected which actions (such as ending the relationship) following a violent episode were viewed as acceptable. Another study demonstrated that negative reactions to receipt of violence were most strongly correlated with the expressed use of dating violence (Bookwala, et al., 1992). Foshee, Bauman and Fletcher (1999) found that adolescents who were perpetrators of dating violence were more accepting of the use of dating violence when compared to adolescents who were not perpetrators. To supplement the information on adolescents it is important to note that Riggs and Caulfield (1997) suggested that violent men were significantly more likely than nonviolent men to believe that violence would result in the winning of an intimate argument. In addition, they found that, as compared to violent men's beliefs, nonviolent men were more likely to believe that the use of violence would bring about a permanent end to the relationship.

Status and Duration of Relationship

The status and length of the dating relationship and number of dating experiences may affect the likelihood of involvement in violence for adolescents. Some study results suggest that up to 35% of violence occurred in short term relationships of less than six months (Bergman, 1992; Roscoe & Callahan, 1985), as compared to six percent of violence, which occurred in relationships of two years or more (Roscoe & Callahan, 1985). Another study suggested that longer relationships have an increased likelihood of violence (O'Keefe, 1997). Reuterman and Burcky (1989) found that adolescents who experienced dating violence reported a higher number of dating experiences.

Pregnancy

Involvement in sexual dating violence has been associated with involvement in other risk factors that often result in unwanted pregnancy: disagreements about sex and sexual activity, alcohol use before sexual encounter, forced sexual contact, increased sexual activity and number of partners, and number of times previously getting someone pregnant (Bergman, 1992; Carlson, 1987; Burcky, Reuterman & Kopsky, 1988; Krieter et al., 1999; Molidor & Tolman, 1998; Valois et al., 1999; Williams & Martinez, 1999).

Health Risks

It has also been reported that adolescent involvement in dating violence is a predictor of increased number of sexual partners and involvement in other serious health risk behaviors (Valois et al., 1999). In addition to straightforward mental, emotional and physical health effects, dating violence against women limits their ability to protect themselves against sexually transmitted diseases, unwanted pregnancy, and undesired sexual intercourse, while increasing their risk for acquiring AIDS/HIV and other sexually transmitted diseases (Valois et al., 1999; Wood, Maforah & Jewkes, 1998).

Self-Esteem Problems

Early on, O'Keefe, Brockopp and Chew (1986) maintained that ongoing violence in dating relationships destroys adolescents' self-esteem. Low self-esteem has been found to be a predictor of involvement in dating violence (Burke, Stets & Pirog-Good, 1988; O'Keefe, 1998; Sharpe & Taylor, 1999; Stets & Pirog-Good, 1987). When controlling for length of relationship, self-esteem was found to be significantly associated with physical dating violence in a sample of undergraduates in Nova Scotia (Sharpe & Taylor, 1999). It was also reported that self-esteem was associated with physical and psychological violence for females in this same study. Recently, youths who reported experiencing date violence and rape also reported lower levels of self-esteem (Ackard & Neumark-Sztainer, 2002). Previous study results indicated that involvement in dating violence caused diminishment in self-esteem (Kasian & Painter, 1992). On the other hand, at least two studies have found that self-esteem is not related to involvement in dating violence (Bird, Stith & Schladale 1991; Makepeace, 1981).

Mental Health Indicators/Disorders

There is some evidence that suggests that mental health disorders, such as anti-social personality disorder, depression, suicide risk, and post-traumatic stress disorder may play a role in adolescent involvement in dating violence. The relationship between mental health indicators and adolescent dating violence has not been explored at length (Williams & Martinez, 1999). Criminologists suggest that delinquent behavior as a child increases the likelihood of involvement in other delinquent behavior, including dating violence, as an adolescent (Giordano et al., 1999). Deviant peer association and later aggression towards a partner was found to be mediated by antisocial behavior in one study (Capaldi et al., 2001). Other results suggest a significant association between dating violence, psychopathology, and physical aggression in young couples (Andrews et al., 2000). Dating violent females were recently reported to have more internalizing symptoms such as withdrawal, anxiety and depression symptoms as compared to non-dating violent females (Chase, Treboux & O'Leary, 2002). Other findings indicate that posttraumatic stress symptoms accounted for the relationship between childhood maltreatment and dating violence across school samples (Wekerle et al., 2001). Findings from one study indicate that dating violence was associated with higher levels of serious disordered eating behaviors (Ackard & Neumark-Sztainer, 2002). In the same study, over 50% of girls and boys who experienced dating violence and date rape also reported suicide attempts and scored lower on measures of emotional well-being when compared to non-dating violent peers. Females who reported dating violence were more likely than those who did not report such involvement to have attempted suicide according to Kreiter and colleagues (1999). Boys with a history of childhood maltreatment were more likely than boys without a maltreatment history to report clinical levels of depression, posttraumatic stress, and overt dissociation, and also had a greater risk of using threatening behaviors and physical abuse against a dating partner (Wolfe, Scott, Wekerle & Pittman, 2001).

Lack of School Success

Lack of success in school has been associated with the likelihood of involvement in dating violence. Bergman (1992) found a relationship between lower high school grade point average and involvement in dating violence. Reuterman and Burcky (1989) found that high school subjects involved in date fighting were more likely to have been suspended or expelled from school, and were more likely to be following a general high school academic program rather than a college preparatory academic program.

FAMILIAL FACTORS

Violence and Abuse in the Family of Origin

Dysfunctional early family involvement has been identified as a predictor of dysfunctional couple functioning in one recent study (Andrews et al., 2000). Dating violence may be a continuation of violence adolescents are reared with, as adolescents who grew up exposed to violence in the home may become desensitized to it (Williams & Martinez, 1999). Research demonstrates that experience with violence in the family of origin may increase adolescent involvement in violent dating relationships and/or model how to interact violently in intimate relationships (Carlson, 1987; Foshee, Bauman & Fletcher, 1999; Gwartney-Gibbs, Stockard & Bohmer, 1987; O'Keefe, Brockopp & Chew, 1986; Simons, Lin & Gordon, 1998; Smith & Williams, 1992). In one of the earlier studies of adolescent dating violence, Roscoe and Callahan (1985) found that 59% of adolescents who reported involvement in dating violence also reported violent treatment in their families of origin. O'Keefe (1998) found evidence that high school students who witnessed violence in the family of origin were more likely to be involved in dating violence either as victims or perpetrators, although not all of the students in her sample were violent with dating partners. Riggs and O'Leary (1996) found that dating aggression was associated with exposure to violence in the family of origin for female college students but not for males. In another study, subjects with violent family backgrounds reported experiencing more aggressive conflict in their dating relationships than subjects who did not have violent family backgrounds (Duggan, O'Brien & Kennedy, 2001). Some studies have failed to find that parental violence is a factor in teen dating violence (Riggs & O'Leary, 1996; Sigleman, Berry & Wiles, 1984; Simons, Lin & Gordon, 1998).

Some authors suggest that previous experience of child abuse/maltreatment may contribute to adolescent involvement in dating violence (O'Keefe, 1998; Wekerle & Wolfe, 1999). Parent-child violence has been shown as one predictor of the use of courtship violence with females but not with males (Tontodonato & Crew, 1992). Wolfe, Wekerle, Reitzel-Jaffe, and LeFebvre (1998) reported that youths who are maltreated prior to age 12 have significantly more verbal and physical conflicts with dating partners than non-maltreated youths in their sample of over 300 15-year-olds. Results from another study indicate that dating violence can be predicted by childhood maltreatment across high school samples with both genders (Wekerle et al., 2001). Other researchers have discovered consistent findings (Marshall & Rose, 1988; Riggs, O'Leary & Breslin, 1990).

Interpersonal Problems with Parents

Problems with parents have been associated with dating violence involvement in a recent study of adolescents. Dating violent females were more likely to report that their parents were less involved in their lives, less open with decision making, and less concerned about their well-being and whereabouts when compared to non-dating violent females, while males did not perceive their parenting to be any different (Chase, Treboux & O'Leary, 2002).

Simons, Lin and Gordon (1998) examined criminology literature and suggested that adolescent dating violence may be a manifestation of anti-social tendencies, which develop in childhood, often as a result of anti-social parents with ineffective parenting strategies. The results of their 3-year longitudinal survey of parents and adolescents in 3 counties provided strong evidence in support of their hypothesis. Experts have found evidence that unskilled parenting and family instability mediated the development of anti-social behavior, which played an important role in use of dating violence with an intimate partner in adolescence (Capaldi & Clarke, 1998; Wekerle & Wolfe, 1999).

Corporal Punishment

Harsh corporal punishment in the family of origin has also been associated with dating violence in adolescents (Foshee, Bauman & Fletcher, 1999; O'Leary et al., 1989; Strauss & Smith, 1990; Simons, Lin & Gordon, 1998). Reuterman and Burcky (1989) found that adolescents who had experienced dating violence were more likely than others to report that their parents had used various forms of violence as a means of disciplining them. Harsh discipline from a father was particularly predictive of involvement in dating violence, and those involved in dating violence were less likely than others to report close relationships with their fathers. They also found that being hit by a mother was not associated with the perpetration of dating violence for females, but was associated for males. In another study, being hit by a father was positively associated with dating violence for either gender (Foshee, Bauman & Fletcher, 1999).

Divorce

One study suggests that divorce in the family of origin may contribute to use of dating violence during adolescence. Billingham and Notebaert (1993) reported that students who come from a divorced family report higher scores of violent behavior on the Violence subscale and they also report higher scores for their dating partners on both the Violence subscale and the Verbal Aggression scale.

SOCIETAL FACTORS

Violence in Schools and Communities

Adolescents are often exposed to violence in their schools and communities (Krieter et al., 1999), which appears to play a role in dating violence involvement (Williams & Martinez, 1999; O'Keefe, 1998; Bergman, 1992), particularly when coupled with the stressor of violence within the family of origin (O'Keefe, 1998). Malik, Sorenson and Aneshensel (1997) found, in their study of over 700 high school students, that weapon ownership, coupled with injuries resulting from community violence, were associated with higher rates of student involvement in dating violence. They concluded that, for high school students, being exposed to violence in one context, such as the community of origin, appears to have crossover effects related to victimization and perpetration in another context, such as involvement in dating violence. Another study suggested that girls who grow up in neighborhoods where more female on female fighting takes place may be more prone towards other delinquent acts, such as participation in and acceptance of dating violence (Giordano et al., 1999). In other words, teen violence in one context may result in violence in other contexts.

Socioeconomic Status

O'Keefe (1998) found that male adolescent involvement in dating violence was mediated by lower socioeconomic status. This supports the findings of a later study suggesting that women reared in economically depressed areas might be more prone to engage in dating violence (Giordano et al., 1999). Others found that subjects who experienced dating violence were more likely to live in rural areas (Reuterman & Burcky, 1989).

Pop Culture

Pop culture may encourage dating violence in adolescents (Bergman, 1992). Teens are often exposed to music and media that perpetuate the use of violence against women as acceptable and sometimes expected. Results reported from 60 African-American boys and girls ranging in age from 11-16 years suggested significant acceptance of violence against women present in the adolescents who were exposed to rap music videos depicting male on female violence (Johnson et al., 1995).

Peer Influences

Reuterman and Burcky (1989) found that reported association with peers who were involved in dating violence increased the probability that a student would report being involved in dating violence him/herself. Wood, Maforah and Jewkes (1998) reported that female peers reinforced the acceptance of and submission to dating violence in their sample of South African teens.

DISCUSSION

It is clear from this literature review that adolescent dating violence is a complex problem associated with many different risk factors at a variety of levels. Social workers have much to contribute to the understanding of school based violence, given the profession's frontline involvement with the problem (Proctor, 2002). Based on the results of this literature review, it is clear that there is not enough knowledge development related to risk factors associated with adolescent dating violence. Social workers must advocate for the development of more empirical knowledge related to adolescent dating violence so that practitioners know where dating violence interventions should be targeted.

Despite the fact that more knowledge development in this area is needed, there is still important information present in the current literature review that school social workers can consider when targeting at-risk student dating violence on campus. For example, because of the evidence presented related to the relationship between low self-esteem and dating violence involvement, it may be pertinent for school social workers to target students with low self-esteem to participate in dating violence prevention programs. In addition, because the current literature suggests that exposure to violence in one context may lead to involvement in other types of violence, school social workers may want to concentrate dating violence interventions on students who have a history of involvement in any kind of violence. Evidence also suggests that students who have interpersonal problems with their parents may have a tendency to become involved in dating violence. Perhaps school social workers could target students who evidence problems with their parents for dating violence prevention programs. Research also demonstrates that those with mental health problems and mental health problem indicators may be at greater risk for involvement in dating violence. Therefore, school social workers should consider assessing students with mental health problems for involvement in dating violence.

CONCLUSIONS

Due to a number of research efforts related to adolescent dating violence, there is now some idea of what risk factors are related to dating violence in adolescent populations. School social workers are in a unique position to help schools modify policies and address conditions on campuses that may contribute to student involvement in dating violence incidences on school grounds. School social workers are also in a position to act as advisors to school administrators to develop practices that will enhance the safety and social development of students by eliminating dating violence on campus.

Although more research is needed, there is a body of research now available indicating that risk factors for dating violence are present at the individual, familial and societal levels. It is important for school social workers to consider the available research when they are thinking of which students to target for dating violence interventions. School social workers need to become involved in dating violence prevention that is based on the current literature so that dating violence can be prevented and treated in adolescence before it leads to a lifestyle that includes violence into adulthood. It is time to acknowledge dating violence in schools as another form of school violence.

REFERENCES

Ackard, D. M., & Neumark-Sztainer, D. (2002). Date violence and date rape among adolescents: Associations with disordered eating behaviors and psychological health. *Child Abuse & Neglect, 26*, 455-473.

Andrews, J. A., Foster, S. L., Capaldi, D., & Hops, H. (2000). Adolescent and family predictors of physical aggression, communication, and satisfaction in young adult couples. *Journal of Consulting and Clinical Psychology, 68*, 195-208.

Astor, R. A., Behre, W. J., Fravil, K. A., & Wallace, J. M. (1997). Perceptions of school violence as a problem and reports of violent events: A national survey of school social workers. *Social Work, 42*, 55-69.

Becky, D., & Farren, P. M. (1997). Teaching students how to understand and avoid abusive relationships. *School Counselor, 44*, 303-308.

Bergman, L. (1992). Dating violence among high school students. *Social Work, 37*, 21-27.

Bethke, T., & DeJoy, D. (1993). An experimental study of factors influencing the acceptability of dating violence. *Journal of Interpersonal Violence, 8*, 36-51.

Billingham, R. E., & Notebaert, N. L. (1993). Divorce and dating violence revisited: Multivariate analyses using Straus's conflict tactics subscores. *Psychological Reports, 73*, 679-684.

Billingham, R. E., & Sack, A. R. (1986). Courtship violence and the interactive status of the relationship. *Journal of Adolescent Research, 1*, 305-325.

Bird, G. W., Stith, S. M., & Schladale, J. (1991). Psychological resources, coping strategies, and negotiation styles as discriminators of violence in dating relationships. *Family Relations, 40*, 45-50.

Bookwala, J., Frieze, L. H., Smith, C., & Ryan, K. (1992). Predictors of dating violence: A multivariate analysis. *Violence and Victims, 7*, 297-311.

Burke, P. J., Stets, J. E., & Pirog-Good, M. A. (1988). Gender identity, self-esteem, and physical and sexual abuse in dating relationships. *Social Psychology Quarterly, 15*, 272-285.

Burcky, W., Reuterman, N., Kopsky, S. (1988). Dating violence among high school students. *The School Counselor, 35*, 353-358.

Capaldi, D. M., & Clark, S. (1998). Prospective family predictors of aggression toward female partners for at-risk young men. *Developmental Psychology*, 34, 1175-1188.

Capaldi, D. M., Dishion, T. J., Stoolmiller, M., & Yoerger, K. (2001). Aggression toward female partners by at-risk young men: The contribution of male adolescent friendships. *Developmental Psychology, 37*, 61-73.

Carlson, B. E. (1987). Dating violence: A research review and comparison with spouse abuse. *Social Casework, 68*, 16-23.

Cascardi, M., Avery-Leaf, S., O'Leary, D., & Slep, A. M. S. (1999). Factor structure and convergent validity of the Conflict Tactics Scale in high school students. *Psychological Assessment, 11*, 546-555.

Chase, K.A., Treboux, D., & O'Leary, K. D. (2002). Characteristics of adolescent's dating violence. *Journal of Interpersonal Violence, 1*, 33-49.

Duggan, S., O'Brien, M., & Kennedy, J. K. (2001). Young adult's immediate and delayed reactions to simulated marital conflicts: Implications for intergenerational patterns of violence in intimate relationships. *Journal of Consulting and Clinical Psychology, 69*, 13-24.

Foshee, V. A., Bauman, K. E., & Fletcher, L. G. (1999). Family violence and the perpetration of adolescent dating violence: Examining social learning and social control processes. *Journal of Marriage and the Family, 61,* 331-342.

Giordano, P. C., Millhollin, T. J., Cernovich, S. A., Pugh, M. D., & Rudolph, J. L.(1999). Delinquency, identity and women's involvement in relationship violence. *Criminology, 37*, 17-29.

Gwartney-Gibbs, P. A., Stockard, J., & Bohmer, S. (1987). Learning courtship aggression: The influence of parents, peers and personal experiences. *Family Relations, 36*, 276-282.

Henton, J., Cate, R., Koval, J., Lloyd, S., & Christopher, S. (1983). Romance and violence in dating relationships. *Journal of Family Issues, 4*, 467-482.

Jackson, S. M., Cram, F., & Seymour, F. W. (2000). Violence and sexual coercion in high school student's dating relationships. *Journal of Family Violence, 15*, 23-36.

Jezl, D. R., Molidor, C. E., & Wright, T. L. (1996). Physical, sexual and psychological abuse in high school dating relationships: Prevalence rates and self-esteem issues. *Child & Adolescent Social Work Journal, 13*, 69-87.

Johnson, J. D., Adams, M. S., Ashburn, L., & Reed, W. (1995). Differential gender effects of exposure to rap music on African American adolescent's acceptance of teen dating violence. *Sex Roles, 33,* 597-605.

Kasian, M., & Painter, S. L. (1992). Frequency and severity of psychological abuse in a dating population. *Journal of Interpersonal Violence, 7*, 350-364.

Krieter, S. R., Krowchuk, D. P., Woods, C. R., Sinal, S. H., Lawless, M. R., & DuRant, R. H. (1999). Gender differences in risk behaviors among adolescents who experience date fighting. *Pediatrics, 104,* 1286-1298.

Makepeace, J. M. (1981). Courtship violence among college students. *Family Relations, 30*, 97-102.

Malik, S., Sorenson, S. B., & Aneshensel, C. S. (1997). Community and dating violence among adolescents: Perpetration and victimization. *Journal of Adolescent Health, 21*, 291-302.

Marshall, L. L., & Rose, P. (1988). Family of origin and courtship violence. *Journal of Counseling and Development, 66,* 414-418.

Molidor, C., & Tolman, R. M. (1998). Gender and contextual factors in adolescent dating violence. *Violence Against Women, 4,* 180-194.

O'Keefe, M. (1998). Factors mediating the link between witnessing interparental violence and dating violence. *Journal of Family Violence, 13,* 39-57.

O'Keefe, M. (1997). Predictors of dating violence among high school students. *Journal of Interpersonal Violence, 12,* 546-569.

O'Keefe, N. K., Brockopp, K., & Chew, E. (1986). Teen dating violence. *Social Work, 46,* 3-8.

O'Keefe, M., & Treister, L. (1998). Victims of dating violence among high school students: Are the predictors different for males and females? *Violence Against Women, 4,* 195-223.

O'Leary, K. D., Barling, J., Arias, I., Rosenbaum, A., Malone, J., & Tyree, A. (1989). Prevalence and stability of physical aggression between spouses: A longitudinal analysis. *Journal of Consulting and Clinical Psychology, 57,* 263-268.

Proctor, E. (2002). Social work, school violence, mental health, and drug abuse: A call for evidence-based practices (Editorial). *Social Work Research, 26,* 67-70.

Reuterman, N. A., & Burcky, W. D. (1989). Dating violence in high schools: A profile of the victim. *Psychology, 26,* 1-9.

Riggs, D. S., & Caufield, M. B. (1997). Expected consequences of male violence against their female dating partners. *Journal of Interpersonal Violence, 12,* 229-240.

Riggs, D. S., & O'Leary, K. D. (1989). Theoretical model of courtship aggression. In M. Pirog-Good, & J. Stets (Eds.), *Violence in Dating Relationships:Emerging Social Issues* (pp. 53-71). New York: Praeger.

Riggs, D. S., O'Leary, K. D., & Breslin, F. C. (1990). Multiple correlates of physical aggression in dating couples. *Journal of Interpersonal Violence, 5,* 61-73.

Ronfeldt, H. M., Kimerling, R., & Arias, I. (1998). Satisfaction with relationship power and the perpetration of dating violence. *Journal of Marriage and the Family, 60,* 70-79.

Roscoe, B., & Callahan, J. (1985). Adolescent's self-reports of violence in families and dating relationships. *Adolescence, 20,* 545-553.

Ryan, K. M. (1995). Do courtship-violent men have characteristics associated with a "battering personality?" *Journal of Family Violence, 10,* 99-120.

Ryan, K. M. (1998). The relationship between courtship violence and sexual aggression in college students. *Journal of Family Violence, 13,* 377-394.

Schwartz, M., O'Leary, S. G., & Kendziora, K. T. (1997). Dating aggression among high school students. *Violence and Victims, 9,* 295-305.

Sharpe, D., & Taylor, J. K. (1999). An examination of variables from a social-developmental model to explain physical and psychological dating violence. *Canadian Journal of Behavioral Science, 31,* 165-175.

Sigelman, C. K., Berry, C. J., & Wiles, K. A. (1984). Violence in college students dating relationships. *Journal of Applied Social Psychology, 5,* 530-548.

Simons, R. L., Lin, K. H., & Gordon, L. C. (1998). Socialization in the family of origin and male dating violence: A prospective study. *Journal of Marriage and the Family, 60,* 467-478.

Smith, J. P., & Williams, J. G. (1992). From abusive household to dating violence. *Journal of Family Violence, 7,* 153-165.

Stets, J. E. & Pirog-Good, M. A. (1987). Violence in dating relationships. *Social Psychology Quarterly, 50,* 237-246.

Straus, M. A., & Smith, C. (1990). Family patterns and primary prevention of family violence. In M. A. Straus, & R. J. Gelles (Eds.), *Physical Violence in American Families* (pp. 507-528). New Brunswick, NJ: Transaction.

Tontodonato, P., & Crew, B. K. (1992). Dating violence, social learning theory and gender: A multivariate analysis. *Violence and Victims, 7,* 3-14.

Valois, R. F., Oeltemann, J. E., Waller, J., & Hussey, J. R. (1999). Relationship between number of sexual intercourse partners and selected health risk behaviors among public high school adolescents. *Journal of Adolescent Health, 25,* 328-335.

Wekerle, C., & Wolfe, D. A. (1999). Dating violence in mid-adolescence: Theory,significance and emerging prevention issues. *Clinical Psychology Review, 19,* 435-456.

Wekerle, C., Wolfe, D. A., Hawkins, D. L., Pittman, A., Glickman, A., & Lovald, B. E. (2001). Childhood maltreatment, posttraumatic stress symptomatology and adolescent dating violence: Considering the value of adolescent perceptions of abuse and a trauma mediational model. *Development and Psychopathology, 13,* 847-871.

Williams, S. E., & Martinez, E. (1999). Psychiatric assessment of victims of adolescent dating violence in a primary care clinic. *Clinical Child Psychology and Psychiatry, 4,* 427-439.

Wolfe, D. A., Scott, K., Wekerle, C., & Pittman, A. (2001). Child maltreatment: Risk of adjustment and dating violence in adolescence. *Journal of the American Academy of Child and Adolescent Psychiatry, 40,* 282-289.

Wolfe, D. A., Wekerle, C., Reitzel-Jaffe, D., & LeFebvre, L. (1998). Factors associated with abusive relationships among maltreated and normal treated youth. *Development and Psychopathology,* 10, 61-85.

Wood, K., Maforah, F., & Jewkes, R. (1998). "He forced me to love him": Putting violence on adolescent sexual health agendas. *Social Science and Medicine, 47,* 233-242.

Perceptions of Bullying and Non-Bullying Children: Results from an Exploratory Study in a U.S. Rural School

William S. Rowe, DSW
Matthew T. Theriot, PhD
Karen M. Sowers, PhD
Catherine N. Dulmus, PhD

SUMMARY. This exploratory study focuses on the differences between children who self identify as bullies versus those who do not. Students (N = 192), grades 3 through 8, from a rural school district in the United States were surveyed as to their experiences with bullying in the school setting. A total of 70 students in the sample identified themselves as bullies. No substantial differences were found between the two

---

William S. Rowe is Professor and Director at the University of South Florida.

Matthew T. Theriot is Assistant Professor, Karen M. Sowers is Professor and Dean, and Catherine N. Dulmus is Associate Professor, The University of Tennessee, College of Social Work.

Address correspondence to: William S. Rowe, University of South Florida, School of Social Work, 4202 East Fowler Avenue, MGY 132, Tampa FL 33620 (E-mail: mrowe@chumal.csa.usk.edu).

The authors would like to gratefully acknowledge the contributions of Pamela Jinks and David Dupper to the project.

[Haworth co-indexing entry note]: "Perceptions of Bullying and Non-Bullying Children: Results from an Exploratory Study in a U.S. Rural School." Rowe, William S. et al. Co-published simultaneously in *Journal of Evidence-Based Social Work* (The Haworth Social Work Practice Press, an imprint of The Haworth Press, Inc.) Vol. 1, No. 2/3, 2004, pp. 159-174; and: *Kids and Violence: The Invisible School Experience* (ed: Catherine N. Dulmus and Karen M. Sowers) The Haworth Social Work Practice Press, an imprint of The Haworth Press, Inc., 2004, pp. 159-174. Single or multiple copies of this article are available for a fee from The Haworth Document Delivery Service [1-800-HAWORTH, 9:00 a.m. - 5:00 p.m. (EST). E-mail address: docdelivery@haworthpress.com].

http://www.haworthpress.com/web/JEBSW

Digital Object Identifier: 10.1300/J394v1n02_11

groups in regard to gender or age, however, a larger percentage of bullying students were found in grades 7 and 8. Differences between the two groups relating to questions concerning empathy for peers and student's sense of helping were found. Results provide some insight into the attitudes and beliefs of children who bully. Expanding our understanding could lead to the development of more effective education and intervention programs for students, parents and teachers.

KEYWORDS. Bullying, rural schools, bullies, victimization

Research has shown that bullying is a pervasive and disturbing problem in schools around the world. In fact, bullying is so prevalent that many individuals have come to accept bullying has simply a normative, albeit negative aspect of peer interaction in the school experience. Perhaps this attitude is best exemplified in the following conclusion drawn by Arnold (1994), ". . . bullying is rooted at one extreme of the range of 'normal' behavior arising in group social interactions amongst children" (p. 183).

Given the mounting evidence that involvement in bullying can have long-term negative consequences on the victim and the bully, these attitudes are especially troubling. Most studies on bullying in schools, however, have been done outside of the United States and with a specific focus on the negative experience of children who have been bullied. In light of increased violence in American schools, it is important to expand our understanding of the nature of bullying, both from the viewpoint of children who exhibit bullying behavior and those who do not. This study provides information to further develop that understanding.

Background and Prevalence

The original work of Dan Olweus, *Aggression in the Schools: Bullies and Whipping Boys* (1978), examined the phenomenon and prevalence of bullying behaviors of primary and secondary students in Norway. As a pioneer in this research, he developed the following definition: "a student is being bullied or victimized when he or she is exposed, repeatedly and over time, to negative actions on the part of one or more other students" (Olweus, 1994). Olweus' work sparked international interest in the pervasiveness, impact, and long-term effects of bullying behaviors in school children of all ages (Smith, Cowie, Olafsson and Liefooghe, 2002). As a result, studies were completed in countries around the globe that focused on identifying the magnitude and significance of bullying within the lives of school-aged children. The degree to which these behaviors could be predicted within the general population of all school children was also studied, as were the effects that bullying, being bullied, or witnessing these behaviors had upon the children during childhood and in later life (Twemlow and Sacco, 1996).

Twemlow and Sacco (1996) suggest that a conservative estimate of the number of children involved in bullying or being bullied is approximately 10% of all school children worldwide. Estimates of children engaging in bullying behaviors or experiencing being bullied vary greatly from country to country, among age groups, and at various socio-economic levels.

Preliminary results from one study (Hoover, Oliver and Hazler, 1992) indicated victimization by bullies is more prevalent in the United States than in European countries. Dake, Price and Telljohann (2003) found that 19% of elementary students within the United States were bullied compared to 11.3% in Finland and 49.8% in Ireland. The prevalence of being a bully similarly ranges from 4.1% to 49.7% in studies done outside of the U.S. compared to 13% to 20% in American studies (Dake, Price, & Telljohann, 2003; Nansel et al., 2001; Pellegrini, Bartini, & Brooks, 1999). One survey of school principals conducted in the 1996-97 school year identified over 200,000 serious fights or public attacks in public schools (National Center for Educational Statistics, 1998). Student surveys indicate even higher rates of aggressive behavior (Kann et al. 1995).

Characteristics of Bullies

Bullies are often depicted as strong, towering boys with clenched fists and an angry face. In terms of personality and emotion, they are often described as tough on the outside yet insecure and fearful on this inside. Educationally, their behavior is often explained as stemming from displaced frustration about poor academic success and repeated school failures. However, research on school bullying has repeatedly and consistently shown the fallacy and inaccuracy of these beliefs. Instead, school bullies may be boys or girls (Olweus, 1993; 1994). Likewise, bullies do not have a lower self-image or lower self-esteem than their non-bullying peers (Rigby & Slee, 1991; Clarke & Kiselica, 1997). Bullies also tend to have average or lower levels of anxiety and insecurity (Olweus, 1993; 1994; Clarke & Kiselica, 1997). Finally, academic performance has little or no influence over the perpetration of bullying behavior (Rigby & Slee, 1991).

Other studies have further characterized bullies as having a genuine lack of empathy (Olweus, 1993; 1994). In terms of popularity, bullying children generally have average popularity in elementary school that then decreases later in middle school and high school (Clarke & Kiselica, 1997). Lastly, bullies are frequently physically larger than their victims, yet they possess an unwillingness to admit that their victim is weaker than they are and, instead, insist that they were provoked (Olweus, 1993; 1994).

Several studies have also identified many worrisome outcomes for children involved in school bullying. For bullied children, Brockenbrough, Cornell and Loper (2002) found that repeated victimization resulted in aggressive attitudes and the likelihood of children to engage in high-risk behaviors such as weapon carrying and fighting. In another study, Smith and associates (2003) reported an association between school and workplace bullying, noting that victims of bullying at school were more at risk of workplace victimization later in life. Regarding bullies, research has found a relationship between childhood bullying and later delinquency and criminality (Olweus, 1993; 1994). Yet, Cullingford and Morrison (1995), in their study of the relationship between bullying while in school and subsequent criminal activity, noted the following: "The question remains as to why some children respond more readily to provocation than others, and why they choose certain methods of retaliation from those available." These are the types of queries that must eventually drive research in this area.

However, our understanding of bullying from the perspective of the children themselves remains limited. As such, before complex developmental questions can be answered or effective interventions designed, it is important to conduct exploratory studies to better understand the attitudes, beliefs, perceptions and behaviors of children who bully and those who do not. This study is a step in this direction. Specifically, this study will identify children who report bullying others, differentiate these children from their non-bullying peers, and then describe their bullying behaviors. As we begin to look at the ethos or culture of bullying as a formative influence, the exploration done here will help to advance the knowledge base in this direction.

METHODOLOGY

Study Design

This study utilized a survey research design to gather information from students as to their self-reported bullying victimization, as well as self-reported bullying behaviors towards other students in their school. The IRB at a large research university in the Southeastern United States granted permission to conduct the research prior to the start of the project. Parental consent was obtained for all student subjects whose participation was voluntary and confidential.

Study Sample

Letters to parents were sent home with students to recruit subjects. Subjects were recruited from three rural public schools (an elementary school, a middle school, and a school that housed grades K-8) located within the same school district in a Southeastern rural region of the United States. The school district is located in a county characterized by high rates of poverty as evidenced by 43% to 61% of students receiving free or reduced lunches and 12% of the population still not having a telephone. The school district students are 98% Caucasian and the dominant culture is Appalachian.

The letter sent home to parents included information related to the study and a consent form for parents to complete to allow their child to participate in the study. A self-addressed stamped envelope was provided for parents to mail the consent form back to the principal investigator at the university. Ultimately, the convenience sample consisted of 192 students in grades three through eight, representing an 18.4% response rate. Data collection occurred in the fall of 2002. A team of researchers conducted data collection in the school setting for all children who met inclusion criteria and for whom written parental consent was obtained. Since all subjects were measured at one point in time, no follow-up was necessary. Thus, attrition was not problematic.

Inclusion criteria were as follows: (a) subjects had to be students enrolled in the school where data collection occurred, and (b) subjects had to be in grades three through eight. Written parental consent was obtained for each subject prior to their participating in the study. In addition, all children completed an individual assent form.

Measure

Each subject completed the Olweus Bully/Victim Questionnaire (Olweus, 1986). This 56-item, self-administered questionnaire, designed for grades 3 through 10, asks questions specific to experiences with and participation in various aspects of bullying in the school setting.

For the purposes of this study and as per the Olweus questionnaire, we defined and explained bullying to the students as being when another student, or several other students, do the following:

- completely ignore or exclude him or her from their group of friends or leave him or her out of things on purpose
- hit, kick, push, shove around, or lock him or her inside a room
- tell lies or spread false rumors about him or her or send mean notes and try to make other students dislike him or her
- and other hurtful things like that.

In addition, we explained that a student is being bullied when the above things happen over and over again, and it is difficult for the student being bullied to defend himself or herself. We further explained that bullying is when a student is teased over and over in a mean and hurtful way, but that bullying was not when teasing was done in a friendly or playful way.

Data Collection Procedures

A team of researchers collected data in the school setting over a period of two days. Students whom parental consent had been obtained were called to the cafeteria during the school day to complete the assent form and questionnaire. Definition of bullying used for this study and directions for completion of the questionnaire were provided. Data collectors were trained to use appropriate and consistent responses to student questions and to utilize the study's definition of bullying. They also assisted students with the reading of questions as necessary. Upon completion of the questionnaires, students were given a pencil and key chain as a thank you gift and sent back to their classrooms. All subjects were assured of the confidentiality of their responses throughout the study. There were minimal physical, psychological, legal, or social risks for participants. To ensure confidentiality and protection of subjects they were instructed not to put their names or any identifying information on the questionnaire.

Data Analysis

All data were coded directly from respondent's answers to specific questions asked on the survey instrument. The two primary categories for comparison are those students who report bullying others and those students who do not report committing such behavior. Students responding positively to perpetrating some form of bullying when asked about specific types of bullying behaviors or actions are included in the bullying group while those students responding that they have not committed any of the nine types of bullying listed in the survey at any time during the previous three months comprise the comparison group.

Most of the data are displayed on three tables. Table 1 and Table 2 show information for both comparison groups while Table 3 focuses exclusively on those students who have bullied others. On all 3 tables, categorical variables are presented in frequencies and percentages while continuous variables are reported as means (± standard deviations). Additional information not reported in the tables is detailed in the text of the Results section.

RESULTS

Although only 40 students responded that they have bullied other students when asked directly in one survey question, 70 students responded positively to perpetrating some form of bullying when asked about specific types of bullying behaviors or actions. The bullying group, therefore, consists of these 70 students compared to 122 in the non-bullying group. Table 1 presents information on the demographic and attitudinal characteristics for the two groups. There does not appear to be any substantial differences in gender, age, or each student's reported number of good friends between the two groups. There is, however, a larger percentage of bullying students in the two most senior grades (grades 7 and 8) compared to the group of non-bullies (35.7% versus 26.2%). Students who have not bullied others also reported liking school more than the students who have bullied others (74.6% versus 65.7%).

Table 2 illustrates the student's perceptions about bullying. Expectedly, there are several important differences between the two

TABLE 1. Demographic and Attitudinal Characteristics (N = 192)

Characteristic	Have Bullied Others in Past Three Months (n = 70) Frequency (%) or Mean ± SD	Have Not Bullied Others in Past Three Months (n = 122) Frequency (%) or Mean ± SD
Gender (n = 191)		
Male	34 (49.3)	58 (47.5)
Female	35 (50.7)	64 (52.5)
Current School Grade Level		
3rd Grade	13 (18.6)	32 (26.2)
4th Grade	10 (14.3)	14 (11.5)
5th Grade	14 (20.0)	22 (18.0)
6th Grade	8 (11.4)	22 (18.0)
7th Grade	11 (15.7)	17 (13.9)
8th Grade	14 (20.0)	15 (12.3)
Age	10.8 ± 1.83	10.5 ± 1.83
Do you like school?		
I dislike school.	7 (10.0)	9 (7.4)
Neutral	17 (24.3)	22 (18.0)
I like school.	46 (65.7)	91 (74.6)
How many good friends do you have?		
None	0 (0.0)	1 (0.8)
1	6 (8.6)	6 (4.9)
2-3	11 (15.7)	27 (22.1)
4 or more	53 (75.7)	88 (72.1)

Column percentages may not total 100% because of rounding. SD = standard deviation

groups. Many of these differences relate to questions concerning empathy for peers and students' sense of helping. For example, a larger percentage of the students who bully reported feeling very little when observing others being bullied or they reported feeling that those students deserved it (17.1% of bullies versus 8.2% of the comparison group). A larger portion of the bullying students also said that they would just watch another student be bullied or that they would think about helping but do nothing (34.8%) than those students who do not bully (24.6%). Not surprisingly, students who bully were also more willing to join in the bullying of another student (25.7% versus 3.3% of students in the non-bullying group). Conversely, more non-bullies

TABLE 2. Summary of Student Perceptions About Bullying (N = 192)

Characteristic	**Have Bullied Others in Past Three Months (n = 70)** Frequency (%)	**Have Not Bullied Others in Past Three Months (n = 122)** Frequency (%)
What do you feel or think when you see another student your age being bullied at school?		
They deserve it.	5 (7.1)	7 (5.7)
I don't feel much.	7 (10.0)	3 (2.5)
I feel sorry for them.	19 (27.1)	30 (24.6)
I feel sorry for them and I want to help.	39 (55.7)	82 (67.2)
How do you usually react if a student your age is being bullied by other students? (n =191)		
I have never noticed this.	21 (30.4)	44 (36.1)
I take part in the bullying.	1 (1.4)	0 (0.0)
I don't act, but I think the bullying is OK.	1 (1.4)	0 (0.0)
I just watch.	8 (11.6)	6 (4.9)
I don't act, but I think I should help the bullied student.	16 (23.2)	24 (19.7)
I try to help the bullied student.	22 (31.9)	48 (39.3)
Do you think you could join in bullying another student whom you didn't like?		
Yes	11 (15.7)	4 (3.3)
Yes, Maybe	7 (10.0)	0 (0.0)
I don't know	13 (18.6)	18 (14.8)
No, I don't think so	10 (14.3)	5 (4.1)
No	17 (24.3)	36 (29.5)
Definitely No	12 (17.1)	59 (48.4)
How often do other students try to stop it when a student is being bullied at school?		
Almost never	18 (25.7)	49 (40.2)
Once in a while	21 (30.0)	20 (16.4)
Sometimes	12 (17.1)	27 (22.1)
Often	11 (15.7)	12 (9.8)
Almost always	8 (11.4)	14 (11.5)

TABLE 2 (continued)

Characteristic	Have Bullied Others in Past Three Months (n = 70) Frequency (%)	Have Not Bullied Others in Past Three Months (n = 122) Frequency (%)
How often do teachers or other adults try to stop it when a student is being bullied at school?		
Almost never	18 (25.7)	36 (29.5)
Once in a while	14 (20.0)	13 (10.7)
Sometimes	10 (14.3)	7 (5.7)
Often	14 (20.0)	24 (19.7)
Almost always	14 (20.0)	42 (34.4)
Overall, how much has your teacher done to counteract bullying? (n = 191)		
Little or nothing	21 (30.4)	38 (31.1)
Fairly little	15 (21.7)	14 (11.5)
Somewhat	13 (18.8)	19 (15.6)
A good deal	11 (15.9)	31 (25.4)
Much	9 (12.9)	20 (16.4)

Column percentages may not total 100% because of rounding.

stated that they would feel sorry for another student being bullied and want to help (67.2% versus 55.7% of bullies). Furthermore, these students also said that they would actually take action to help a bullied student (39.3% versus 31.9% of bullies).

Concerning the actions and reactions of teachers and school personnel, a larger percentage of the students who bully felt like adults tried to stop bullying at school only sometimes or less (60.0% versus 45.9% of non-bullies) while more of the students who did not bully felt like teachers often or almost always tried to stop bullying at school (54.1% versus 40.0%). This relationship is consistent regarding students' overall impressions of how much teachers do to counteract bullying. The students in the non-bully group believe that teachers have done a good deal or more to counteract bullying (41.8%). Fewer students in the other group share this belief (28.8%). It should be recognized, however, that the approximately 50% of students in both groups believe that teachers have done little or fairly little to counteract bullying.

Table 3 reports information on specific types of bullying behavior and their frequency. The most common type of bullying is calling others

TABLE 3. Frequency and Type of Bullying Committed in Past Three Months (N = 70)

Type of Bullying	**Has Not Happened in Past 3 Months** Freq. (%)	**Happened Only Once or Twice** Freq. (%)	**Happened 2-3 Times a Month** Freq. (%)	**Happened About Once a Week** Freq. (%)	**Happened Several Times a Week** Freq. (%)
Called Others Mean Names, Made Fun of, or Teased Them	28 (40.0)	27 (38.6)	6 (8.6)	4 (5.7)	5 (7.1)
Intentionally Excluded or Ignored Others	36 (51.4)	23 (32.9)	4 (5.7)	3 (4.3)	4 (5.7)
Hit, Kicked, Shoved, or Assaulted Others	45 (64.3)	14 (20.0)	4 (5.7)	5 (7.1)	2 (2.9)
Spread Lies or False Rumors About Others	52 (74.3)	11 (15.7)	2 (2.9)	3 (4.3)	2 (2.9)
Took or Damaged Money or Items	59 (84.3)	5 (7.1)	2 (2.9)	1 (1.4)	3 (4.3)
Threatened or Forced Others to Do Things (n = 68)	50 (73.5)	12 (17.6)	2 (2.9)	4 (5.9)	0 (0.0)
Said Comments or Called Others Names Based on Race or Color	56 (80.0)	9 (12.9)	2 (2.9)	2 (2.9)	1 (1.4)
Bullied Others with Sexual Comments, Names, or Gestures	53 (75.7)	8 (11.4)	5 (7.1)	2 (2.9)	2 (2.9)
Bullied Students in Other Ways (n = 69)	54 (78.3)	9 (13.0)	4 (5.7)	0 (0.0)	2 (2.9)

Column percentages may not total 100% because of rounding.

mean names or teasing them. Approximately 60.0% of bullying students report doing this in the past three months. Since 7.1% of bullies said that they do this several times a week, this is also the most frequent bullying act. The second most common and frequent type of bullying is intentionally excluding or ignoring others. Among students who bully, 48.6% reported committing such behavior while 5.7% said they do this several times a week. The only other act reported by at least 30% of the bullying sub-sample was hitting, kicking, or otherwise physically assaulting another student (35.7% reported this behavior). The least common (and second least frequent) type of bullying is the use of racist comments or racial name-calling. Only 20.0% of bullying students said that they have done this in the past three months and only one student (1.4%) has done bullying of this nature several times a week.

Though not reported on the tables, it is worth noting that, among the students who have committed acts of bullying, seventeen of these students (24.3%) stated that a teacher has talked with them about their bullying in the past three months. Along the same lines, fifteen students in the bullying group (21.5%) said that an adult at home has talked with them about their bullying during this time period.

DISCUSSION

The percentage of students in this sample who reported bullying their peers in the past three months (36.5%) is considerably higher than figures reported in other U.S. studies. As cited in this paper's opening section, prevalence estimates on student's participation as bullies have generally ranged from 13% to 20% (Pellegrini, Bartini, & Brooks, 1999; Nansel et al., 2001; Dake, Price, & Telljohann, 2003). In comparison, then, the prevalence of bullying among children in this sample would be almost double that in these other pieces of research.

Since the definitions of bullying and the length of the research periods differ from study to study, comparisons between the collected studies should be made cautiously. Regardless of these contrasts, however, the substantial number of self-reporting bullies in this study must be acknowledged. With greater than one-third of the students committing bullying behaviors, this size and scope of the bullying problem for these children would seem to be tremendous.

Furthermore, the high prevalence of bullying in this sample is consistent with Olweus' (1993) hypothesis that bullying may be a bigger problem in rural areas than in large cities. In his extensive study of children in Norway, Olweus found that there was more communication about bullying between teachers, parents and children in the big cities. These results, according to Olweus, suggest a greater awareness about bullying issues in the larger cities compared to less-populated, more rural areas.

The lack of empathy that has been highlighted in other studies is also evident here. On a handful of questions concerning student's feelings while watching peers being bullied, a larger percentage of the bullying children reported feeling very little for the victims or feeling that the victim deserved it. This feeling that the bullying was somehow warranted or deserved fits with the characterization of bullies as believing victims provoke bullying behavior.

The most common bullying behaviors reported here were among the most commonly reported from victims in the study done by Nansel et al. (2001). In their study, being belittled about looks and speech was the most common form of bullying followed by the spread of false rumors and then physical attacks. The ordering for the present study moves from teasing and name-calling to intentional exclusion and then physical assault. Bullying with racial insults or racial name-calling was the least common in both studies.

Implications for Education

As if the soaring prevalence of bullies was not enough to justify the development of immediate and effective interventions, there are other important implications to consider regarding the bullying problem in schools. Having already discussed the lasting impact that bullying may have on the bullies and the victims, it is necessary to recognize the effect that bullies may have on all school children.

Bullying, in many ways, can be viewed as a contagion. Children who witness school bullying may become less sensitized to violence and aggression as young adults (O'Connell, Pepler, & Craig, 1999). This could lead to lower empathy in later life (Rigby & Slee, 1991). Socially, bullies possess many of the characteristics that make them powerful models for teaching behavior to peers (O'Connell, Pepler, & Craig, 1999). These characteristics for effective modeling include the bully's position as a powerful figure within the school and the similarity in traits between bullies and other students. Finally, whenever bullying goes unreported or unpunished at school, the message is sent that there is no negative consequence for aggressive behaviors (Bandura, 1977; O'Connell, Pepler, & Craig, 1999).

Interventions targeted at school bullying problems have traditionally involved only the bully and victim (Garrity & Jens, 1997). For the reasons stated above, these interventions have met with limited success. Instead, the more effective interventions utilize a school-wide approach designed to change both individual behaviors as well as the overall climate of the school (Garrity & Jens, 1997). Olweus (1978; 1993; 1994) showed that a school-wide intervention reduced bullying problems by 50%. Other studies have likewise demonstrated decreased bullying and positive changes in the school through the use of such interventions (see Clarke & Kiselica, 1997). Specific to interventions targeting bullies, the bully's need for power and attention can be viewed as an opportunity to develop pro-social leadership qualities (Garrity & Jens, 1997). To this end, Garrity and Jens state that the best tactic for clinical work with bullies is "no-nonsense behavioral corrections with pro-social development of interventions to foster replacement behaviors for the power needs of the bully" (p. 1054).

Limitations

This exploratory research provides beginning knowledge as to self-reported bullying behaviors among children in a rural school setting. As new research directions are constructed, the limitations of this study should be considered and possibly addressed in future work. First, generalizability is limited by the lack of random assignment, low response rate, no control group, subjects coming from only one region of the country, and the lack of diversity among students in the school district. The questionnaire used in this study also limited statistical analysis. Since the purpose of this study was exploratory, with the results of the data focused on student self-report behaviors of bullying, the myriad of psychosocial factors that may be involved in bullying and being bullied were not examined.

CONCLUSIONS

This exploratory study has helped identify some of the differences between children who self identify as bullies versus those who do not. It provides some insight into the attitudes and beliefs of children who bully. Expanding our understanding could lead to the development of more effective education and intervention programs for students, parents and teachers. School-based social workers as well as others have generated potentially effective programs and policies for reducing school based bullying. Some of these include recommendations like "schools must create a positive climate; discuss bullying openly; refuse to accept the behavior; develop consistent, non-shaming consequences; keep records on aggressive actions; involve student witnesses, parents and teachers; increase hallway and playground monitoring; create support programs for victims that teach problem solving and assertiveness skills; and help bullies become more empathic" (Garrett, 2001, p. 74).

These can be effective only if we are able to more fully understand the attitudes, beliefs and motivations of children who bully as well as their developmental sequelae. Further study must be conducted with children from all cultural, geographic and socio-economic backgrounds to identify key elements that support these pervasive destructive phenomena.

REFERENCES

Arnold, F. (1994). Bullying, a tale of everyday life: Reflections on insider research. *Educational Action Research, 2* (2), 183-193.

Bandura, A. (1977). *Social learning theory.* Englewood Cliff, NJ: Prentice Hall.

Brockenbrough, K. K., Cornell, D. G., & Loper, A. B. (2002). Aggressive attitudes among victims of violence at school. *Education and Treatment of Children, 25* (3), 273-287.

Clarke, E. A., & Kiselica, M. S. (1997). A systemic counseling approach to the problem of bullying. *Elementary School Guidance and Counseling, 31* (4).

Cullingford, C., & Morrison, J. (1995). Bullying as a formative influence: the relationship between the experience of school and criminality. *British Education Research Journal, 21* (5), 547-56.

Dake, J. A., Price, J. H., & Telljohann, S. K. (2003). The nature and extent of bullying at school. *Journal of School Health, 73* (5), 173-181.

Garrett, K. J. (2001). Reducing school-based bullying. *Journal of School Social Work, 12* (1), 74-90.

Garrity, C., & Jens, K. (1997). Bully proofing your school: Creating a positive climate. *Intervention in School and Clinic, 32* (4), 235-244.

Hoover, J. H., Oliver, R., & Hazler, R. (1992). Bullying: Perception of adolescent victims in the midwestern USA. *School Psychology International, 13*, 5-16.

Kann, L., Warren, C. W., Harris, W. A., Collins, J. L., Douglas, K. A., Collins, M. E., Williams, B. L., Ross, J. G., & Kolbe, L. J. (1995). Youth risk behavior surveillance-United States, 1993. *Morbidity and Mortality Weekly, March 24, 1995, 44, No. SS-1*, 1-66.

Nansel, T. R., Overpeck, M., Pilla, R. S., Ruan, W. J., Simons-Morton, B., & Scheidt, P. (2001). Bullying behaviors among US youth: Prevalence and association with psychosocial adjustment. *Journal of the American Medical Association, 285* (16), 2094-2100.

National Center for Education Statistics (1995, October). *Student victimization in schools.* Washington, DC: Department of Education.

O'Connell, P., Pepler, D., & Craig W. (1999). Peer involvement in bullying: Insights and challenges for intervention. *Journal of Adolescence, 22* (4), 437-452.

Olweus, D. (1978). *Aggression in the schools: Bullies and whipping boys.* Washington DC: Hemisphere Publishing Corporation.

Olweus, D. (1986). *The Olweus Bully-Victim Questionnaire.* Mimeo. Bergen, Norway: University of Bergen.

Olweus, D. (1993). *Bullying at school: What we know and what we can do.* Oxford, United Kingdom: Blackwell Publishers.

Olweus, D. (1994). Annotation: Bullying at school: Basic facts and effects of a school based intervention program. *Journal of Child Psychology and Psychiatry, 35* (7), 1171-1190.

Pellegrini, A. D., Bartini, M., & Brooks, F. (1999). School bullies, victims, and aggressive victims: Factors relating to group affiliation and victimization in early adolescence. *Journal of Educational Psychology, 91* (2), 216-224.

Rigby, K., & Slee, P.T. (1991). Bullying among Australian school children: Reported behavior and attitudes to victims. *Journal of Social Psychology, 131*, 615-627.

Smith, P. K., Cowie, H., Olafsson, R. F., Liefooghe, A. P. D. (2002). Definitions of bullying: A comparison of terms used, and age and gender differences, in a fourteen-country international comparison. *Child Development, 73* (4), 1119-1133.

Smith, P. K., Singer, M., Hoel, H., & Cooper, C. L. (2003). Victimization in the school and the workplace: Are there any links? *British Journal of Psychology, 94,* 175-188.

Twemlow, S. W., & Sacco, F. C. (1996). A clinical and interactionist perspective on the bully-victim-bystander relationship. *Bulletin of the Menninger Clinic, 60* (3), 296-314.

School-Based Violence Prevention Programs: A Review of Selected Programs with Empirical Evidence

Irma Molina, MSW
Stan L. Bowie, PhD
Catherine N. Dulmus, PhD
Karen M. Sowers, PhD

SUMMARY. School violence in the United States is an issue of grave concern for educators, students, parents, and communities. Many schools have responded to the problem by initiating prevention interventions without empirical evidence of effectiveness, assuming it is better to do something rather than to do nothing. In some cases though, more harm than good may result when such intervention strategies and programs are implemented only for the sake of doing something in response to the problem. The literature review examines research on school vio-

---

Irma Molina is a doctoral student, Stan L. Bowie is Assistant Professor, Catherine N. Dulmus is Associate Professor, and Karen M. Sowers is Professor and Dean with The University of Tennessee, College of Social Work.

Address correspondence to: Irma Molina, MSW, The University of Tennessee, College of Social Work, 313 Henson Hall, Knoxville, TN 37996 (E-mail: imolena@utk.edu).

[Haworth co-indexing entry note]: "School-Based Violence Prevention Programs: A Review of Selected Programs with Empirical Evidence." Molina, Irma et al. Co-published simultaneously in *Journal of Evidence-Based Social Work* (The Haworth Social Work Practice Press, an imprint of The Haworth Press, Inc.) Vol. 1, No. 2/3, 2004, pp. 175-189; and: *Kids and Violence: The Invisible School Experience* (ed: Catherine N. Dulmus and Karen M. Sowers) The Haworth Social Work Practice Press, an imprint of The Haworth Press, Inc., 2004, pp. 175-189. Single or multiple copies of this article are available for a fee from The Haworth Document Delivery Service [1-800-HAWORTH, 9:00 a.m. - 5:00 p.m. (EST). E-mail address: docdelivery@haworthpress.com].

http://www.haworthpress.com/web/JEBSW

Digital Object Identifier: 10.1300/J394v1n02_12

lence and provides a review of selected school-based violence prevention programs with beginning empirical support of their effectiveness. The authors stress the importance of schools implementing school-based violence prevention programs that have produced empirical evidence of effectiveness. *[Article copies available for a fee from The Haworth Document Delivery Service: 1-800-HAWORTH. E-mail address: <docdelivery@haworthpress.com> Website: <http://www.HaworthPress.com>*

KEYWORDS. School, violence, prevention, program interventions, empirical

School violence in the United States is an issue of grave concern for educators as well as parents. News about school violence has produced fears and anxieties in schools and communities, especially following the Columbine shooting of April 1999. The schools, which were once viewed as a safe place where children can learn, have turned out to be the new breeding grounds for this growing epidemic. In 1998, for instance, 43 of every 1000 children were victims of nonfatal violent crime while at school or on their way to and from school (Mytton, DiGuisepi, Gough, Taylor, & Logan, 2002). Teachers and school administrators are victims of school violence as well, and are concerned for their personal safety while working at school (Petersen, Pietrzak, & Speaker, 1996). According to the Hammond's (1998) Testimony on Youth Violence, preliminary findings from the Centers for Disease Control and Prevention (CDC) show that in recent years, the average age of homicide offenders and victims has grown younger and younger. Data also suggest that youth violence has grown worse because their fighting has become more lethal. Homicide remains the second leading cause of death for young Americans between the ages of 15 and 24 and the leading cause of death for African Americans in this age group.

The scope of concern about school safety not only includes chances of serious violence like shootouts, but also less serious forms of peer hostility, such as physical aggression such as shoving and pushing, face-to-face verbal harassment, public humiliation, rumor mongering, and bullying (Juvoven, 2001). Although men are more engaged in violent behavior, data reveal that more and more girls are also engaging in violent behavior (Coombs-Richardson, 2000; Tuckson et al., 2000).

Recent figures from the mid 1990s showed that the overall incidence of both weapon carrying and fighting-two risk factors strongly associated with violence-decreased among adolescents. Between 1993 and 1997, the risk of serious violence in school, which is greater for urban than for suburban or rural students, declined 29% overall. The 26 violent deaths associated with schools that took place in 1998-99 represented a 40% drop from the previous year (Tuckson et al., 2000). There are indications that violent crime in schools is geographically concentrated. Data taken from a U.S. Department of Education survey of school principals that asked about the number and types of crimes reported to police from the 1996-97 school year showed that 60% of the violence occurred in 4% of the schools (Cantor & Wright, 2002).

Although data indicate that serious violence is not a problem for many schools, and that only a small percentage of schools seemed to have this type of crime, it also indicates that for a small percentage of schools, violence is extremely high. The number and types of crimes reported to the police by principals for the 1996-1997 school year included serious violence, including murder, suicide, robbery, rape, and assault or fights with weapons. They also included fighting or physical attacks without weapons, property crimes, vandalism, and petty theft. Weapon carrying was found to be higher in schools with a higher percentage of low socioeconomic status (SES) students in the school, larger schools, and schools with higher levels of violence around the school (Price & Everett, 1997). Although most adolescents have never been victims of violent crime, an appreciable number of them have reported being assaulted, robbed, or threatened with violence (Connor, 2002). The prevalent type of school violence was verbal threats by students, followed by organic problems of students (Fetal Alcohol Syndrome, "crack babies"), followed by pushing or shoving, sexual harassment, punching or hitting, kicking, the presence or use of guns, classroom/building vandalism, rumor/peer escalation of violence, and the use of knives/ice picks/razors.

In the past, bullying was not considered to be part of the school violence phenomenon in the United States and was thought to be part of a normal developmental process among children. Bullying is now the subject of numerous studies and is being examined in light of new data pointing out that it is clearly a type of aggression that is harmful to many school-age children. Research findings show that there are consistent relations between bullying and violent behavior. It is not a normative aspect of youth development, but rather a marker for more serious violent behaviors, including weapon carrying, frequent fighting, and fighting-related injury (Nansel, Overpeck, Haynie, Ruan, & Scheidt, 2003). Although boys are more exposed to bullying than girls, girls are more exposed to indirect and more subtle forms of bullying (Olweus, 1994).

Violence concerning male-female relationships has also become a point of concern (Hilton, Harris, Rice, Krans, & Lavigne, 1998; Avery-Leaf, Cascardi, O'Leary, & Cano, 1997).

The causes of violence as perceived by teachers and school administrators are oftentimes the lack of parental supervision/ involvement and a lack of rules or family structure. Exposure to violence in the mass media was also blamed by some authors (Petersen, Piezrak, & Speaker, 1996; Price & Everett, 1997). Children do not achieve the prosocial skills needed when they do not have role models at home to display the appropriate behavior, or when they are exposed to inappropriate modeling. When they do not find emotional and moral stability at home, they turn to gangs where they can meet their needs for social acceptance and are consequently socialized to its norms and values.

Several factors have been shown to predict a child's (7-14 years old) risk for violence. These include individual factors (e.g., children who have been victims of violence or witnesses to violence, poor academic skills or learning problems, substance abuse); family factors (e.g., poor parenting, lack of supervision, inconsistent discipline); and societal and/or community factors (e.g., social acceptance of violence, high rates of crime) (Cooper, Lutenbacher, & Faccia, 2000). The individual, family, and community factors all combine to produce this societal problem.

A national study on school violence and prevention (Petersen, Pietrzak, & Speaker, 1996) found that students most frequently seen as perpetrators were males, came from a Caucasian or African American background, and were the same age or older than their victims. Perpetrators were most frequently in middle or high school, lived in unstable single-parent homes, had below average academic success, and were generally involved with drugs or alcohol. The most frequent victims, on the other hand, were males, from a Caucasian or African American background, who were the same age or younger than the perpetrator. They were usually students most likely to be in middle or high school from unstable single parent homes. Their academic success was viewed as below average and their gang affiliation was largely unknown, as was their involvement with drugs or alcohol. High schools with the highest levels of violence tended to be located in urban areas and have a high percentage of minority students, compared to high schools that reported no crime to the police. They also tended to be located in lower SES areas with high residential mobility.

Numerous prevention programs have been developed by schools to reduce the number of violent incidents and to teach children the necessary knowledge, attitudes and skills to deal with this situation. Oftentimes, schools with high levels of violence also reported high use of prevention measures and tended to combat violence after the issue had become problematic (Cantor & Wright, 2002; Petersen, Pietrzak, & Speaker, 1996). They place more emphasis on programs geared toward changing individual behavior, such as behavior modification while schools with lesser rates of violence tended to place higher priority on preventive instruction. Schools with lower levels of risk were less likely to have implemented a program or report plans to do so (Price & Everett, 1997). Schools with serious crime problems were also more likely to have a violence prevention program in place, often using the nature of reported crimes as a framework for their prevention planning. Many of these programs were not integrated into the curriculum and only addressed incidences of violence after the fact and were thus not effective. The most commonly used strategies in this category include the use of metal detectors, the use of security personnel, random or scheduled locker searches, crisis management services, increased lighting, peer education, cognitive and social skills training, conflict resolution skills/peer mediation, cameras, police dogs, programs to increase parental involvement, and so forth.

Although the efficacy of these prevention programs still has yet to be documented, schools use them anyway as a reactive stance to the incidence of school violence. There is limited data, therefore, to inform policy makers as to which strategies work best with specific populations. As Farrell, Meyer, Kung, and Sullivan (2001) noted, "no matter how well intentioned, the widespread implementation of programs of unknown effectiveness is unlikely to have a significant impact on this serious problem."

More harm than good may be done to children with aggressive or violent behaviors if interventive strategies and programs are implemented only for the sake of doing something in response to this problem. Some school authorities might think that doing something is better than not doing anything at all. A number of school-based violence prevention programs have been implemented over the last decade, with some positive empirical support for effectiveness. Selected programs are outlined below.

SELECTED SCHOOL-BASED VIOLENCE PREVENTION PROGRAMS AND THEIR EFFECTIVENESS

Peacemakers Program

Shapiro, Burgoon, Welker, and Clough (2002) documented the efficacy of the Peacemakers Program, a school-based intervention for students in grades four through eight. The program included a primary prevention component delivered by teachers and a remedial component implemented by school psychologists and counselors with referred students. The intervention was based on a 17-lesson curriculum which takes about 45 minutes to conduct and emphasized the importance of infusing program content into student's everyday life by helping them learn to recognize potentially problematic situations and then recall and use the psychosocial skills called for by the situation. The goal of the program was for Peacemaker's principles and strategies to become part of the culture of the school.

The program attempted to strengthen participant aspirations for non-violent behavior and strengthen student motivation to learn the psychosocial skills by teaching anger management and conflict avoidance techniques, conflict resolution techniques, self-perception training, structured problem-solving techniques, assertiveness training, communication skills, and narrative psychotherapy. The study included 2,000 students in an urban public school system, with pre and post program assessment. The program resulted in positive change in 6 of the 7 aggression-related variables examined, including knowledge of psychosocial skills, self-reported aggressive behavior, and teacher-reported aggression, with a 41% decrease in aggression-related disciplinary incidents and a 67% reduction in suspensions for violent behavior. The no-treatment control group students over time increased their aggression, compared to the decreased aggression in the Peacemakers group.

SMART Talk

Bosworth, Espelage, and DuBay (1998) used a multimedia, computer-based school intervention program called SMART Talk. The computer program uses games, simulations, cartoons, animation, and interactive interviews to enable young adolescents to learn new ways of resolving conflict without violence. Ninety-eight seventh graders in Tuscon, Arizona completed the 175-item Teen Conflict Survey (pretest) and 83% of them participated in the posttest 4 weeks later. The

Teen Conflict Survey was used to collect baseline data on the following issues: knowledge and attitudes regarding non-violent and violent strategies of conflict resolution, self-efficacy as it relates to conflict resolution and anger management, intentions to use nonviolent strategies in conflict situations, self-reported caring and noncaring behaviors, self-esteem, impulsitivity, nonviolent role models, and peer influence. The dependent variables were knowledge, self-knowledge, prosocial behavior, confidence, intentions, trouble behavior, and computer use. Results showed that most students' self knowledge on how certain behaviors may contribute to the escalation of a conflict situation increased from 43% (pretest) to 77% (posttest). Students who reported helping another student solve a problem doubled from 15% (pretest) to 30% (posttest). There was also a decrease in name calling from 45% to 23%. Student's intentions to use nonviolent strategies increased from 10% to 67%, and trouble behavior decreased from 32% to 23% at home, 44% to 33% at school, and 54% to 6% in the community. SMART Talk was also found to be popular with both males and females.

Fighting Fair Model

The Fighting Fair Model curriculum was implemented in Florida. The curriculum teaches students to deal with conflict positively and to replace aggressive behaviors with constructive ones. The rules for the Fighting Fair curriculum are the following: (1) identify the problem, (2) focus on the problem, (3) attack the problem, (4) listen with an open mind, (5) treat a person's feelings with respect, and (6) take responsibility for your actions. Three classes (one class each from grades four, five, and six) were selected as the experimental group and three control classrooms (one class from each of grades four to six) were chosen randomly. The experimental effect was measured by a pre and post teacher-administered survey of attitudes and knowledge and written evaluations by school staff of aggressive behaviors. Students provided multiple-choice responses to the survey, the responses being categorized from most prosocial to antisocial response. Pre-test and post-test survey scores improved for the treatment group while the mean scores of the treatment group changed little. The written reports by the school staff also decreased for both groups. No reported incident of fighting occurred among subjects in either the experimental or control group during the project implementation period (Powell, Muir-McClain, & Halasyamani, 1995).

BRAVE

In Maryland, a peer mediation project named BRAVE (Baltimoreans Reducing All Violent Encounters) was implemented for two years at one elementary school (K-5) located in a neighborhood with a high incidence of drug trafficking and violence. Peers, teachers, and administrators nominated student mediators. They underwent training sessions that taught listening and communication skills, problem identification and solutions. Student mediators patrolled in pairs in the hallways, cafeteria and the playground, wearing patrol belts that identified them as mediators. The mediators guided disputants toward a solution or compromise by facilitating communication between them. The project coordinator, a trained parent or faculty member, monitored the mediation session. During the two years of the project, disputants signed agreements in 93% of the incidents. Follow-up by the project coordinator indicated that 95% of the agreements were honored for the remainder of the school year. Although no information about a comparison group was obtained, the project reduced disciplinary suspensions, reduced referrals to the principal's office from 93% to 80%, improved faculty attendance from 92% to 95%, and improved student attendance from 91% to 93%. In addition, the perception of less fighting suggested a favorable influence of the project on the school atmosphere (Powell, Muir-McClain, & Halasyamani, 1995).

Prothrow-Stith Curriculum

Farrell and Meyer (1997) examined the impact of a school-based curriculum designed to reduce violence among urban sixth-grade students in 6 middle schools within the Richmond Public Schools. Outcome measures were administered at the beginning (T1), middle (T2), and end of the school year (T3). The curriculum's implementation was staggered to meet the school system's objective that every sixth grader complete the program. Within each school, classrooms were scheduled to participate in the programs during either the fall or spring semester. The curriculum was based on the Prothrow-Stith curriculum, which focuses on imparting knowledge about the ways in which the host, agent, and environment contribute to youth violence. The Prothrow-Stith curriculum was modified for use with middle school students using concepts from *The Friendly Classroom for a Small Planet.* The 18 sessions focused on building trust (2 sessions); respect for individual differences (2 sessions); the nature of violence and risk factors (3 sessions); anger management (3 sessions); personal values (2 sessions); and non violent alternatives to fighting (3 sessions). The curriculum emphasized prosocial behavior and norms. Four prevention specialists trained in conflict resolution implemented the curriculum. The frequency of violent behavior was assessed with the Violent Behavior Scale from the Behavioral Frequency Scales.

Fall participants reported a lower frequency of being threatened by someone with a weapon than spring participants. Among boys, those who participated in the program in the fall reported significantly lower rates of fighting than boys in the delayed-treatment group. This effect was not significant for the girls. Boys who participated in the fall tended to report lower rates of violent behavior at T2 and T3 than boys who participated in the spring. Girls showed a trend in the opposite direction. The one exception was physical fighting. By the end of the school year, the frequency of fighting in the delayed-treatment group had decreased to the level of the fall participants. Boys overall reported significantly higher frequencies than girls across measures, including the Violent Behavior Scale, physical fighting, threatening someone with a weapon, being threatened by someone with a weapon, and the Problem Behavior Scale. The differential impact on girls and boys was a result of the fact that indirect aggression, which girls are most likely to employ, was not addressed in the curriculum.

The study concluded that the fact that boys in the delayed-treatment group showed a greater rate of increase in the frequency of problem behaviors at T2 than boys who participated in the program in the fall suggests that the first year of middle school may be a critical time to intervene.

Mastery Learning Intervention and The Good Behavior Game

Dolan et al. (1993) assessed the impact of two interventions: the Good Behavior Game (GBG), which was aimed at reducing aggressive and shy behaviors, and the Mastery Learning (ML), designed to improve poor reading achievement, an antecedent for later depressive symptoms as well as a correlate of aggressive and shy behaviors. The GBG and ML are universal interventions that were carried out in 19 schools in 5 urban areas in Baltimore City, from fall to spring of first grade. Intervention and control classrooms were used. The GBG a classroom team-based behavior management strategy that promotes good behavior by rewarding teams that do not exceed maladaptive behavior standards. A team could win if the total number of team checkmarks did not exceed four at the end of the game period. The winning teams received tangible rewards like stickers or erasers and later they engaged in rewarding activity like extra recess or class privileges. The ML intervention consisted of an extensive and systematically applied enrichment of the reading curriculum. Critical aspects of the program included a group-based approach to mastery, a more flexible corrective process, and material support. Measures included teacher ratings, peer nominations, and standardized achievement test measures in the fall and spring of first grade in both intervention and control classrooms.

Results showed that the GBG had an impact for boys on aggressive behavior as nominated by peers, but it had no effect on peer nominations of aggressive behavior among girls. The frequencies of peer-rated aggressive girls were markedly lower even before the GBG. For both boys and girls, GBG had the greatest impact on children who began the school year with more aggressive ratings by teachers. The GBG also had an impact on shy behavior as rated by teachers for both boys and girls. However, its impact on peer nominations of shy behavior was limited to the shy behavior item, i.e., "*has few friends*" for girls. The results for the ML intervention indicate that it raised reading achievement test scores for both boys and girls through the end of first grade. The ML intervention primarily benefited boys at the lower end of the achievement continuum. For girls, ML enhanced achievement among already high-achieving girls by boosting them into the top achievement groups. The study concluded that the GBG was found to be an effective intervention for reducing aggressive behavior among first-grade children, and the ML intervention was found to be effective intervention for improving reading achievement among first grade children. For girls only, there was weak evidence that ML improved shy behavior as rated by teachers.

A Combined Intervention

Sprague et al. (2001) investigated the effects of a one-year universal intervention package aimed at improving the safety and social behavior of students in nine treatment and six comparison elementary and middle schools in the Pacific Northwest. Treatment and comparison schools were not randomly selected but rather chosen by local administrators. The project included 4 major intervention strategies aimed at building personnel and students. Technical assistance was provided; the entire staff of each treatment school received an eight-hour in-service implementing the Second Step curriculum, and an additional four hour session of the Effective Behavioral Support Model. The EBS Model is a multiple system, whole school approach to addressing the problems posed by antisocial students and coping with challenging forms of student behavior. It is a system of training, technical assistance, and evaluation of school discipline and climate. Schools taught lessons throughout the year about rules on "safety," "respect" and "responsibility" and posted rules about those patterns of behavior. Second, each school established a consistent system of enforcement, monitoring, and positive reinforcement to enhance the effect of rule teaching and maintain patterns of desired student behavior. Data-based feedbacks on school regarding their responses to the "Assessing Behavior Support in Schools" were also given. Finally, the Second Step Violence Prevention Curriculum was installed in each treatment school. Research has shown it to be effective in increasing positive social skills and reducing aggressive playground behavior.

Results showed that all treatment schools reported reductions in office discipline referrals in the intervention year when compared to the baseline year and showed greater improvement relative to comparison schools. With regard to school safety, no meaningful differences were detected in the ratings based from the Oregon School Safety Survey. In the treatment schools, the school discipline team was asked at midyear to rate the status of several features of Effective Behavioral Support. The checklist asked raters to indicate whether an item is "in place," "in progress," or "not started" across the areas of school-wide, common area, classroom, and individual student systems. Treatment middle schools reported 50% of school wide, 2% common area, 48% classroom, and 30% individual student item as "in place." Elementary treatment schools reported 57% of school wide, 33% common area, 63% classroom, and 42% individual student items as "in place." The highest ratings were obtained in the school-wide and classroom systems. Students were also given a test to assess their ability to define essential skills (e.g., empathy). All grade levels in all schools improved on this measure after instruction.

The average percent correct in the baseline was 46% and average scores increased to 55% across all grades. As an additional indictor of the qualitative effects of intervention, focus group interviews with teachers, administrators, and parents were conducted at four treatment and four comparison groups. The four comparison groups reported a lack of comprehensive approaches to school-wide discipline. Discipline procedures were more reactive than preventive and generally applied most often to at-risk students. They also reported the need for a consistent, school-wide approach to behavioral management but noted a lack of technical support and training in this area. Treatment schools described consistent use of teaching school behavior expectations both school-wide and in classrooms.

Olweus

Olweus (1994) systematically evaluated an intervention program that he developed with the campaign against bully/victim problems in Norwegian schools. The goal of the program was to reduce existing bully/victim problems as much as possible and to prevent the development of new problems. The program focused on creating a school environment characterized by warmth, positive interest, and involvement from adults, on one hand, and firm limits to unacceptable behavior on the other. In cases of violations of rules, nonhostile, nonphysical sanctions were applied. The intervention program is based on an authoritative adult-child interaction, or child rearing model. The program utilized teachers and other school personnel like psychologists, social workers, and school counselors, as well as students and parents in the implementation. The measures used were translated into the school, class, and individual levels.

The results showed that there were marked reductions in the level of bully/victim problems for the periods studied. Reductions were obtained for both boys and girls and across all cohorts compared. There were also consensual agreements in the classes that the bully/victim problems have decreased considerably. The reductions in terms of percentages of students reporting being bullied or bullying others amounted to 50% or more in most comparisons. There was also a clear reduction in general antisocial behavior as well as improvement regarding the various aspects of the "social climate" of the class, such as improved order and discipline, more positive social relationships, and more positive attitudes toward school work and the school. At the same time, there was an increase in student satisfaction with school life. For several variables, the effects of the intervention program were more marked after 2 years than after 1 year. The intervention program not only affected existing victimization problems, but it also reduced the number of new victims. The program had thus both primary and secondary prevention effects.

CONCLUSION

This paper was an examination of school violence in the United States and some of the limited evidence-based programmatic endeavors that were developed and implemented to address the problem. It included a thorough assessment of the phenomenon of school violence–the dramatic violence that results in serious injury and death, as well as the increasing problem of less serious, nonfatal violent crime that has proven to be harmful to school aged children. This includes bullying and physical peer hostility such as shoving, pushing, face-to-face verbal harassment and humiliation, and so forth. The events at Columbine High School in April 1999 made it clear that the consequences of the less dramatic types of peer hostility in schools can have tragic consequences, oftentimes stemming from a raging desire for revenge by the victim(s) of the bullying and hostility.

Some of the prevalent demographic patterns associated with school violence were discussed. The data make it clear that specific patterns of school violence are emerging, including younger and younger victims and perpetrators, a heightened level of school violence by females, the fact that school violence tends to be geographically concentrated, and the manner in which male-female relationships are increasingly contributing to escalating levels of school violence. Variables related to family socioeconomic status, family socialization, and academic achievement levels were also examined in relation to predictors of school violence.

Finally, the paper examined some school-based program models that featured empirical evidence of positive outcomes. Some of the key characteristics of the successful programs were the use of behavioral management techniques (e.g., anger management, conflict avoidance); computer-assisted interactive games and activities that promoted positive decision-making; curriculum-based structured conflict resolution strategies; use of peer mediators; cognitive development strategies that emphasized improved academic performance and/or understanding of environmental contributors to school violence; and the use of violence reduction models that utilized adult authoritarian figures combined with student peers.

Much work remains to be done to properly address the problem of school violence. As pointed out above, some innovative programs have, indeed, been developed and are currently being tested with appropriate statistical methodologies. Unfortunately, far more many violence reduction and anti-bullying programs operated by schools have great public relations value, but very little data to demonstrate the effectiveness of outcomes or inform policy makers on where public resources should be focused for addressing the problem. The obvious solution is to continue to develop, test, and adjust current programmatic approaches until the most effective models are isolated to work in specific environments and with specific populations. This is the only way that schools will transform back to peaceful learning environments where students can focus on their personal and career development, as opposed to daily stressors and fears from their peers. The future viability of American schools, the students, and the communities-at-large will depend on whether this goal is successfully achieved.

REFERENCES

Avery-Leaf, M. A., Cascardi, M., O'Leary, K. D., & Cano, A. (1997). Efficacy of a dating violence prevention program on attitudes justifying aggression. *Journal of Adolescent Health, 21* (1), 11-17.

Bosworth, K., Espelage, D., & DuBay, T. (1998). A computer-based violence prevention intervention for young adolescents: Pilot study. *Adolescence, 33* (132), 785-795.

Cantor, D., & Wright, M. M. (2002). *School crime patterns: A national profile of US public high schools using rates of crime reported to police.* Report on the Study on School Violence and Prevention, Rockville, MD. (ERIC Document Reproduction Service No. 471 867)

Connor, D. (2002). *Aggression and antisocial behavior in children and adolescents.* New York: Guilford Press.

Coombs-Richardson R. (2000). *Violence in schools: Causation and prevention.* Paper presented at the Annual Convention of the National Association of School Psychologists, New Orleans, LA, March 28-April 1, 2000. (ERIC Document Reproduction Service No. 440 317).

Cooper, W., Lutenbacher, M., & Faccia, K. (2000). Components of effective youth violence prevention programs for 7 to 14 year-olds. *Archives of Pediatrics and Adolescent Medicine, 154*, 1134-1139.

Dolan, L., Kellam, S., Hendricks Brown, C., Werthamer-Larsson, L., Rebok, G., Mayer, L., Laudolff, J., & Turkkan, J. (1993). The short-term impact of two classroom-based preventive interventions on aggressive and shy behaviors and poor achievement. *Journal of Applied Developmental Psychology, 14*, 317-345.

Farrell, A., & Meyer, A. (1997). The effectiveness of a school-based curriculum for reducing violence among urban sixth-grade students. *American Journal of Public Health, 87* (6), 979-984.

Farrell, A., Meyer, A., Kung, E., & Sullivan, T. (2001). Development and evaluation of school-based violence prevention programs. *Journal of Clinical Child Psychology, 30* (1), 207-220.

Fishbaugh, M. S. E.; Berkeley, T. R., Schroth, G. (2003). *Ensuring Safe School Environments: Exploring Issues-Seeking Solutions.* Mahwah, NJ: Lawrence Erlbaum Associates, Inc.

Hammond, W. (1998). Testimony on youth violence, before the Committee on Education and the Workforce House Subcommittee on Early Childhood, Youth and Families. Retrieved October 28, 2003 from *http://www.hhs.gov/asl/testify/t980428c.html.*

Hilton, N., Harris, G., Rice, M., Krans, T., & Lavigne, S. (1998). Antiviolence education in high schools. *Journal of Interpersonal Violence, 13* (6), 726-742.

Juvonen, J. (2001). School violence: Prevalence, fears and prevention. *Rand Education Issue Paper.* Retrieved October 30, 2003 from *http://www.rand.org/publications/* IP/IP219/.

Mytton, J., DiGuiseppi, C., Gough, D., Taylor, R., & Logan, S. (2002). School-based violence prevention programs. *Archives of Pediatrics and Adolescent Medicine, 156*, 752-762.

Nansel, T., Overpeck, M., Haynie, D., Ruan, W., & Scheidt, P. (2003). Relationships between bullying and violence among US youth. *Archives of Pediatrics and Adolescent Medicine, 157*, 348-353.

Olweus, D. (1994). Annotation: Bullying at school: Basic facts and effects of a school-based intervention program. *Journal of Child Psychology, 35* (7), 1171-1190.

Petersen, G., Pietrzak, D., & Speaker, K. M. (1996). *The enemy within: A national study on school violence and prevention.* Paper presented at the annual meeting of the Association of Teacher Educators, St. Louis, MO, February 24-28, 1996. (ERIC Document Reproduction Service No. ED 394 907).

Powell, K., Muir-McClain, L., & Halasymani, L. (1995). A review of selected school-based conflict resolution and peer mediation projects. *Journal of School Health, 65* (10).

Price, J., & Everett, S. (1997). A national assessment of secondary school principal's perceptions of violence in schools. *Health and Education Behavior, 24*, 218-229.

Rollin, S., Ulrey, C., Potts, I., & Creason, A. (2003). A school-based violence prevention model for at-risk eighth grade youth. *Psychology in the Schools,* 40 (4), 403-416.

Shapiro, J., Burgoon, J., Welker, C., & Clough, J. (2002). Evaluation of the Peacemakers Program: School-based violence prevention for students in grades four through eight. *Psychology in the Schools, 39* (1), 87-100.

Sprague, J., Walker, H., Golly, A., White, K., Myers, D., & Shannon, T. (2001). Translating research into effective practice: The effects of a universal staff and student intervention on indicators of discipline and school safety. *Education and Treatment of Children, 24* (4), 495-511.

Tuckson, R., Callan, C., Elster, A., Brown, R., Fleming, M., Lyznicki, J., & Grosso, V. (2000). *Youth and violence.* A Report by the Commission for the Prevention of Youth Violence. Retrieved October 28, 2003 from http://www.ama-assn.org/violence.

Index

BOOK ORDER FORM!

Order a copy of this book with this form or online at:
http://www.haworthpress.com/store/product.asp?sku=5324

Kids and Violence

The Invisible School Experience

____ in softbound at $29.95 (ISBN: 0-7890-2586-8)
____ in hardbound at $49.95 (ISBN: 0-7890-2585-X)

COST OF BOOKS ________

POSTAGE & HANDLING ________
US: $4.00 for first book & $1.50 for each additional book
Outside US: $5.00 for first book & $2.00 for each additional book.

SUBTOTAL ________

In Canada: add 7% GST. ________

STATE TAX ________
CA, IL, IN, MN, NJ, NY, OH & SD residents please add appropriate local sales tax.

FINAL TOTAL ________
If paying in Canadian funds, convert using the current exchange rate, UNESCO coupons welcome.

❑ **BILL ME LATER:**
Bill-me option is good on US/Canada/ Mexico orders only; not good to jobbers, wholesalers, or subscription agencies.

❑ **Signature** ________

❑ **Payment Enclosed: $** ________

❑ **PLEASE CHARGE TO MY CREDIT CARD:**

❑ Visa ❑ MasterCard ❑ AmEx ❑ Discover
❑ Diner's Club ❑ Eurocard ❑ JCB

Account # ________

Exp Date ________

Signature ________

(Prices in US dollars and subject to change without notice.)

PLEASE PRINT ALL INFORMATION OR ATTACH YOUR BUSINESS CARD

Name
Address
City State/Province Zip/Postal Code
Country
Tel Fax
E-Mail

May we use your e-mail address for confirmations and other types of information? ❑ Yes ❑ No We appreciate receiving your e-mail address. Haworth would like to e-mail special discount offers to you, as a preferred customer. **We will never share, rent, or exchange your e-mail address.** We regard such actions as an invasion of your privacy.

Order From Your **Local Bookstore** or Directly From
The Haworth Press, Inc. 10 Alice Street, Binghamton, New York 13904-1580 • USA
Call Our toll-free number (1-800-429-6784) / Outside US/Canada: (607) 722-5857
Fax: 1-800-895-0582 / Outside US/Canada: (607) 771-0012
E-mail your order to us: orders@haworthpress.com

For orders outside US and Canada, you may wish to order through your local sales representative, distributor, or bookseller.
For information, see http://haworthpress.com/distributors

(Discounts are available for individual orders in US and Canada only, not booksellers/distributors.)

Please photocopy this form for your personal use.
www.HaworthPress.com

BOF05